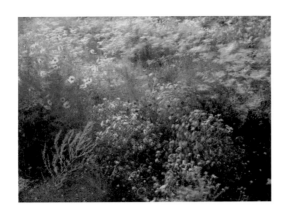

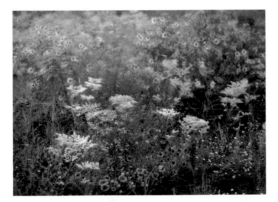

National Audubon Society
Guide to
NATURE PHOTOGRAPHY

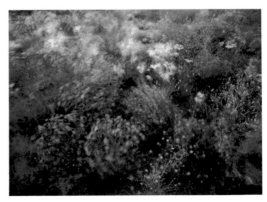

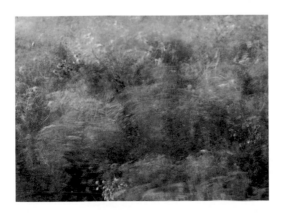

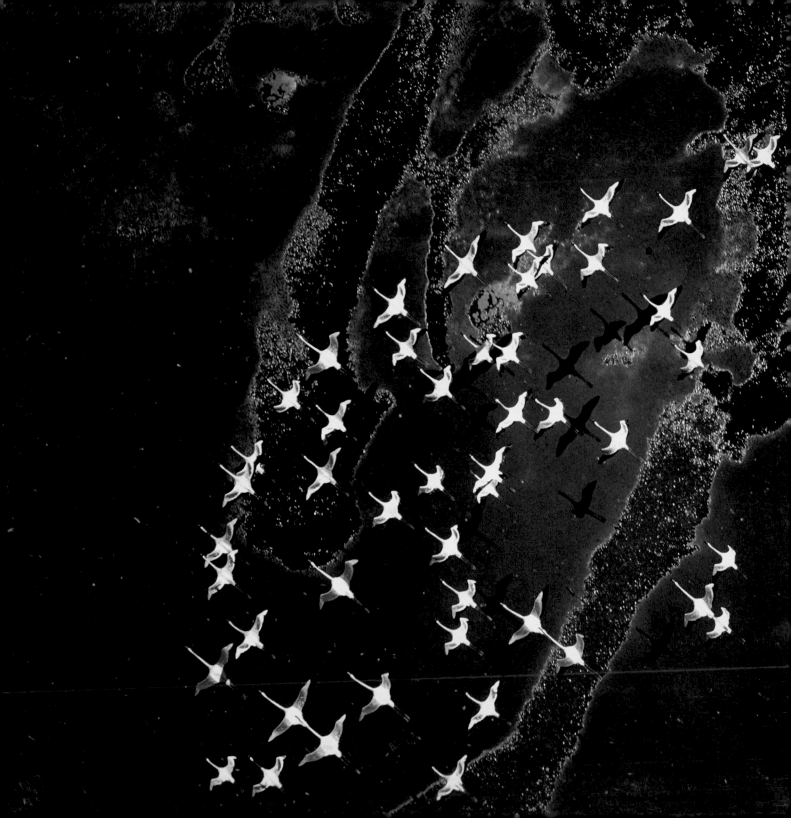

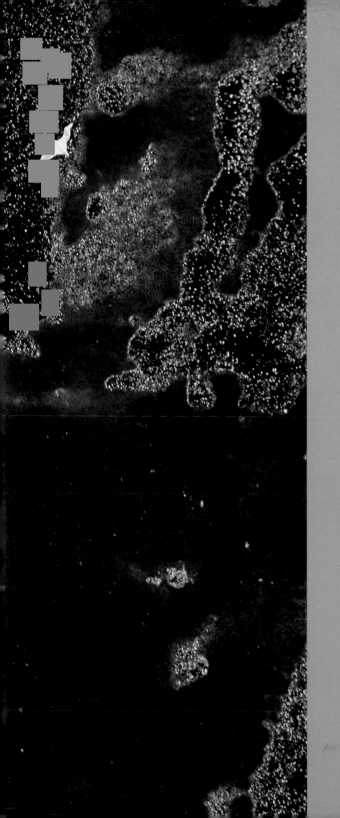

National Audubon Society
Guide to
NATURE PHOTOGRAPHY

Tim Fitzharris

FIREFLY BOOKS

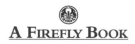

A FIREFLY BOOK

Published by Firefly Books Ltd., 2003

First printing, revised edition, 2003
First paperback edition published 1996
First edition published 1990

U.S. Cataloging-in-Publication Data
(Library of Congress standards)

Fitzharris, Tim, 1948-
National Audubon Society guide to nature photography : revised edition / Tim Fitzharris.
[192] p. : col. ill. , photos. ; cm.
Includes bibliographical references and index.
ISBN 1-55297-808-7 (pbk.) ISBN 1-55297-818-4 (bound)
1. Nature photography. I. National Audubon Society. II. Title.
778.9/3 21 TR721.F58 2003

National Library of Canada Cataloguing in Publication

Fitzharris, Tim, 1948-
National Audubon Society guide to nature photography / Tim Fitzharris. - revised ed.
Title of previous edition: Nature photography : National Audubon Society guide.
Includes bibliographical references and index.
ISBN 1-55297-808-7 (pbk.) ISBN 1-55297-818-4 (bound)
1. Nature photography. I. National Audubon Society II. Title.
TR721.F574 2003 778.9'3 C2003-901040-6

Published in Canada in 2003 by
Firefly Books Ltd.
3680 Victoria Park Avenue
Toronto, Ontario, M2H 3K1

Published in the United States in 2003 by
Firefly Books (U.S.) Inc.
P.O. Box 1338, Ellicott Station
Buffalo, New York, 14205

Designed and produced by Tim Fitzharris and Joy Fitzharris
Printed and bound in China

Photo Captions
Half-title Page: Wind-tossed wildflowers, Eldorado, New Mexico
Title Page: Lesser flamingos over Lake Magadi, Kenya

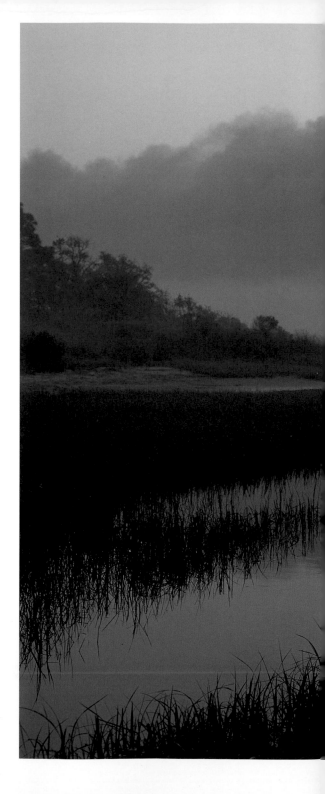

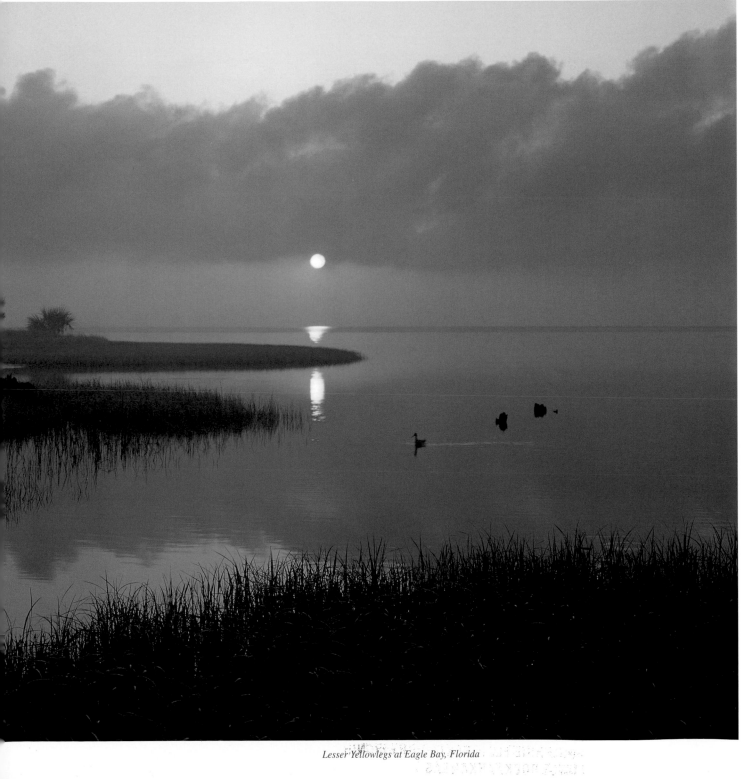

Lesser Yellowlegs at Eagle Bay, Florida

For Sean

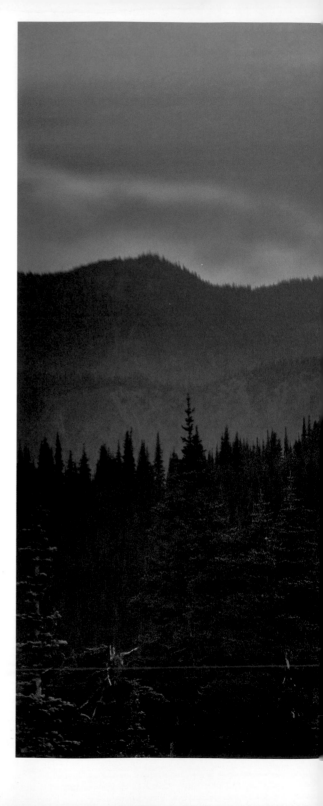

Books by Tim Fitzharris

AAA National Park Photography

Rocky Mountains: Wilderness Reflections

Virtual Wilderness

The Sierra Club Guide to Close-up Photography in Nature

Nature Photography Hotspots

The Sierra Club Guide to 35 mm Landscape Photography

Wild Bird Photography: National Audubon Society Guide

Fields of Dreams

Wild Wings: An Introduction to Birdwatching

Forest: A National Audubon Society Book

West Coast Wildlife (written by Bruce Obee)

Canada: A Natural History (with John Livingston)

Wildflowers of Canada (with Audrey Fraggalosch)

The Adventure of Nature Photography

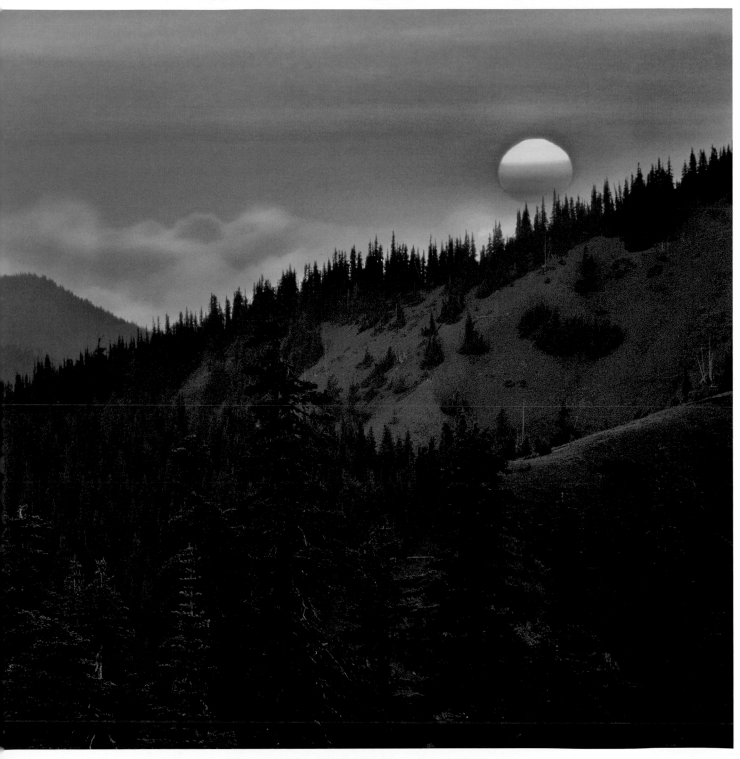

Sunset over Hurricane Ridge, Olympic National Park, Washington

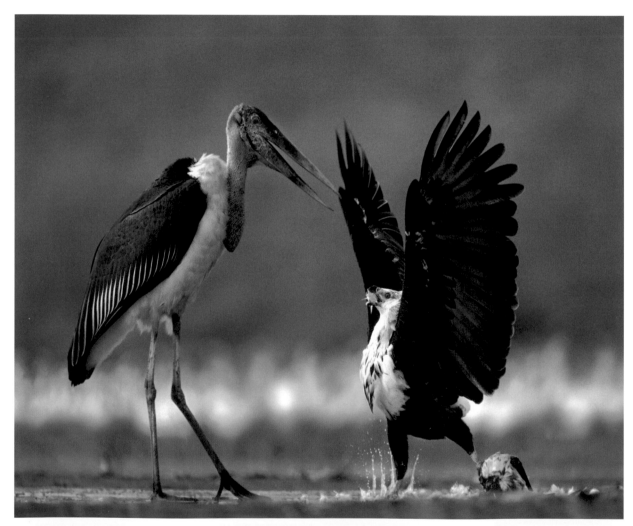

Marabou stork and African fish eagle fighting over a flamingo carcass, Lake Bogoria, Kenya

National Audubon Society

THE AUDUBON MISSION is to conserve and restore natural ecosystems, focusing on birds, other wildlife and their habitats for the benefit of humanity and the earth's biological diversity.

Through its education, science and public policy initiatives, Audubon engages people throughout the U.S. and Latin America in conservation. Audubon's Centers and its sanctuaries and education programs are developing the next generation of conservation leaders by providing opportunities for families, students, teachers and others to learn about and enjoy the natural world. The science program is focused on connecting people with nature through projects like Audubon at Home and Great Backyard Bird Count. Audubon's volunteer Citizen Scientists participate in research and conservation action in a variety of ways, from monitoring bird populations and restoring critical wildlife habitat to implementing healthy habitat practices in their own backyards. Audubon's public policy programs are supported by a strong foundation of science, environmental

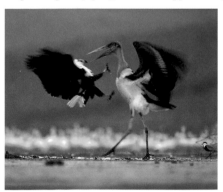

education and grassroots engagement. Working with a network of state offices, chapters and volunteers, Audubon works to protect and restore our natural heritage.

To learn how you can support Audubon, call (800) 274-4201, visit our website at www.audubon.org or write to Audubon, 700 Broadway, New York, New York 10003.

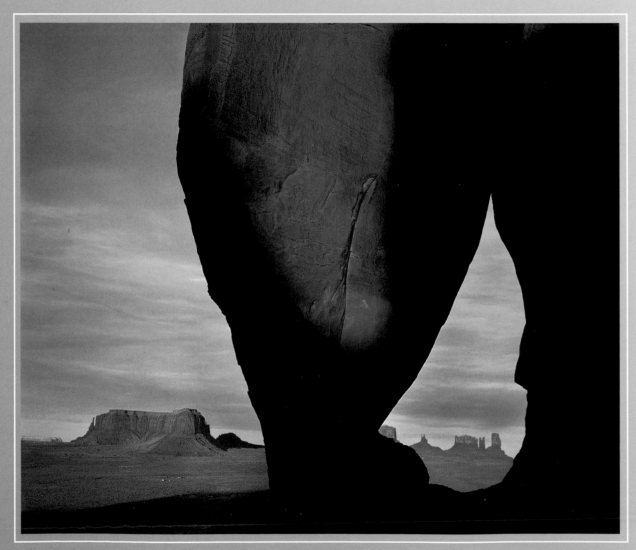

Teardrop Arch, Monument Valley, Arizona

Contents

Introduction
The Craft and Art of Nature Photography

Cottonwood leaves in Pine Creek, Zion National Park, Utah (right).
Surrounded by the rainbow-hued walls of Zion Canyon soaring 3,000 feet above, this diminutive composition of scattered leaves among floating prisms of natural oil could be overlooked easily. Small, seemingly undramatic elements are tractable vehicles for recording impressions and feelings about the natural world. Your choice and approach to subject matter can be a reflection of how you view yourself and the world. Pentax 645, Pentax 80–160 f/4.5 lens, extension tube, Singh-Ray circular polarizer, Fujichrome Velvia, two seconds at f/16.

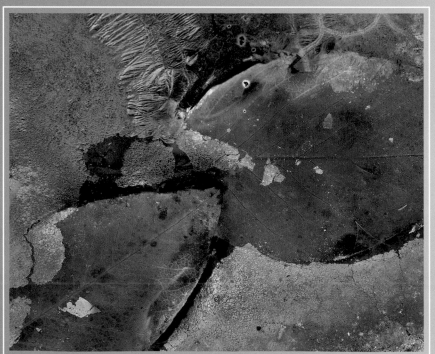

NATURE PHOTOGRAPHY MEANS different things to different people. It is for all of us an acting-out of the instinctive urge to hunt and gather, even to claim territory. On another level it is an expression of our appreciation of beauty. The philosophy, experience and practice of nature photographers allow each to be placed for the moment somewhere along this continuum between subject matter and theme, between craft and art. This book should help photographers with a knowledge of photography's basic principles find their way along this route and enjoy its numerous attractions.

My interest in nature photography began with a love of the wilds rather than of photography. When I began in 1970, wildlife photography was not yet a popular pastime and initially I pursued my interest in nature by hunting. As for many people, trying to kill the things I found fascinating seemed ridiculous. So I took up wildlife photography, purchasing a new, preset Soligor 400mm f/6.3 lens for a little over $100. With this I could enjoy all the attractions of hunting with none of the unpleasantness —a reason to be outdoors, wonderful equipment to tinker with, the thrill of the chase and a trophy at the end that could be projected on a wall for friends to admire. I became a convert and am still an avid follower more than three decades later. I have since discovered that nature photography's attraction goes well beyond hunting with a camera.

Photographing wild creatures is a challenging undertaking with infinite possibilities. When shooting a bird or mammal, the approach is mostly determined by the subject. There are logical, hard-to-ignore prerequisites that concern us when filming whales, giraffes or butterflies. We want to capture expression in the eyes, definition of specialized limbs or how the subject gets its food. These subject-generated issues are not so compelling when working with inanimate trees, sand dunes or breaking waves. Instead, the approach is guided more by influences from within — a philosophy, a mood, a telling experience, a visual sensation. This engagement with self-expression is at once easier (who's to say you're wrong?) and more challenging (does anyone care?) than satisfying the more apparent and objective criteria of subject-based imagery. Depending on mood, inspiration and encounters with compelling subjects and settings, most of us move back and

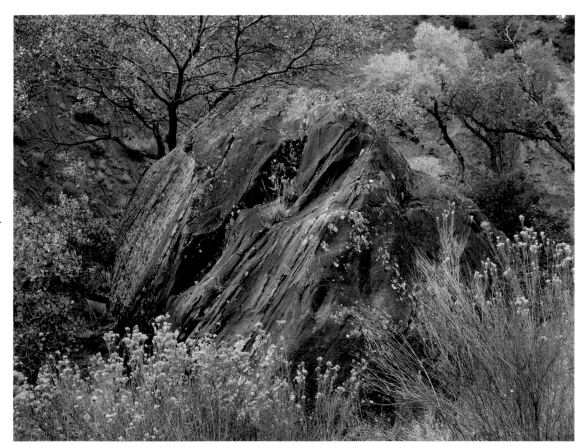

forth between crafting photographs and expressing our artistic urges.

This is not the book to find detailed advice on how to run your high-tech equipment. Most of the time, this preoccupation is only peripheral to making pictures. Photography isn't complicated — a camera is a basically simple machine for capturing images on a light-sensitive surface. The technical advances of the last three decades have not made cameras more responsive or creative picture-making easier, although they have

Granite boulder, Zion Canyon, Zion National Park, Utah (above). *Soft light from an overcast sky, rosy tones reflected from surrounding sandstone ramparts, and pastel tints of autumn's desert palette coalesce in a simple study of color and texture. Pentax 645 N11, Pentax 45–85mm f/4.5 lens, polarizing filter, Fujichrome Velvia, one second at f/22.*

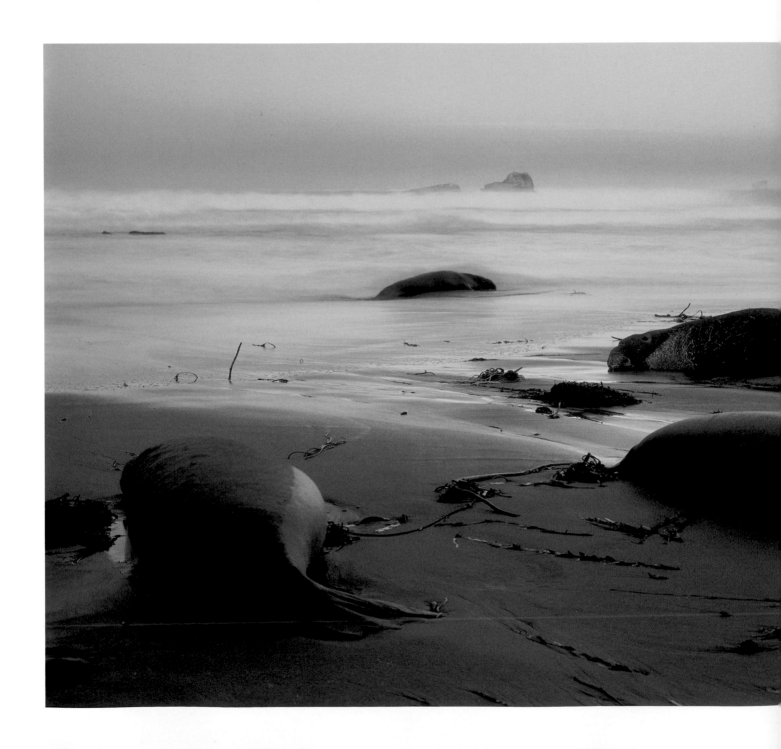

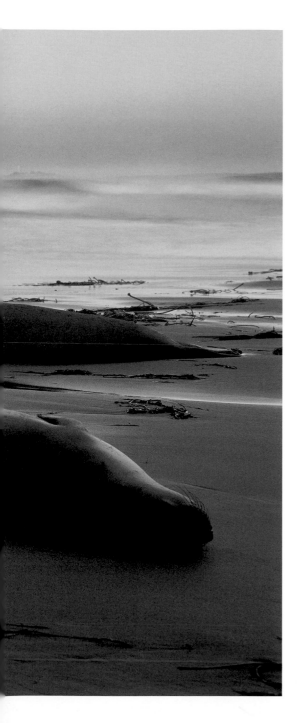

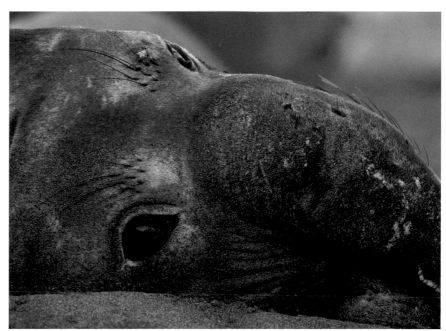

enticed consumers en masse to buy new equipment. This book is intended in part as an antidote to the "buy more" trend — its aim is to help you make the best pictures in the most direct, practical, economical, intuitive way possible.

At a time when the earth's natural resources and wild places are being destroyed at a pace unmatched in human history, you could choose few better ways to spend your life or your leisure time than photographing nature. No matter the result of your picture-taking efforts, the act itself serves as an example to family members, friends and even the larger community of a philosophy that marries the values of beauty and survival.

Elephant seals, Point Piedras Blancas, Big Sur, California (left and above). Nearly extinct in the 1880s, elephant seals have recovered thanks to protection from commercial hunting. More than 2000 pups are born each year at this idyllic spot on the central California coast.

Part One

The Right Equipment

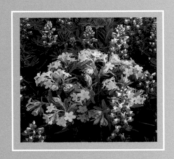

Basic Kit

Essential Equipment for Photographing the Natural World

MOST SERIOUS AMATEUR and professional nature photographers rely on single-lens reflex (SLR) cameras to handle all of their picture taking needs whether it be shooting grizzly bears in Alaska, volcanoes in Hawaii or butterflies in the Texas Hill Country. The SLR allows you to view the scene directly through the lens by means of a pentaprism which delivers an accurate image to the viewfinder, a feature especially important when shooting small subjects at close range. Just prior to exposure, a mirror that reflects the scene through the pentaprism to the eye, flips up and out of the way to allow light to strike the film. This happens almost instantly, allowing you to keep continuous sight of the subject, a boon when trying to capture moving wildlife. Most single-lens reflex cameras permit lens interchange, a feature that makes it possible to photograph the panorama of an alpine vista with a wide-angle lens and a moment later to capture a bird with a telephoto or record drops of dew lined up on a blade of grass.

You can record the world of nature with either a traditional film camera or a digital camera. Digital cameras capture the subject on a light sensor and save it as pixels (tiny, computer-coded bits of light) on a compact memory card similar in function to a computer storage disk.

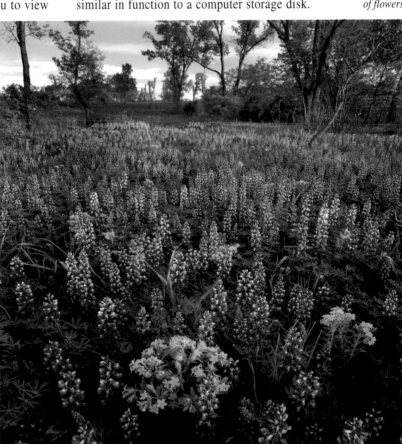

Lupine field, Indiana Dunes National Lakeshore, Indiana (left). *This photograph was made with an SLR camera at close range. The accurate viewing system allowed me to carefully frame the array of flowers to capture the most effective pattern. Due to the interchangeable lens system, I was able to shoot with an ultra wide-angle lens to create a sense of depth. Mounting the camera on a tripod made it convenient to adjust exposure settings and steady the scene while I considered the composition. Pentax 645, 35mm, f/3.5 lens, Singh-Ray circular polarizer, Fujichrome Velvia, two seconds at f/22.*

Digital Camera Advantages

For enlargements up to large wall-calendar size, the best digital cameras produce results equal to or better than traditional film cameras in image resolution, highlight and shadow detail, and grain/noise. With a digital camera, exposure and composition can be verified on a small screen immediately after exposure (rather than waiting for film to be developed) allowing you to reshoot on the spot if corrections are needed. Digital images can be easily modified on your computer. You can dodge, burn, adjust color and brightness, and enhance sharpness with image editing software (Adobe Photoshop being the standard).

Once the image is adjusted to your satisfaction, you can print it on a photo-quality desktop printer and, with just a bit of practice, end up with enlargements superior to those produced in a professional, custom film lab. Digital SLR cameras (DSLRs) currently cost several times as much as their film counterparts. To use them effectively, you also need to invest in a high-speed computer, imaging software and a photo-quality printer. But you never need buy a single roll of film or pay for processing.

Advantages of Film Cameras

Except for the low initial cost of the camera, there are few advantages to shooting with film. When loaded with transparency film, traditional cameras produce a physical image that can be easily and quickly viewed in high detail (once the film is developed) without the need of a cumbersome computer, monitor and power supply. Film images can be digitized with desktop scanners and edited on the computer with the same facility as images from digital cameras.

Stretching Mallard Drake, Witty's Lagoon, Vancouver Island, British Columbia (below). This photo could have been made with either a professional level digital or film camera with similar results at enlargements up to wall calendar size. I approached this wary drake in silence from a floating, mobile blind. The shallow depth of field of the telephoto lens produced an out-of-focus background that throws the arabesque bird into strong relief. Canon F1, Canon 500mm f/4.5 L lens, Kodachrome 64, 1/60 second at f/4.5.

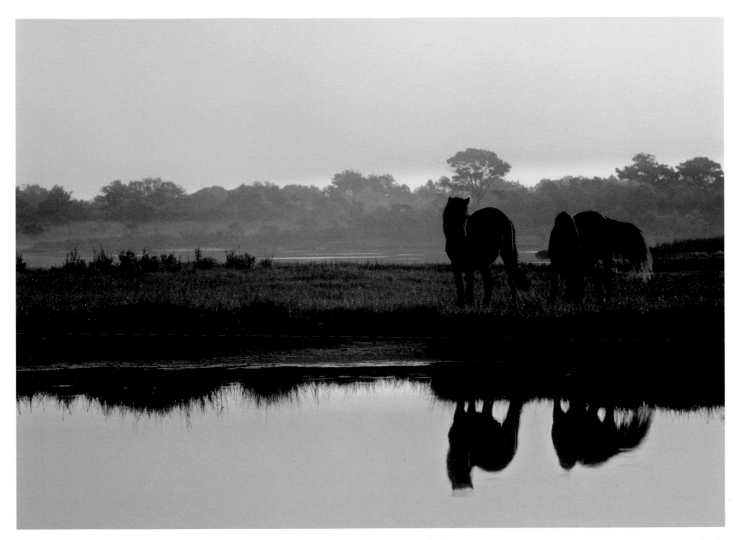

If you are just getting started with nature photography, buy into a brand that makes SLR and DSLR models that accept the same lenses (e.g. Nikon, Canon, Sigma, Contax). If you wish to test the waters first, buy an entry level film SLR. Later you can upgrade to a more expensive digital model without having to buy new lenses. Get a DSLR with the highest pixel count you can afford — although most shooters needn't go beyond a six-megapixel camera which can be used to make professional-quality prints up to wall calendar size. If you enjoy shooting landscapes, give preference to models with full-frame sensors. Due to their partial-frame sensors, many

Wild ponies, Assateague Island National Seashore, Maryland (above). A lightweight tripod was essential to steady this exposure made at a slow shutter speed with a telephoto lens. Pentax 645, 80–160mm f/4.5 zoom lens, Fujichrome Velvia, 1/2 second at f/16.

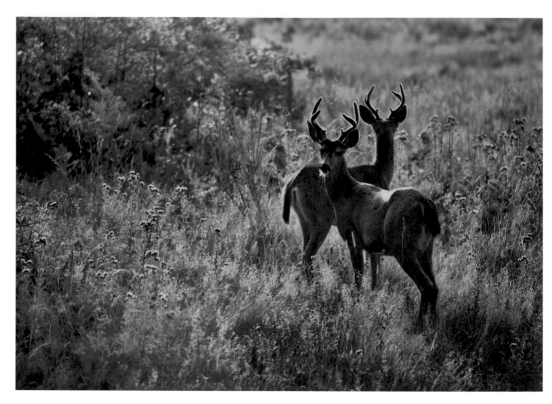

Black-tailed deer, Vancouver Island, British Columbia (right). For a few seconds, these velvet-antlered bucks presented this eye-catching choreography. A motor drive and smooth-panning tripod head allowed me to quickly frame the composition and take a few steady shots. Canon T90, Canon 500mm f/4.5 L lens, Kodachrome 64, 1/250 second at f/4.5.

Scarlet paintbrush and daisies, Big Sur Coast, California (far right). A lightweight tripod (Manfrotto Carbon Fiber One 441) made it easy to position the camera on the steep bluff where these blooms were growing. Pentax 645 N11, 80–160mm f/4.5 lens, Singh-Ray circular polarizer with color intensifier filter, Fujichrome Velvia, 1/2 second at f/16.

DSLRs multiply focal length by about 1.6X, effectively eliminating extreme wide-angle focal lengths. Full-frame sensors retain actual lens focal length, but they are expensive and not widely available. At present, Canon is the SLR/DSLR brand of professional choice due to its selection of super-telephoto lenses equipped with image stabilization, a feature of great benefit when shooting wildlife.

THE BASICS: CAMERA AND TRIPOD

The backbone of any nature photographer's system is the 35mm format single-lens reflex camera. New or used, it really doesn't matter as long as the camera has depth-of-field preview, motor-driven film advance (or high-speed image capture with digital cameras), and can make use of a cable shutter release. Other crucial features (lens interchange and through-the-lens exposure metering, for instance) are standard features on practically any 35mm SLR/DSLR. Depth-of-field preview is necessary for judging picture composition prior to exposure; high-speed film transport gives you the best chance of capturing nature in its multitude of ever changing, always moving configurations; a cable release is often necessary to avoid camera shake during exposure, something that will prevent you from attaining sharp images.

A tripod should be your first additional purchase once you have acquired a basic camera and lens. A tripod is necessary for shooting most subjects in the dramatic but weak light of dawn and dusk when exposure times are too long for you to hold the camera steady. It is also indispensable for attaining sharp images if shooting with telephoto lenses or close-up equipment when even minor movements of the camera during exposure become exaggerated, resulting in blurred pictures. The most suitable tripods have tubular legs (for sturdiness), are tall enough to bring the camera to eye-level with the center column seated, have legs that spread independently for easy setup on uneven terrain, and have clip-lock levers controlling the extension of leg sections (concentric controls get easily jammed by dirt and even water). Ballheads (rather than pan/tilt heads with levers) make the best links between tripod and camera. They are compact, don't get snagged on vegetation, and allow you to lock the camera in any position quickly by tightening a single control. (For more information on tripods see the next chapter.) The camera body and tripod are integral to shooting every type of nature subject. Once you have these two items, you can expand your system according to your special interests and budget.

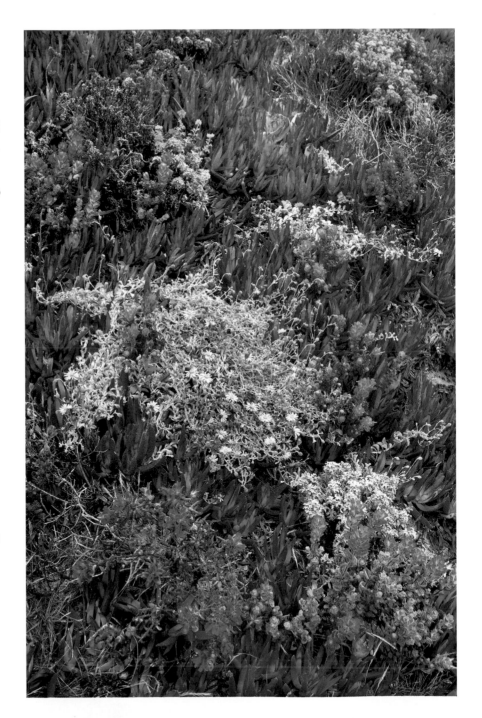

Beach at Jughandle State Reserve, Mendocino Coast, California (below). A telephoto zoom lens allowed precise framing of this scene taken from precipitous terrain where camera positions were restricted.

Elephant seal bulls, Point Piedras Blancas, California (far right). A close-up of these behemoths was made with a 500mm lens and 1.4X teleconverter (effectively 700mm).

Big Lenses for Wildlife

Making professional caliber wildlife images (including birds) requires the biggest financial investment. Wild animals are generally not afraid of photographers, and given the chance, they will tolerate us at close range in areas where hunting is proscribed year-round. Even so, frame-filling pictures of most species are not possible without using a telephoto lens. As a graduate of the high mobility school, I prefer smaller, lighter telephotos in the f/4 to f/5.6 maximum aperture range, specifically a 300mm for large animals and handheld shots of subjects in motion and a 500mm for small and/or wary creatures. The best and most expensive telephoto lenses have glass elements described as ED (extra low dispersion) or APO (apochromatic). The ultimate in supertelephoto lens quality resides in Canon's IS (image stabilizer) lenses which reduce or eliminate camera shake during exposure, producing the most consistently sharp telephoto images of any camera system. If you're interested in one of these, you might want to start thinking about a second mortgage. (For more information on buying and using telephoto lenses see page 32.)

Ideally, your wildlife shooting kit will be rounded out with a 1.4X teleconverter (increases focal length of the prime lens by 1.4) and an extension tube of around 25mm (allows extra-close focusing for songbirds, chipmunks, butteflies and other small creatures).

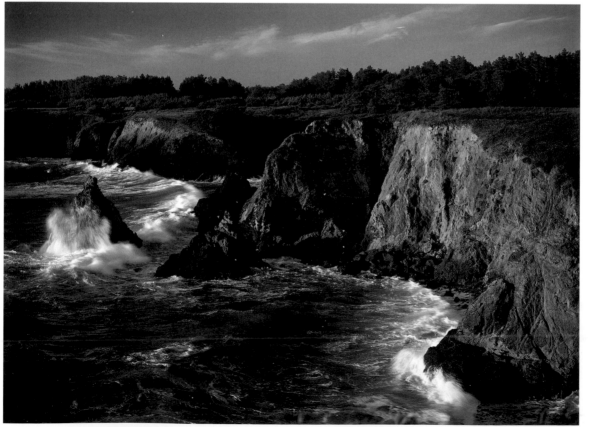

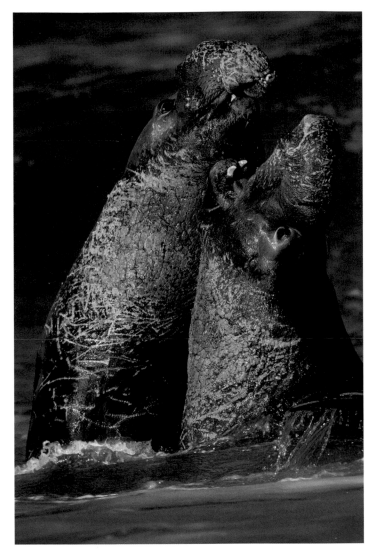

lenses you have, but you will want to cover all of the territory between about 18mm and 200mm with two or three lenses (the fewer the better). For wide-angle focal lengths, lenses with aspherical elements produce the best quality. Internal focusing (IF) lenses provide great convenience when using polarizing and graduated filters which otherwise must be readjusted each time you change focus. It also saves aggravation (and money) if all of your lenses use the same size filters.

You will need two types of filters: First, a screw-on polarizing filter to darken blue skies, modify reflections from water, and eliminate reflections from foliage for increased color saturation; Second, a series of split and graduated neutral density filters to bring the contrast range of the landscape within, or closer to, the contrast range of the film or digital sensor. This is often the only way to achieve good detail and color in both the lightest and darkest parts of the image. Neutral density filters are square and fit into adjustable holders that screw onto the front

To Shoot the Landscape

Here, we are closer to earth in terms of a financial commitment. Zoom lenses are preferred for landscape work because they allow you to precisely magnify the scene for the best composition. It's not important what combination of

Equipment List
(In Order of Purchase)

35mm SLR or DSLR with interchangeable zoom lens (80–200mm approximately)

Tripod with ballhead

Cable shutter release

25mm extension tube

Circular polarizing filter

Modular photo vest

Fold-up reflector (2 sides — silver + white)

Wide-angle to short telephoto zoom lens (24–80mm approximately)

Split neutral density filters (one- and two-stop)

1.4X teleconverter

Ultrawide-angle lens (17–20mm range)

500 or 600mm super- telephoto lens

50mm extension tube

Macro flash and bracket

Extra camera body

California poppies and eriophyllum, Tehachapi Mountains, California (right). This floral tapestry was recorded by a 90mm lens with specialized tilt and shift movements. This feature allowed me to match the plane of sharp focus with that of the most important elements in the composition — the poppy blooms scattered about the meadow. This in turn made possible the use of a brief shutter speed that arrested subject motion and produced a detailed image. Sophisticated equipment, however, does not get exclusive credit for this image (on a calm day a standard lens would have yielded nearly the same result). Skill and experience were needed to recognize, define and accentuate the graphic properties of the setting. Canon T90, Canon 90mm TS lens, Kodachrome 64, 1/350 second at f/8.

of the lens. Two filters of one-stop and two-stop densities are usually sufficient. Cokin produces the most popular and least expensive filters of this type, while Singh-Ray supplies the best quality and the most extensive selection.

INTRIGUED WITH TINY CRITTERS?

Nature's miniature world is home to some of the most beautiful and easily photographed subjects — dew drops, wildflowers, butterflies, spiders. You cannot make frame-filling records of these subjects with standard lenses. You either need to buy special close-up adapters to extend the focus range of your existing optics (least expensive) or buy macro lenses that are specially designed for this type of work (more convenient). Both approaches yield excellent results.

Add-on close-up accessories include screw-on supplementary filters — simple meniscus lenses that work just like magnifying glasses. (Two-element supplementary lenses are recommended for top quality.) These accessories cost little more that a few rolls of film and give you access to the greatest variety of nature subjects for the least amount of money. Extension tubes provide another relatively inexpensive way to get close.

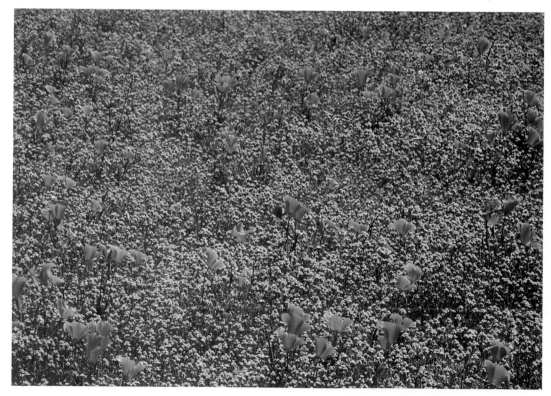

These hollow tubes, available in a variety of stackable sizes, are fitted between the prime lens and camera body. They generally yield better quality images and a greater range of magnification than supplementary lenses. They work best when used with prime lenses of normal to telephoto length.

Fixed focal-length macro lenses focus from infinity to a close-up range

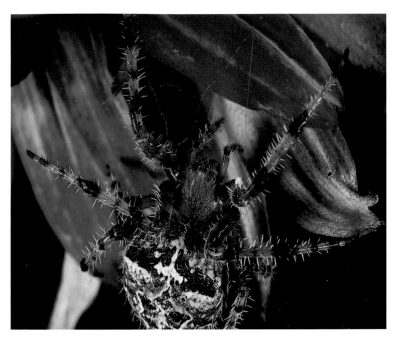

that generally provides enough magnification to take a frame-filling picture of a bumblebee. No need to fiddle with accessories; shoot the landscape on one frame and a butterfly on the next without taking your eye from the viewfinder. Zoom or telephoto lenses with macro capability do not yield this much magnification, being suitable for portraits of animals the size of chipmunks and larger. For animals smaller than a bumblebee, more specialized techniques and equipment are necessary.

Another essential piece of close-up gear is a reflector to modify lighting conditions. A portable, fold-up reflector with one side silver for maximum reflection and the other side white for a more subtle effect, is inexpensive, easy to

carry, and yields professional-looking results. Unlike electronic flash, you can see the effects in the viewfinder before you take the picture. Reflectors made by Flex-fill are popular and widely available. (For more about close-up photography see page 169.)

This is only an outline of the range of equipment you need to photograph the natural world. These suggestions should keep you on track until you get a better feeling for the subject, how you wish to work, and the types of imagery you are interested in producing. Technical marvels that are generally over-engineered and over-designed, modern cameras and lenses are only tools for taking photos of nature's world. Great images will be made by you, not the equipment.

Orb-weaver spider, Santa Fe, New Mexico (left). This little fellow appeared in my bathtub one morning. I transferred it to a daisy plucked from the garden and made the portrait indoors with a handheld camera. The scene was illuminated by the brief light of an electronic flash. Canon EOS Elan 11, Canon 28–105mm lens with 25mm extension tube, 2 electronic flash units with Kleenex tissue diffusers, Fujichrome Provia 100F, 1/60 second at f/22.

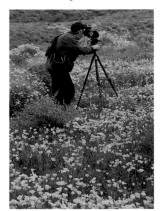

Tripods

The best tripod features for nature photography

American oystercatcher, Little Estero Lagoon, Florida (below). A tripod is essential to steady the super-telephoto lenses used for wary wildlife species. Here I set up the tripod as low as possible, which offered an angle on the bird that threw the background out of focus. Effortless framing was achieved with a gimbal head (Wimberley Sidekick). Canon EOS 3, 500mm f/4 IS Canon lens, Fujichrome Provia 100F, 1/500 second at f/5.6.

RUBY BEACH ON OLYMPIC National Park's Pacific Coast is holy ground for photographers, a remote landscape shrine where the faithful quietly appear on foggy mornings. The tide is out and sheens of sand stretch hundreds of meters to the water's edge and for as far as you can see to the north and south. Big rocks and looming granite stacks are arranged in the sand among mirrored pools, their naked bases adorned by blue mussels in neat ranks and seastars tangled in orgies of pastel color. While fog writhes under

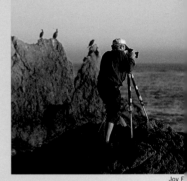

Joy F

the beam of a rising sun, I wander this beach, searching for angles. My tripod goes up for ten minutes at a stretch to fix the camera on each revelation. It is stationed precariously atop a jumble of boulders, next it is half submerged in a tidal pool, then spread low on a slope of mushy sand as I kneel to record pebbles and a gull feather. Many times it is on and off my shoulder, extended, retracted, pulled and prodded, soaked and muddied. After two hours, the wind stirs and the fog retreats, leaving the beach exposed to the sun's glare. I shoulder my gear and begin the climb back up the trail.

For nature photographers, a tripod is nearly as important as a camera and lens. Rarely are top quality images made without one. It is essential for stabilizing telephoto lenses for shooting wildlife and macro lenses for recording insects and wildflowers. For scenic work, a tripod makes possible the long exposures needed to

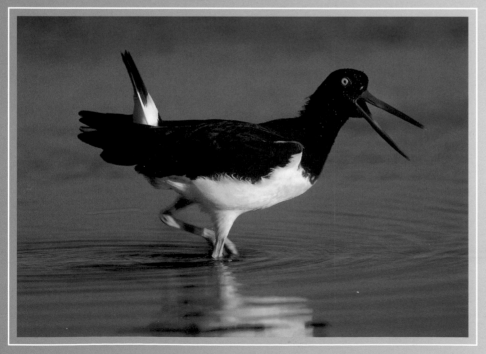

achieve sharp focus throughout the image field. Its controls require repeated adjustment, on the whole nearly as much as camera and lens. To capture nature's fleeting dramas, they must be precise, quick, and sure.

This may be beneficial for macro specialists but for general nature work this is not advisable. A long center column is valuable in landscape work to bring the camera up to eye-level when you are working on a steep slope or perhaps atop a

APPROPRIATE SIZE

When fully extended the tripod with camera mounted should come to eye-level with the center column seated. (Eye-level is about five inches less than your height.) A manufacturer's specifications for tripod height do not include the tripod head which gives about a five-inch boost, nor the position of the camera's viewfinder which adds a further three inches or more. The lower the tripod can be set up the better. Some tripods drop right to ground level when fully spread if the center column is removed.

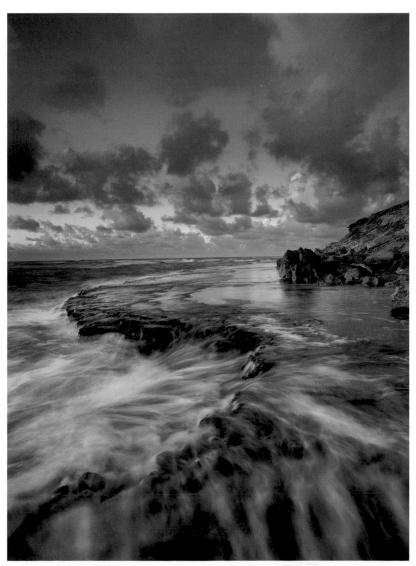

Keoneloa Bay, Kauai, Hawaii (left). To ensure image sharpness a tripod was necessary to steady the camera during this extended sunrise exposure. I was able to set up the tripod quickly and securely on this uneven coral shelf because the legs spread independently, allowing them to be secured on almost any surface no matter how uneven. Salt water causes minimal harm to tripods as long as the working mechanisms and other corrosive parts are kept lubricated. Pentax 645 N11, 33–55mm f/4.5 lens, Singh-Ray circular polarizer, one-stop split neutral density filter (to darken sky), Fujichrome Velvia, two seconds at f/22.

Prickly pear cactus and paint-brush near Luchenbach, Texas (below). To get this ankle-level view of springtime Texas, I used a tripod (Manfrotto Carbon One 441) that permitted me to remove the center column and re-insert it parallel to the ground. Unlike the more standard practice of re-inserting the column upside-down, this method gives ready access to the viewfinder (no squeezing yourself between the legs to take a peak at your subject). Pentax 645 N11, 80–160mm f/4.5 lens, Singh-Ray circular polarizer, Fujichrome Velvia, 1/2 second at f/11.

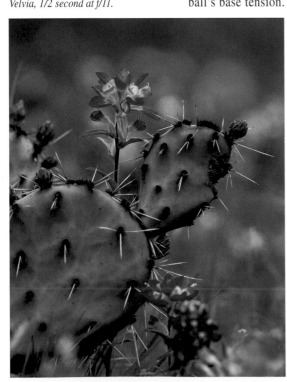

boulder with the tripod set up below you. It's valuable in wildlife shooting to raise the camera position a few inches to avoid a foreground inter-ference such as a twig or leaf. The best center columns are ones that are shorter (eight to nine inches) or ones that can be removed and mounted horizontally on the tripod legs.

TRIPOD HEADS

A compact, fast-working ball-and-socket head with panning capabilities is best for nature pho-tography. The head should have comfortable knobs for both locking the head and setting the ball's base tension. When locked down the head should not creep in response to the camera's weight even when using a heavy lens. There are good ballheads on the market in the $200 to $400 range.

SPECIAL HEADS FOR SUPER-TELEPHOTO LENSES

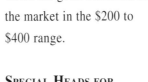

For large and heavy tele-photo lenses, a gimball-type head provides quick, sure, fingertip control of aiming, tracking, and panning (see photo page 30). Such heads are made by Wimberley (www.tripodhead.com) in

two sizes. For lenses 600mm f/4 and larger, the full size Wimberley provides the most stability and best balance, but this head is large and heavy and primarily used by wildlife specialists who do not move around much when shooting. Due to its smaller size and weight, the Wimberley Sidekick is the best choice for those who enjoy working with a variety of subjects. The less expensive Sidekick attaches to a regular ballhead and offers advantages similar to the full-size gimbal head. To work properly, the Sidekick must be mated with a ballhead that has a panning mechanism.

LIGHTNESS MORE IMPORTANT THAN STABILITY

A massive tripod may impart a comforting sense of stability when you first lower a 600mm f/4 into its saddle, but out on the range you will find the big tripod seldom desirable. Both amateurs and professionals get more keepers in the bag and have more fun doing it when they err on the side of lightness. When shooting wildlife, I change positions often in response to the animal's behavior for improved magnification, lighting, background, foreground or subject view — a tiresome exercise even with a light outfit. I usually collapse the tripod and spread the legs a little wider for more stability so that I can shoot from a kneeling position. This provides a desir-able near eye-level view of most species — from wild turkeys to mule deer. When set low, the tripod is less conspicuous, stronger than at

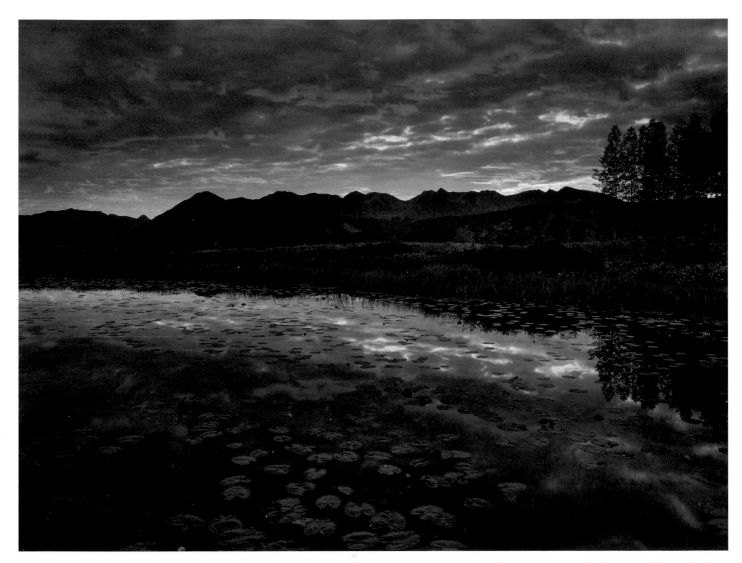

full-extension, and it is also out of the wind. For most landscape and macro subjects, a big, sturdy tripod provides no practical advantage over a small one, except under windy conditions.

The lightest tripods have legs made of carbon fiber. As a bonus this material is stiffer and absorbs vibration better than metal. Such tripods are several times more expensive than metal counterparts, but it is an investment that most nature photographers find worthwhile. A tripod should provide plenty of support if its maximum load limit exceeds the weight of your heaviest

Sunrise on Molas Pass, San Juan Mountains, Colorado (above). *Traveling light with a small, carbon-fiber tripod allows easier access to remote locations. For landscapes, a big heavy tripod serves little purpose.*

Forget Your Beanbag?

Beanbags are the easiest and most solid way of positioning your tripod close to the ground or stablizing a telephoto lens on the hood or roof of your car. Beanbags mold to the shape and angle of the camera to keep it solidly in place. With two gallon-size bags, you can position the camera at ground level up to about eight inches (depending on the size of the camera and lens). You can jerry-rig a beanbag with a shopping stop at most groceries, large or small: You'll need a one-gallon freezer baggy (two if you want to double up for extra strength) and a couple of pounds of dried beans. Sunflower seeds work just as well and they're lighter and great for attracting birds. Add the ballast until the bag is nearly full and still flexible. Squeeze out excess air, zip up and you're ready to start shooting.

Gimbal-type head (below). *The Wimberley Sidekick (contact www.tripodhead.com) is a compact gimball head that attaches to a ballhead for steadying super-telephoto lenses. It allows smooth panning and framing with but a fingertip.*

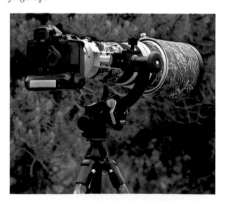

lens/camera combination by five or six pounds. (My 500mm f/4 lens with EOS 3, power booster, Wimberley Sidekick, and ballhead weigh nearly 20 pounds.)

QUICK IS BEST

You will erect your tripod frequently in awkward spots — river banks, boulder fields, bramble patches, sand dunes and beaver ponds — and you will need to make many adjustments before you begin shooting. To complicate matters, many subjects — setting suns, sipping butterflies, bugling elk — are often fleeting and call for quick tripod setups. In this important respect, some tripod features are more desirable than others. Ballheads should have quick-release mechanisms for fast switching of cameras and lenses. Ballhead knobs should be large and comfortable and require little

Tripod Features for Nature Subjects

Camera should come to eye level when tripod is fully extended and center column seated

Quick-release platform for quick mounting of camera

Carbon-fiber construction is lightest, strongest, sturdiest, warmest but also costliest

Ball-and-socket head for quick, one-hand adjustment

Collar that allows lateral insertion of center column

Three-step, push-button leg-spread controls are most convenient

Standard (non-concentric) control knob for tightening center column

Center column should be about nine inches long

Clip-lock, three-section legs (not more) for quick set-up

Legs should spread independently (no center braces) for versatile set-up on uneven terrain

Inconspicuous dark or camouflage finish

Tripod should collapse as low as possible to access ground-level subjects

Tripod should support the heaviest lens/camera combination plus about five pounds

Tripod shown: Manfrotto 441 with Kirk ballhead BH1 (not strong enough for super-telephotos)

effort to lock and unlock. Three-section tripod legs afford faster adjustment of height than four-section ones, which are normally only advantageous when small collapsed size is important (e.g. backpacking, carry-on luggage). The legs should spread independently (no central struts). The leg-length locking mechanisms should ideally be clips that snap open and shut rather than concentric twist rings. The fastest leg spread controls are three-position, spring-loaded, push buttons. The center column lock should be a simple knob rather than a concentric ring (a drawback of Gitzo tripods).

INCONSPICUOUS COMFORT?

Most photographers carry the tripod with camera and lens attached over their shoulders when moving between locations. If you work from a bag, the weight of the tripod on your shoulder soon becomes uncomfortable. Metal tripods also are cold to handle when the mercury drops. Both problems can be eliminated by attaching a set of camouflaged Tri-pads (see www.rue.com/tripods.html) to the upper leg sections. I make my own with a length of foam pipe insulation (available in hardware stores) and a roll of fabric camouflage tape (often available at

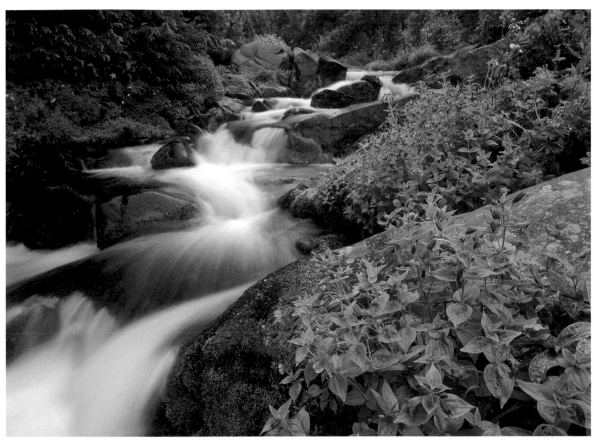

Wal-Mart). Camouflage material hides you from wary subjects and passersby whose curiosity may interrupt concentration, frighten the subject, or cause a traffic jam if you are working roadside.

Careful consideration of your shooting style and subject interests will lead you to selecting an appropriate combination of tripod features, size and price. Visit camera stores to try out various models before making a decision. Your choice of tripod is usually just as important as your selection of a camera.

Paradise River, Mount Rainier National Park, Washington (above). On breezy days tripods are a boon when photographing scenes with vegetation. You can establish the shot and then bide your time between periods of calm while the tripod holds your set-up in place.

Super-telephoto Lenses

Ideal features of the most useful (and expensive) lenses for wildlife

Yellow-headed blackbird, Stone Lake, New Mexico (below). This springtime crooner was photographed with a 500mm lens and 1.4X teleconverter from a floating blind at a distance of about 15 feet. For small subjects a teleconverter is often added to a super telephoto lens to achieve adequate magnification.

IN THIS CHAPTER YOU'LL find out what I think is important in a super-telephoto lens, the big gun in the wildlife photographer's arsenal. The howitzer you now own or are thinking of buying may not have all the features I describe below, but the more the better.

HOW LONG?

Anything shorter than 500mm is too short and anything longer than 600mm is too long. Both focal lengths have plenty of reach and work well with 1.4X and 2X teleconverters. A 500mm f/4 is about four or five pounds lighter than a comparable 600mm and so affords more mobility and less fatigue. It's usually about 25 percent less expensive than its big brother, maximum apertures being equal. The 600mm has greater reach, which comes in handy for small and/or skittish subjects. However, it's not unusual to find yourself over-magnified with either focal length. If you're restless and puny (like me) and like to get off the beaten path, then the 500mm is your focal length. If you can crush lens barrels on your forehead, are enamored with tight framing, and have the patience to remain still until the subject strikes the right pose or wanders into the right light, then get the 600mm. Some of these lenses cost thousands of dollars, even if purchased second-hand. You can save a lot by

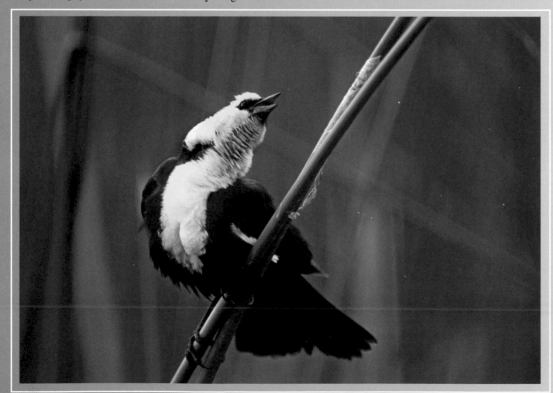

combining a 300mm or 400mm lens with 1.4X and 2X teleconverters but image quality will be compromised at comparable magnifications. The reduction in light transmission caused by the teleconverters will limit your choice of film and your ability to shoot in the weak but attractive light of early morning and late afternoon.

What About Zooms?

Variable-aperture zoom lenses reaching into the super-telephoto range are becoming more common. Unfortunately, the long end of the range, which is most useful for wildlife photography, usually delivers the poorest quality image at the smallest aperture. Nevertheless, these lenses certainly can be used to make professional quality pictures. The addition of a teleconverter, however, so serviceable with prime focal lengths, introduces both a decline in image quality (about ten percent with a 1.4X and twenty percent with a 2X) and a reduction in maximum aperture.

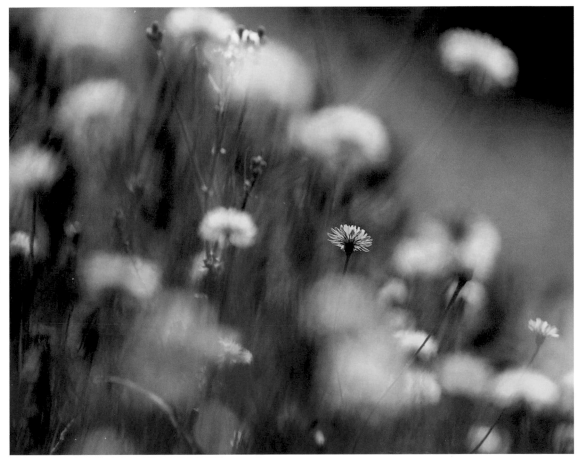

What Brand?

If you are starting from scratch, or are willing to lose more on trading in your equipment than you have on your NASDAQ stock portfolio, then Canon is far and away the brand of choice in the super-telephoto field. Other manufacturers (Nikon, Pentax, Minolta, Leica) make super-telephotos of comparable optical quality but few match the speed of Canon's auto-focusing system and none offer comparable (if any) image

Sow-thistle, Chuckanut Bay, Washington (above). Super telephotos are not just for wildlife subjects. They are great special effects tools for compressing landscape views, isolating water patterns at seaside, or creating abstract impressions of wildflower meadows, as shown here. In this image I shot at maximum aperture for the least depth of field in order to blur all of the blossoms except one.

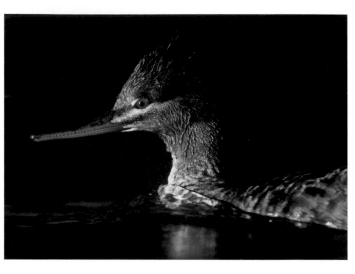

Red-breasted merganser, Esquimalt Lagoon, Vancouver Island (right). *The development of professional quality digital sensors and high-speed film has reduced the need for a telephoto lens with a maximum aperture greater than f/5.6. These slower lenses are not only less expensive but they are also more enjoyable to use. Being smaller and lighter, they allow you to operate in the field more productively with greater ease. The drawback is that auto-focus is usually lost when using teleconverters — in practice a worthwhile trade-off. I approached this speedy swimmer with a relatively light 500mm f/4.5 lens and 1.4X teleconverter mounted on the deck of a floating blind.*

Joy Fitzharris

stabilization or DOE (diffraction optical element) technology, both of which are valuable to wildlife photographers and are discussed later in the chapter. If you are using a non-Canon system, don't despair, your plight is shared by legions of renowned professionals who take fabulous pictures despite the hardware handicap.

How Fast?

Lens speed (i.e. maximum aperture) isn't as important as it was a few years ago thanks to the development of fine-grained films such as Fujichrome Provia 100F, an ISO 100 jackrabbit that sprints to ISO 200 and even ISO 400 without breathing heavily. Unpushed, this film delivers sunny early morning and late afternoon shutter speeds of 1/250 and 1/500 second at f/5.6 — exposure times adequate to freeze the movement of most wildlife subjects as well as put the brakes on camera-shakes. Super-telephoto apertures of f/4 and larger deliver faster automatic focusing and/or automatic focusing with teleconverters mounted, two advantages which are occasionally worth the extra glass.

How Close?

The closer your telephoto focuses, the easier it is to make frame-filling studies of puffins, hummingbirds, chipmunks, prairie dogs, fox pups, and many other fascinating subjects. Don't take this characteristic for granted, as many big lenses cannot record subjects of this size without adding an extension tube. In itself this is not a difficult procedure, but a tube reduces the amount of light reaching the film (which may compromise shutter speed choice), it may not link fully with the camera's auto-focus system, and it restricts focusing range to close-up subjects. So, as often as not, you keep the tube in your pocket until you get close enough to actually need it. The problem is I can never remember which pocket I put the thing in (Gosh, the sandpiper is looking right at me now!) and when I finally get the camera body released (Uh oh, he's flexing his wings!) and I'm ready to lock on the tube (Hurry it up, will ya!), the front-heavy lens teeters over in a slow-motion swan dive as the subject takes wing (Drat!). Your super-telephoto should focus close enough to just about fill the vertical frame with a human face including ears. If it doesn't do this you're in for some aggravation in the field.

PRECIOUS GLASS

Super-telephoto focal lengths are prone to chromatic aberration — a blurring of the color spectrum which degrades image quality. Optical engineers correct this problem at some expense with the use of special low-dispersion (apochromatic) glass. It is given various names depending on the manufacturer: APO, LD, UD and ED are all indications that the lens will produce professional caliber imagery. Canon's recent development of diffractive optical elements (designated by DO) not only eliminates chromatic aberration but results in lenses that are three-quarters the size and two-thirds the weight of conventional models.

STEADY YOURSELF

Image stabilization (IS) reduces camera/lens movement and vibration (including that generated by the reflex mirror) during exposure, resulting in an effective increase in shutter speed of two to three stops. (At present Canon is the only manufacturer offering super-telephoto lenses with this feature.) IS effectively turns your 600mm f/4 into a super-fast 600mm f/2 without losing any depth of field. I routinely get excellent results with a hands-on, tripod-mounted 500mm at the following speeds: 1/30 second with prime lens only, 1/60 second with 1.4X teleconverter and 1/125 second with the 2X teleconverter. I don't hesitate to shoot at even slower speeds under weak light. Other professionals report similar, if not better, results. Of

Hippopotamus, Mara River, Kenya (below). *Image stabilization (IS) or vibration reduction (VR) telephoto lenses permit you to make sharp images at shutter speeds two to three stops slower than with conventional optics. This is great in low-light situations when tight framing of a moving subject, such as this hippo, makes it necessary to keep your hands on the camera for framing and triggering.*

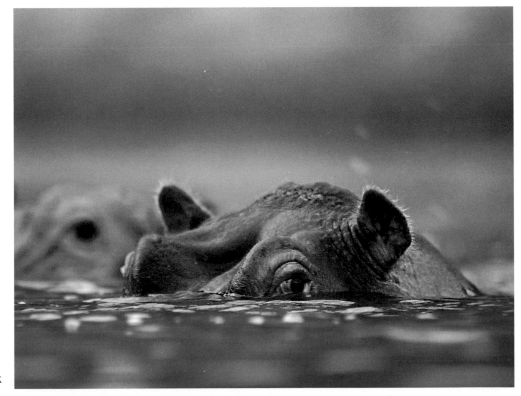

Elephant seals, Big Sur Coast, California (below). These bulls offered an ideal situation for auto-focus — contrasty subjects moving not too fast for the system to track and no intervening foliage to confuse the sensors.

course, these shutter speeds have no value in freezing action, but by reducing camera shake they significantly extend the shooting period for static subjects at the beginning and end of each day, peak times for both wildlife activity and beautiful light. Moreover, IS generally improves the sharpness of super-telephoto images taken at even higher speeds.

AUTO-FOCUS

Sometimes it works, sometimes it doesn't. Fortunately, you can turn off auto-focus in situations

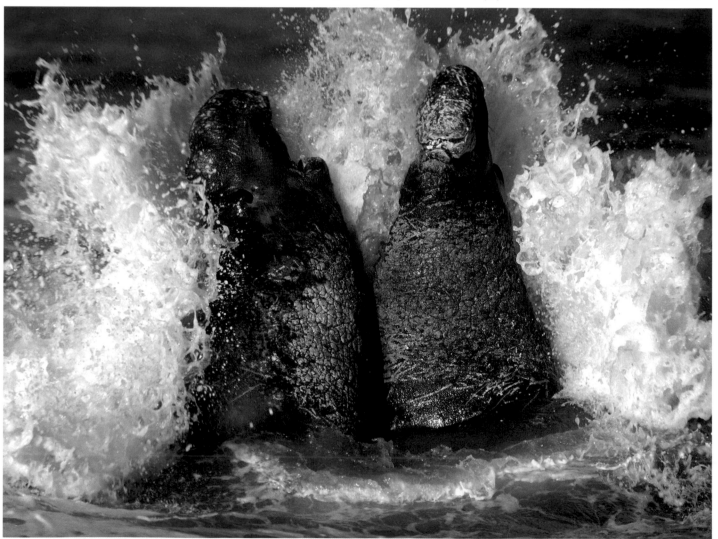

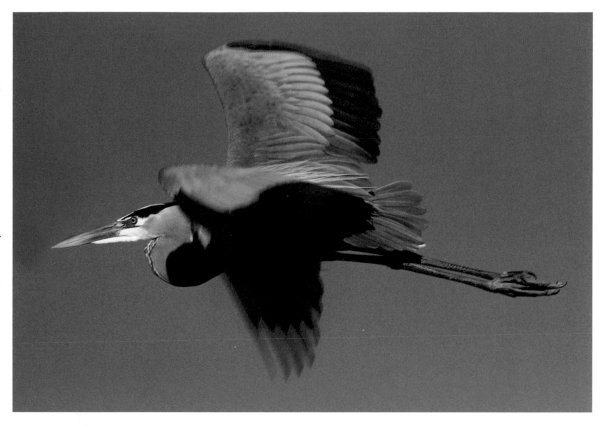

where it isn't working well and leave it on in others. However, for the switchover to work most effectively in the field, the auto-focus system must offer permanent, instantaneous, manual override. No searching for a niggly button when the sensor refuses to lock onto the subject or isn't discriminating enough to sharpen-up moose's eye, just start twisting the focus ring.

Lens Color

Black super-telephotos are classy and white ones are intended to reflect heat but neither paint job is suitable for nature work. As you would expect, camouflage is the lens finish of choice for nature photographers. Camouflage makes you marginally less conspicuous when homing in on wary subjects, but its value doesn't end here. This froggy dressing prevents curious bystanders from spotting your industrial-strength optic and wandering over to find out what all the fuss is about; the fuss they make scares off your rabbit or groundhog. Cover your lens with camouflage tape (available in gun shops and sporting goods stores — get the fabric kind). Not willing to gunk up your lens with gooey tape? Canon 600mm and 500mm investors can order custom-fit, Neoprene skins from www.birdsasart.com.

Shoot in All Kinds of Weather

Water-resistant super-telephoto lenses and cameras (professional models made by Canon) now allow you to shoot during persistent periods of precipitation without bringing out a pesky parasol or protective plastic.

Great blue heron, Venice Rookery, Florida (above). This slow-flying giant was recorded with a tripod-mounted 500mm lens and 1.4X teleconverter. I activated the central focusing sensor only for fastest auto-focus response. Smooth tracking of the heavy lens was made easy with a gimbal head (Wimberley Sidekick) added to the standard Kirk BH1 ballhead.

Working in the Field

Managing your equipment in the field for more enjoyment and greater productivity

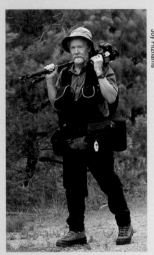

The Wave at Coyote Buttes, Vermillion Cliffs Wilderness, Arizona (below). A seven-mile hike is the only way to access these formations. The route traverses rugged terrain with photo opportunities the whole route. Using the "full-nelson" to carry your tripod is a comfortable way to make good time yet stop occasionally to shoot.

FOR ABOUT SIX MONTHS each year I'm in the field shooting. I expose on average five rolls of 220 film per day when shooting scenic and/or macro subjects. If I am photographing wildlife in 35mm format I go through double this amount of film. Weather and travel permitting, I photograph at sunset and sunrise without fail. I take down and set up my tripod and change lenses thousands of times. I go through half a pint of lens cleaner and about 20 yards of duct or gaffer tape every year. I drive thousands of miles, mostly on back roads and state highways, and hike hundreds more through forests, along beaches, and up mountain sides. If this seems like a lot of work, it isn't. After three decades, I still think of my shooting trips as vacation time filled with stimulating activities and sometimes great adventures. Described here are the bones of a system that I use for managing my equipment in the field. It's premised on making the greatest number of professional quality photos in the least amount of time with the greatest ease. This chapter deals with landscape and other general concerns (for wildlife tips, see Part Four).

EASIER TRIPOD TRIPPING

When on the trail I carry my tripod (with camera mounted) over my shoulder so that I am ready to shoot in but a few seconds.

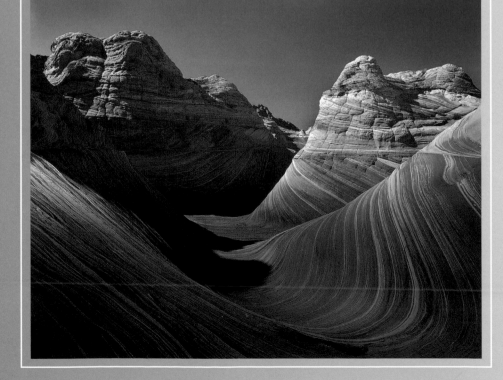

Unfortunately on a hike longer than a mile or so, the weight bearing down on one shoulder creates a strain or your spine, hips and side even if you shift the burden periodically from shoulder to shoulder. In such situations you need to apply the *tripod full nelson* to your opponent. This deft move entails grasping your assailant by the throat (either the tripod head or the camera's lens or grip) and one leg (let the other two legs flop open a little) and swing the culprit up over the shoulders in one smooth motion. This centers the weight on your spine and even provides some rest for your arms. It works better when the camera is affixed with a small lens but larger telephotos can also be hoisted in this fashion.

INVEST IN A VEST

For years I worked from shoulder bags and backpacks. The shoulder bags were difficult to carry for long distances and the backpacks kept my equipment so inaccessible that I often found myself passing up photo ops to avoid aggravation. When photographing, I often wandered so far from my bag that I couldn't find it without a systematic search. At the end of a fast-paced shooting session, my pack would be a mess with little of the equipment remaining in the carefully organized compartments. Everything would have to be tidied and put away before I could close up

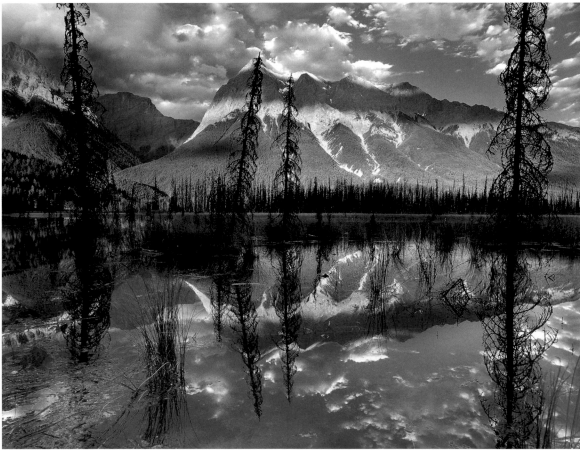

Yoho National Park (above). To achieve this arrangement of tree silhouettes I had to wade into the lake beyond the fringing shore vegetation. By carrying my equipment in a vest, I had everything at my fingertips for quick access. *Pentax 645, 45–85mm f/4.5 lens, one-stop split neutral density filter, Fujichrome Velvia, one second at f/22.*

Sunset at Bean Hollow Beach, California (below). *In situations like this, where contrast levels are difficult to judge, you want to be able to swap filters rapidly. Keeping filters organized in fumble-free pouches and cases (see photos on page 45) will boost productivity and reduce anxiety while working. Here, I slotted in a two-stop, hard-edge split neutral density filter to hold back sky density in this one second exposure.*

and move on to a new site, wasting energy and valuable shooting time. This was especially vexing if nice lighting conditions were fleeting.

When I started using a vest about six years ago, all these problems disappeared and my work became more productive and enjoyable. It seemed like I had grown extra hands and hired an assistant. Many photographers use lightweight cloth vests which are better than bags but don't protect your equipment adequately, especially during travel. My vest preference is the Lowepro Street and Field model which is built of material

similar to a regular bag or backpack and the only vest I know of that offers nearly the same degree of protection. Tamrac makes a modular belt system (as does Lowepro) which is great for carrying less than a full complement of equipment.

The Lowepro system consists of a vest harness to which you can quickly attach and arrange a variety of pouches, compartments, and lens cases to suit your particular shooting and equipment situation. Each module is made of dense, closed-cell foam covered inside and out in durable rain-shedding nylon. Unfortunately some modification is required to get the most out of the system. The pouch lids are designed with both a drawstring and a plastic squeeze-clip. Neither are easy to open or close when you need to work fast and change lenses often. To speed things up I cut off both with scissors and replace them with strips of Velcro — not as secure but generally adequate and a breeze to use. To the vest harness you should attach Lowe-pro's deluxe padded waist belt which also holds several pouches. This allows

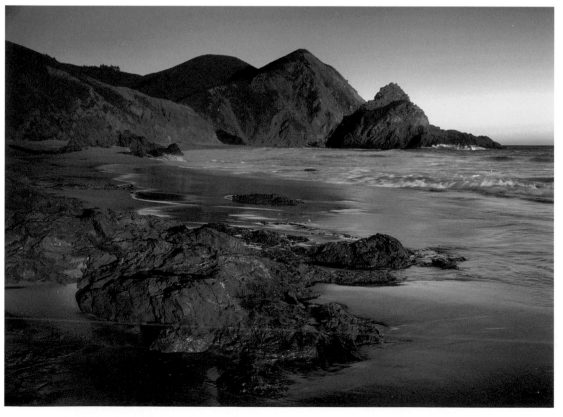

your hips to take on a lot of the load (just like with a backpack) saving strain on the back and shoulders during long hikes. Get pouches (not lens cases) that are the same size to fit the largest lens (telephoto zoom) you intend to carry in the vest. When you take a lens off the camera it can go right into the pouch of the lens you are exchanging. Using this system keeps everything in the right place and close at hand. It allows you to move about freely and readily access equipment on any terrain including marshes, swamps, lakes and ocean beaches. When you get

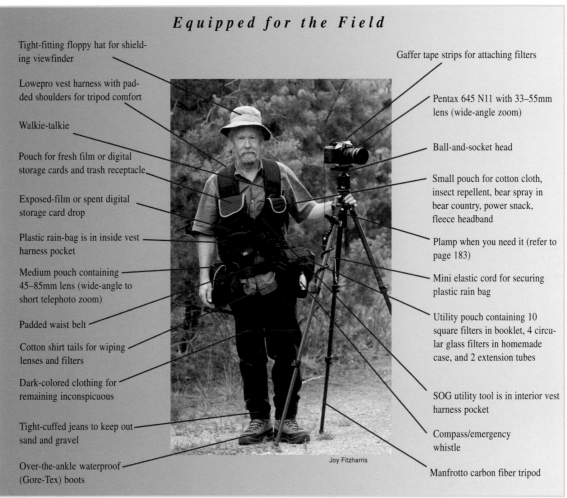

Equipped for the Field

Tight-fitting floppy hat for shielding viewfinder

Lowepro vest harness with padded shoulders for tripod comfort

Walkie-talkie

Pouch for fresh film or digital storage cards and trash receptacle

Exposed-film or spent digital storage card drop

Plastic rain-bag is in inside vest harness pocket

Medium pouch containing 45–85mm lens (wide-angle to short telephoto zoom)

Padded waist belt

Cotton shirt tails for wiping lenses and filters

Dark-colored clothing for remaining inconspicuous

Tight-cuffed jeans to keep out sand and gravel

Over-the-ankle waterproof (Gore-Tex) boots

Gaffer tape strips for attaching filters

Pentax 645 N11 with 33–55mm lens (wide-angle zoom)

Ball-and-socket head

Small pouch for cotton cloth, insect repellent, bear spray in bear country, power snack, fleece headband

Plamp when you need it (refer to page 183)

Mini elastic cord for securing plastic rain bag

Utility pouch containing 10 square filters in booklet, 4 circular glass filters in homemade case, and 2 extension tubes

SOG utility tool is in interior vest harness pocket

Compass/emergency whistle

Manfrotto carbon fiber tripod

Joy Fitzharris

back to the car, there's no need to repack equipment as you would with a cloth vest, simply lay the entire contraption in the trunk or on the seat. If flying, you can stuff your loaded vest into a carry-on bag or pack it in a suitcase to be checked.

Using a Lowepro vest harness is not cheap — my landscape outfit (I have a separate one for wildlife) costs about the same as an entry level SLR. For more information go to the website www.lowepro.com.

Film Drop

Lowepro offers a handy pouch (with one teensy snag) for storing exposed film while you are out shooting. It has a secure one-way slot at the top

Tape to the rescue (top right).
I store a supply of gaffer or duct
tape strips, used for attaching
square filters to the lens, right on
my camera for fast access. I use
hockey tape to secure a cable
release cord to buffer the plug
and socket against accidental
damage. To save time I keep the
release permanently attached to
my landscape/macro camera.

Easy rain protection (bottom
right). This rain-guard system is
so small and light that I forget I
have it until it starts to sprinkle.
The plastic bag goes over the
camera and is snugged up with a
small elastic cord permanently
attached to a tripod leg.

through which you quickly push the cassettes.
This pouch also has a side zipper which you are
supposed to use to extract shot film and it's only
a matter of time until you forget to re-zip, resulting in cassettes dropping in your wake as film
goes in one end of the pouch and out the other.
After losing a few rolls this way I sewed the zipper closed (you could also use glue). Now I pull
the films back out through the top — about as
easy as fooling with the zipper — and all my
hard-earned shots stay in the vault.

DUCT AND GAFFER TAPE

I haven't used a standard filter holder in seven
years. Instead I rely on one-inch pieces of duct or
gaffer tape to attach rectangular filters to the
front of the lens.
Each piece of tape
lasts for several
shooting sessions.
With duct tape you
sidestep the prob-
lem of vignetting,
common with filter
holders. You can
attach as many fil-
ters as you want
and each can be
angled separately
over the scene,
something impos-

sible to do with
the Cokin holder.
I keep a bunch of
tapes (with one
edge folded over
for easy grab-
bing) stuck to
both camera and
tripod.

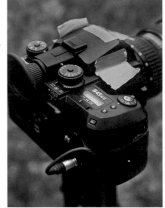

FUMBLE-PROOF FILTER FILES

I regularly use
eight different
rectangular/
square filters
(most are split
neutral density).
Keeping these or-
ganized and
accessible when
balanced atop a

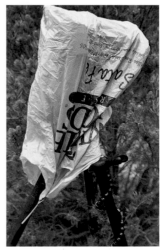

rock or standing waist-deep in a cattail swamp is
easily accomplished with the help of a CD case.
These cases (normally sold anywhere CDs are
sold) are small, zippered booklets with page slots
perfect for holding filters (see photo page 45).
You just flip though the booklet until you come
to the filter you want. The best one I've found
was purchased in the automotive department of
Wal-mart. It holds ten filters and the page slots

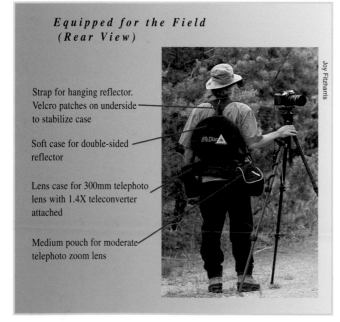

Equipped for the Field (Rear View)

Joy Fitzharris

Strap for hanging reflector.
Velcro patches on underside
to stabilize case

Soft case for double-sided
reflector

Lens case for 300mm telephoto
lens with 1.4X teleconverter
attached

Medium pouch for moderate
telephoto zoom lens

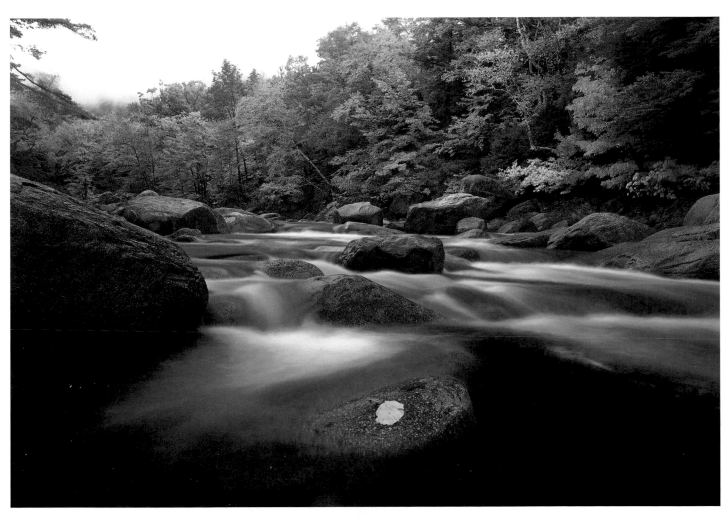

are stiff and cloth-covered for protection and fast, smooth access.

For circular glass filters I have an equally nifty storage system. I take the leather pouches that come with my filters (Singh-Ray brand), cut about one-third off the top of each case (this eliminates the flap), and then loosely tape four of them together (with duct tape). Thus I have a compact case with four, fast-access, snug, well-padded slots for filters (see photo page 45).

REFLECTOR ACCESSOR

I use a double-sided (40-inch silver/white) Photoflex brand reflector for adding fill-light to macro subjects (normally with the white side) and occasionally for brightening the foreground

Swift River, White Mountains National Forest, New Hampshire (below). Wet foliage and overcast light are great for color saturation but make sure you take precautions to keep your equipment dry and out of the water. I shot this solitary leaf from mid-stream between showers wearing chest waders and a vest.

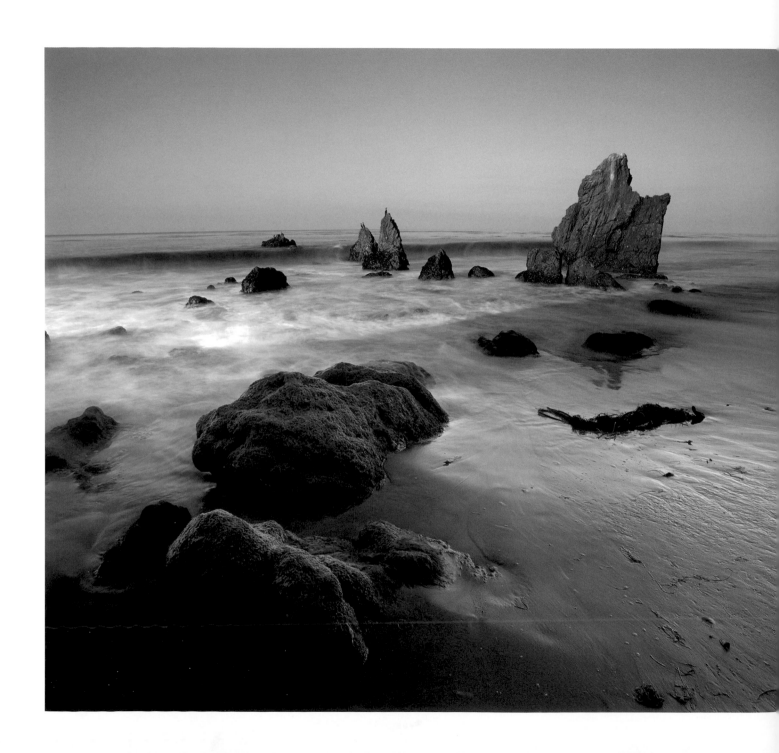

of landscapes (either side depending on conditions). I keep the reflector in its original nylon case on my back hanging by its strap from my vest harness (Velcro patches keep it in place — see photo page 42). When needed I reach over my shoulder and pull the case around to the front to get at the reflector. When I'm done I replace it in the same way (the Velcro grabs the case when I swing it back). This system usually works without a hitch. If the wind is blowing the case will come loose and flop about. On blustery days, I leave the reflector behind.

PLAMP ON HAND

The Plamp (see photo page 41) is used to stabilize wind-jostled plants in order to take the blur out of wildflower shots. When in wildflower country during spring and summer, I keep one of these lightweight, snaky gizmos wrapped around a tripod leg. You never know when you might run into an irresistible blossom.

WHEN IT STARTS TO RAIN

I normally don't try shooting in the rain unless I have someone to stand beside me and hold an umbrella. Otherwise, I fix some temporary protection over my equipment (most all SLR cameras and lenses have zero tolerance for moisture) and make for a sheltered spot to await better conditions. I keep a regular plastic grocery bag (the flimsy kind with handle loops) stuffed into a small pocket in my vest. When rain falls, I slip the bag over the camera mounted on the tripod (the rest of my equipment is protected in the vest) and speedily secure it with a mini elastic bungee cord that is permanently taped to a tripod leg (see photo page 41).

COMMUNICATION ELATION

If you shoot alone it's a wise precaution to have a cell phone with you in case you get into trouble, especially if you are shooting near the ocean or cliffs. If you work with a partner, walkie-talkies generally help to coordinate activities or keep you in touch should you choose to split up to cover more territory. On my shooting junkets I travel in a motorhome with my wife and children. When on the trail I carry a small Motorola radio (five-mile range is best) to tap into home base. Most of the time I use it to alert my wife that I'll be back soon and that I'm really hungry, but it regularly comes into more important use. For example, sometimes I return from a shoot when it's already dark. If I'm bushwhacking, it's easy to get off course (or completely lost). In such cases I ask someone to beep the RV horn so that I can home in on the sound. You'll find all kinds of handy uses for a radio in your own situation. You can buy a single, ultra-compact five-mile range radio for about the price of half a dozen rolls of film.

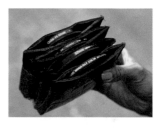

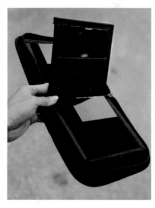

Filter storage (top and above). These pouches offer an effective and inexpensive way to store filters. Your own system should offer the twin benefits of protection and fast access.

El Matador Beach, Malibu, California (far left). Quick access to numerous filters allowed me to try several combinations while waiting for the sun to appear on the eastern horizon. Pentax 645 N11, 33–55mm f/4.5 lens, one-stop split neutral density filter, Singh-Ray circular polarizer with color intensifier, Fujichrome Velvia, two seconds at f/22.

Winter Photography

Preparing yourself, your equipment and your mind for the special challenges of cold weather

Mountain lion (below). Snow is a natural reflector, bouncing light into shadow areas to reduce contrast for better color saturation and detail. The portrait of this born-in-captivity subject was made from a kneeling position with a lowered tripod to achieve intimate eye-level framing. Waterproof, sturdy outer pants will keep you warm and dry during ground-level shooting sessions.

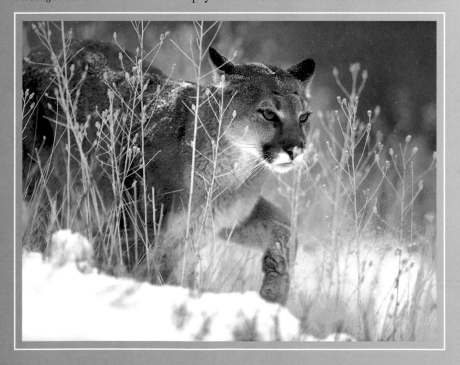

THE WINTER SEASON CALLS for modifications to how you dress, how you handle your equipment, and how you approach the picture making process itself.

Staying comfortable during an outdoor sub-freezing shooting session is as much a matter of remaining cool as it is keeping warm, made difficult due to the changing activity level of the process. For a few minutes we may be hiking up a hill or plowing through deep snow. Then all physical exertion ceases as we consider the scene that confronts us. One minute we may be hot and sweating, the next we're clammy and shivering.

WINTERIZING YOUR BODY

To remain comfortable, you first need to be dressed so that you can regulate easily the escape of body heat. Second, you must anticipate activity levels in order to make timely adjustments to your clothing. These suggestions work well for sessions lasting up to half a day in very cold temperatures below zero degrees Fahrenheit. When it's not quite so cold, reduce the weight and number of undergarments. If you are new at this, start cautiously (cold weather can kill you) with excursions lasting about an hour until you become familiar with your personal needs.

ZIPPERS NOT LAYERS

Dressing in layers is a familiar practice for anyone accustomed to working or playing outdoors. Primarily, you insulate yourself to cope with the worst of anticipated weather conditions. Should you become too warm, you can take off a garment or two; when you get cold, you do the reverse. To be avoided is overheating to the point of perspiring which, in addition to being uncomfortable, causes rapid heat loss by both convection and evaporation. This approach works for hikers and backpackers, but it isn't very practical for nature photographers. Already burdened with equipment, we need to keep our load clear of extraneous garments and our hands free to deal with numerous shooting tasks. Instead of layers that can be taken off and put on, we need layered, stay-put garments that can be vented efficiently and easily. This means clothes with big, strategically located zippers.

OUTER SHELL

The front line in your defense against winter should be a loose-fitting, non-insulated, wind-breaking and water-shedding, breathable parka (Gore-Tex or a similarly performing fabric is recommended). It should have a two-way front zipper (one that can be zipped down from the top and up from the bottom). The top zipper should zip up and over your chin like a turtle neck. The parka's skirt should cover your bum. Zippers under the armpits are valuable for quickly venting heat from

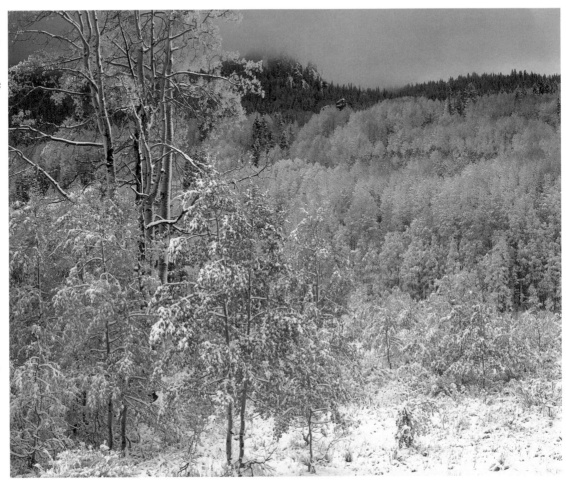

this area. A hood with an elastic drawstring is especially valuable. Velcro closures for zipper flaps and cuff straps are preferable to snaps, which clog with snow.

PANTS

Much of your shooting, be it wildlife, macro subjects, or landscapes, will be done at low level while you are kneeling on snow or ice. You need

Aspen parkland, Gunnison National Forest, Colorado (above).
Although the bold palette of warmer seasons may be absent during winter, colors appear vibrant when set against the whiteness of fresh snow. Your best opportunity to capture this magic is first thing in the morning when the atmosphere is still, light is soft, and the snow has not been affected by the sun.

sturdy, water-shedding, lightly insulated pants with reinforced knees and elastic cuffs (ski or snowboarding trousers are often perfect). The pants should have a suspendered bib front and back to prevent heat loss around your waist and lower back. There should be a front zipper extending from crotch to chest and a zipper along the outside of each leg, preferably to above the knee. To eliminate the need for gators, the pant legs should have stout elastic loops on the cuffs that go under your boots to keep the pants from riding up in deep snow. (You may have to add this feature yourself.)

Head Gear

As seventy percent of heat is lost through the head, this area is the master valve for temperature control and you should give due consideration to how you insulate it. Many extreme weather veterans recommend a balaclava, a hood that completely covers the head, with eye and mouth openings. These are fine for windy subzero temperatures but I find them ticklish and not very temperature versatile in less extreme conditions. I prefer a tailored, polypropylene fleece-lined Gore-Tex hat with velcro chin straps, insulated ear flaps (which can go up and down as needed), and a flexible bill (for shading the viewfinder). When it's extremely cold or windy I lower the flaps, raise the hood, and zip-up the inner turtleneck and outer parka to cover chin and mouth. This funnels warm, exhaled breath up and over my nose to prevent frost bite to this sensitive appendage. If it's not too cold I wear a baseball cap with a headband that I let dangle about my neck or install over the cap and around my ears when more protection is needed.

Bison bull, Waterton Lakes National Park, Alberta (below). *Frosty temperatures give added interest to wildlife subjects, decorating fur and feathers with white and silver accents. It's usually best to base exposure readings on a close-up reading of an average subject.*

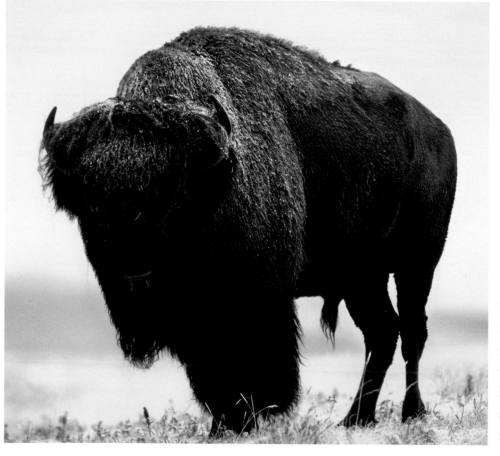

FOOT GEAR

If you keep your head warm, you won't have much of a problem with your feet. Ideal boots rise over the ankle and are made of breathable, waterproof, insulated Nubuck leather (or similar performing material), waterproof Gore-Tex liners and Vibram soles. Usually one pair of heavy wool or moisture-wicking polypropylene fleece socks will provide ample insulation, provided your boots are not tight-fitting.

OTHER ESSENTIALS

A full suit of moisture-wicking long underwear (Capilene or similar material) is necessary for warmth and to draw sweat away from your body. Over this I normally wear a regular wool or silk shirt with pockets for stowing my wallet and personal items, then a zippered sweater or jersey (wool or polar fleece of varying weight depending on weather conditions) with a turtleneck collar, next my bib overalls, then the outer parka shell. There are numerous websites where you can buy and find out more about outdoor expedition-quality apparel. One of my favorites is www.rei.com.

WARM HANDS/NIMBLE SHOOTING

Although commonly recommended, I don't find silk glove liners or gloves with the finger tips removed either warm or dexterous. The best way to keep your hands and fingers skipping nimbly about the camera controls, even in extreme conditions, it to use abbreviated idiot strings on a heavy pair of mittens or gloves (polar fleece-lined, Gore-Tex with traction palms). You simply work the camera bare-handed, slipping your paws back into the gloves (which dangle conveniently from your wrists) whenever they need a warm-up. The attachments should be kept as short as possible (affix the cuffs of your gloves directly to the cuffs of your parka with double-sided Velcro tabs). This enables you to curl up

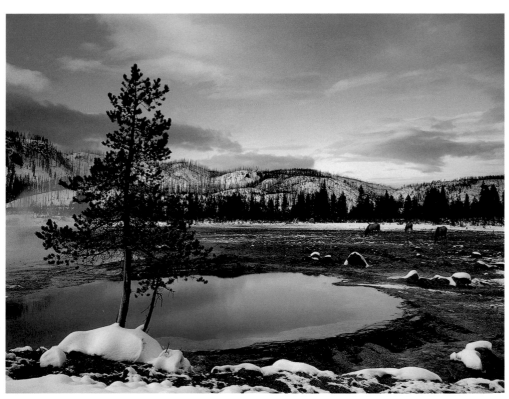

Elk at Saphire Pool, Yellowstone National Park, Wyoming (above). *In midwinter, "magic light" shooting periods can last nearly the day long. Battery exhaustion happens quickly in cold temperatures. For uninterrupted shooting carry an extra set of batteries in an insulated inner pocket to be switched in and out as needed. For this photo I used a one-stop, split neutral density filter to hold the rich color of the sky in this softly illuminated afternoon scene.*

Snowy aspens near Gothic, Colorado (below). Graphic patterns abound in forested regions after an overnight snowfall. Isolate the strongest part of the design (here the branches) with a telephoto zoom lens. Soft light from overcast skies combined with natural fill light from reflected snow lends painterly effects to most winter subjects. Pentax 645, 80–160mm f/4.5 lens, Fujichrome Velvia, 1/4 second at f/22.

your fingers and squirm your hand into the glove unassisted. For extreme temperatures keep small chemical hand-warming packets in your gloves. (When the mercury falls you can put these in your boots, too.) These packets are inexpensive, widely available and last all day.

ANTICIPATE THERMAL CHANGES

Operating this multi-zippered, ready-vented garment system is simple. If you are working behind the camera with little physical exertion, you likely will have most or all of your zippers and flaps closed, depending on ambient temperatures. When you need to move from one shooting location to another, open zipper vents *before* you begin your hike. Then, when you start to feel cool, make minor adjustments as you go along depending on internal heat buildup and weather conditions. There's usually no need to take anything off or on, just work your zippers to avoid both sweating and chilling. Your major controls are the big central zippers on your parka and bib overalls and the headgear configuration.

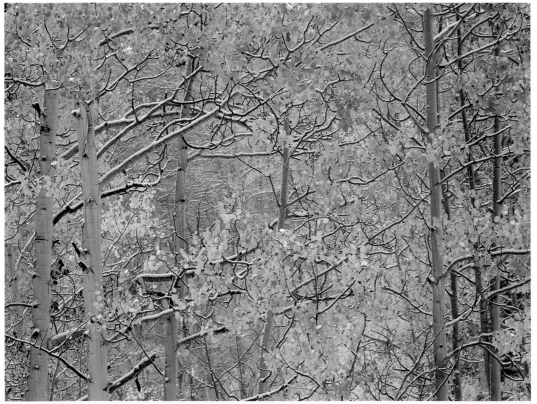

ENERGY SNACKS

It makes you feel more energetic to stoke your furnace periodically with high energy snacks — trail mix, energy bars. I bring along one energy bar (Luna bars are great) for every two hours I plan to be out.

WINTERIZING YOUR EQUIPMENT

Cold weather creates two main problems for equipment. The first is battery failure — easily solved by keeping a spare set of batteries in an inner pocket close to your body inside the insulating layer. If you have two identical camera bodies, simply pocket the entire battery pack from the camera you are leaving behind so you can switch packs in and out in a jiffy. If your camera is able to use lithium batteries, these will provide by far the best performance of any energy cells, especially in freezing temperatures.

Another problem arises when you go back into a warm area (either indoors or into a heated vehicle). Water vapor will condense on any equipment surfaces exposed to air, including interior components. This moisture can foul electronic components or initiate corrosion of other parts. Avoid this by keeping a large, heavy duty trash bag in your vest or camera bag. Before exiting the cold, put your entire vest or camera case inside the plastic bag and close it tightly. Leave the contents inside until they feel about the same temperature as other objects indoors.

Long Johns for Your Tripod

If not insulated, metal tripods make shooting difficult by drawing heat from your hands every time you have to adjust a leg or set up in a new spot. This can be avoided by wrapping the legs with pipe-insulating foam or commercial Tripads (discussed fully on page 31).

Winterizing Your Brain

Winter temperatures not only affect the physical operations of you and your equipment, they also have an affect on the light energy generated by your subjects, which you need to consider in conceiving and realizing the image.

Exposure

With most of the world cloaked in ice and snow, you can no longer trust your light meter, programmed as it is for average, middle-toned subjects. To retain these high-key tones, you must normally open up one or two stops (depending on how much of the composition is occupied by snow and/or ice) from the light meter indication, or lock-in exposure parameters read from an average subject nearby (e.g. a persons's clothing, a tight clump of tree trunks, or the clear northern sky about 45° above the horizon).

Subject Contrast

Another cold-weather hallmark is reduced subject contrast. Snow and ice work as natural reflectors to throw light into shaded portions of

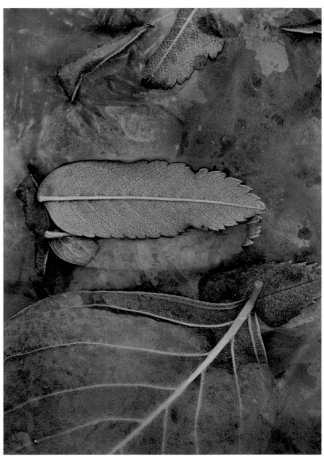

Frosted leaves near Bellingham, Washington (above). To relax and explore the numerous photo opportunities of wintertime, you need to be warm and comfortable. Wearing the right clothing and adjusting it to match your activity level will allow you to operate effectively in almost any weather. Here, frost spreads a delicate silver patina over a retiring still life of icebound leaves.

Sundance Range from Vermil-lion Lakes, Banff National Park, Alberta (below). During northern winters, the sun stays low in the sky the day long, of-fering extended periods of warm, low-contrast light that projects added drama onto both land-scapes and wildlife. This landscape view was made a couple of hours after sunrise.

the scene. This usually benefits picture quality and makes it unnecessary to use fill-flash or handheld reflectors. It is sometimes beneficial to use your split neutral density filters upside down in order to darken and retain detail in snowy areas positioned low in the composition. Simi-larly, a polarizing filter must be used with caution as it may add so much density to blue skies that they become nearly black.

LIGHT QUALITY

In northern latitudes during winter the sun re-mains close to the horizon the day long providing extended opportunities for low contrast, side-lit shooting of both wildlife and landscapes. The dramatic rosy colors of sunrise and sunset simi-larly hang in the sky longer making possible more considered and deliberate compositions and a leisurely bracketing of exposures.

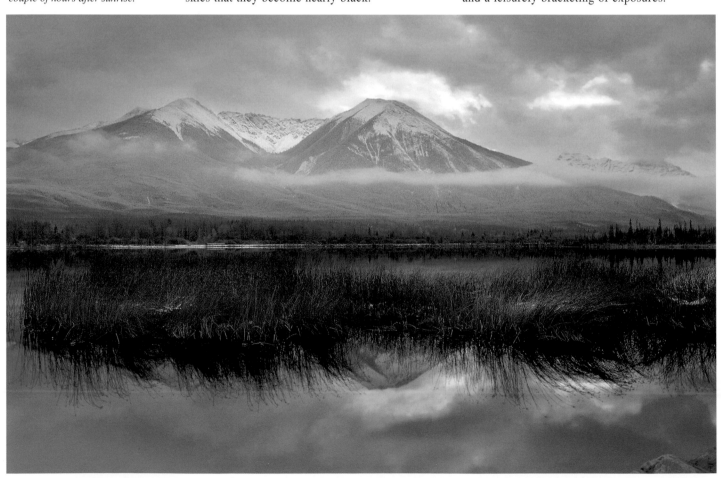

SUBJECT CHOICES

In general the abundance of attractive nature subjects in winter does not on first consideration seem to match that of other seasons — many birds and mammals are in hibernation or have migrated elsewhere. The color palette of northern landscapes is lacking in fresh greens and the exciting, warm hues of the spectrum. But winter provides its own attractions. Juxtaposed against snow's pure white, even muted colors assume added chroma. Reflections of sunlight off ice crystals and sparkling snowbanks can be incorporated theatrically into compositions. Deep and drifting snow spreads sculpted dunes over landscapes devoid of surface features in other seasons. Although wildlife numbers are lower, animals that are in evidence are usually calmer and easier to approach. Fur and feathers are embellished with frost and flakes and snow-blanketed terrain is decorated with tracks. Animals caught in action trail spumes of flying powder and snort clouds of photogenic vapor. Frigid temperatures and scarcity of natural food makes backyard birdfeeders buzz with hungry visitors and draws concentrations of animals to hot springs and feeding areas. Plummeting mercury generates moody atmospheric effects — fog, haze, and falling snow — which can be used to enliven both wildlife and landscape compositions. Frost, ice rime and icicles likewise add interesting features to solid forms, both animate and still. In short, winter offers plenty of special effects to stimulate your imagination and set your trigger finger twitching. Stay warm and happy shooting!

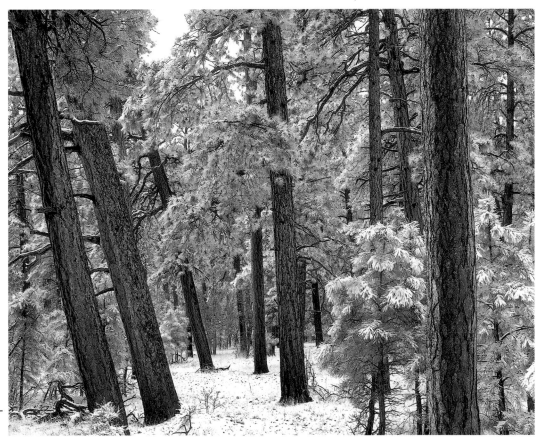

Ponderosa pine forest, Grand Canyon National Park, Arizona (above). To determine exposure in this scene, I made a close-up reading of a lighter-toned trunk, used this as my base setting, and bracketed 1/2-stop above and below. Camera position was chosen to record an arrangement of trunks that funneled attention into the forest. Pentax 645, 45–85mm f/4.5 lens, Fujichrome Velvia, 1/15 second at f/22.

Nature Photography's Year

Month-by-month guide to the best North American shooting sites

Point Piedras Blancas, Big Sur, California (below). Pleasantly cool weather, varied seascapes, and an enormous elephant seal rookery are the attractions at this coastal hotspot.

White Ibis, Ding Darling National Wildlife Refuge, Florida (far right, top). Southern Florida is a bird-shooter's paradise during the winter.

NORTH AMERICA'S NATIONAL parks, wildlife refuges, wilderness preserves, national forests, and other public lands are the most exciting locations for nature photography in the world. Nowhere else can you find such abundant and dramatic combinations of wildlife and scenery. Not only is the potential for taking beautiful pictures unmatched elsewhere, but an infrastructure of roadways, lodges, campgrounds and stores makes access and logistics a relatively simple matter. Most parks and refuges are patrolled by rangers who safeguard both the natural resources and the visiting public. They also provide expert guidance to attractions, trails and natural history. This chapter describes a dozen continent-spanning excursions that promise pleasant weather, comfortable accommodation and the double lure of breathtaking landscapes and confiding creatures. Any of them should provide a comfortable, exciting and productive photography experience.

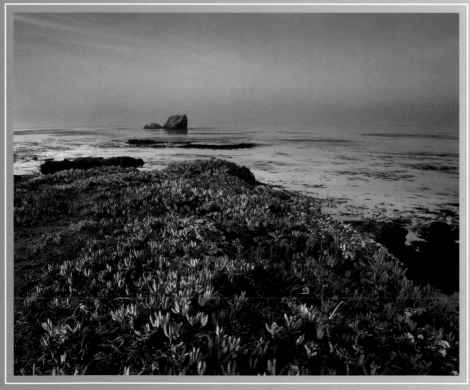

JANUARY: BIG SUR COAST

California's Big Sur Coast (between Monterey and San Luis Obispo) boasts big-time marine wildlife and sweeping beaches. Inland you will find old growth redwood forests, twisting canyons and waterfalls. Sandy beaches a few miles north of San Simeon are breeding locales for Northern elephant seals. You can see these refrigerator-sized pinnipeds from the Pacific Coast Highway which hugs a sparsely settled shoreline. Away from the main rookeries are secluded coves where you can shoot seals at close range. Additional subjects include monarch butterflies (Andrew

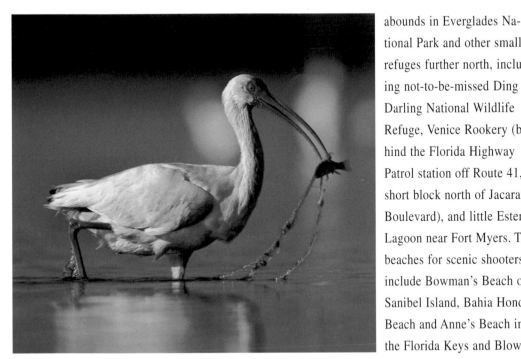

abounds in Everglades National Park and other smaller refuges further north, including not-to-be-missed Ding Darling National Wildlife Refuge, Venice Rookery (behind the Florida Highway Patrol station off Route 41, a short block north of Jacaranda Boulevard), and little Estero Lagoon near Fort Myers. Top beaches for scenic shooters include Bowman's Beach on Sanibel Island, Bahia Honda Beach and Anne's Beach in the Florida Keys and Blowing Rocks Beach on Jupiter Island.

MARCH: GRAND CANYON

Arizona's Grand Canyon provides key elements for great landscape photography: strong color, incredible landforms and, with any luck, dramatic skies. In March, snowfalls are not uncommon and you may be able to

Molera State Park), seabirds and harbor seals sunning themselves on rocky shoals. If you are lucky, you may spot an endangered California condor cruising overhead or scavenging dead animals on the beach. There are plenty of motels, restaurants from rustic to elegant, and state and private campgrounds.

FEBRUARY: SOUTH FLORIDA

In South Florida, winter weather is predictably warm and sunny. Between shoots, you can stretch out on a sandy patch of snow-white beach. The photographic attraction here is primarily wildlife (herons, egrets, pelicans, ibises, spoonbills, anhingas, alligators, turtles) which

Winter Alternatives

• *Yellowstone National Park, Wyoming:* Cold but exciting shooting from snowmobiles of wildlife and snowy landscapes (December through March).

• *Big Bend National Park, Texas:* Superb mountain/desert scenery and great (rain-dependant) wildflowers in February/March — call ahead.

• *Sonoran Desert, Arizona:* Beautiful high-desert scenery and vegetation with pleasant weather, snow possible in January, wildflowers (rain-dependent) in February/March.

Grand Canyon from South Rim, Arizona (below). Late winter offers pleasant if cool weather, dramatic skies, and a chance dusting of snow to enliven canyon contours.

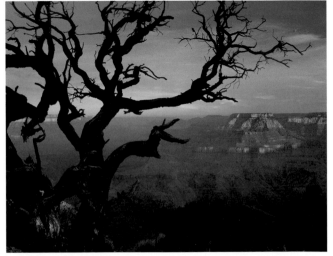

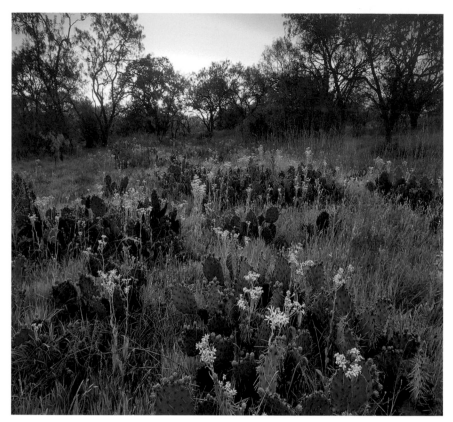

Squaw weed and prickly pear cactus, Texas Hill Country (above). When conditions are right, the floral displays during April on the Edward's Plateau are unsurpassed.

Bison calf, Custer State Park, South Dakota (right). Prairie wildlife is the key attraction at this beautiful drive-through park near Badlands National Park. Colorful eroded terrain and big skies provide plenty of interest for landscape enthusiasts.

where a collection of monstrous mesas and jutting pinnacles tinted in fiery hues awaits the lens.

APRIL: TEXAS HILL COUNTRY

Texas Hill Country bursts into color during wildflower season. The big show is put on by paintbrushes and Texas bluebonnets which festoon this rolling, oak-upholstered landscape in saturated patches of blue and scarlet. You will also find tempting masses of asters, daisies, wine cups, gaillardias, primroses and others (Texas boasts over 5,000 wildflower species). There are good opportunities for shooting white-tailed deer (common everywhere) and wild turkey at South Llano River State Park campground. For a wildflower forecast (blooming times and abundance varies) contact the Lady Bird Johnson Wildflower Center at 512-292-4200. The area is sprinkled with quaint mom and pop eateries, varied accommodations, and campgrounds. Austin is the most convenient fly-in spot.

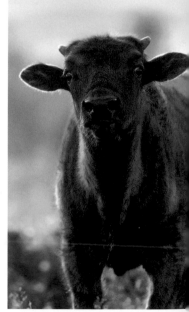

photograph these plunging cliffs and the surrounding deserts and forests with accents of white for heightened color. The canyon runs east to west so that both the rising and setting sun illuminates its cavernous 3,000 feet deep interior. Flagstaff, Arizona, and Las Vegas, Nevada, are good for airport staging. The North Rim is closed until May due to heavy snow but there is plenty of photographic potential on the more accessible south rim. If you need warmer weather and a change of scene, drive south to Sedona, Arizona, a tourist enclave in the heart of red rock country

MAY: VANCOUVER ISLAND

Vancouver Island is a natural history jewel off the southwest coast of British Columbia. Air transport to either Vancouver or Victoria will leave an easy drive to all major attractions. At this time of year, the rumpled hinterlands are enlivened with the blooms and buds of red alder, big-leaf maple and Pacific dogwood together with numerous wildflower species. Photograph old growth temperate rain forests at numerous locations, including Cathedral Grove. Shoot the dramatic beaches and marine wildlife of Pacific Rim National Park on the Island's outer coast or photograph seals, sea lions and orcas in the vicinity of Race Rocks near Sooke. For the latest information on Vancouver Island's natural history attractions, contact the BC Provincial Parks at 250-387-4550.

JUNE: BADLANDS NATIONAL PARK

Once you've shot all the attractions at Badlands National Park in South Dakota, it's an easy two-hour drive to a couple of other hotspots — Wind Cave National Park and Custer State Park. At Badlands your viewfinder will be filled with stretches of native prairie peppered with wildflowers and the odd buffalo sandwiched between eroded badlands washed in tints of yellow, rose and rust. June offers the chance of dramatic afternoon thunderstorms which intensify landscape color and create stagey lighting effects and fiery sunsets. Wind Cave National Park and Custer State Park are magnets for wildlife enthusiasts. These rolling hills, wrapped in coniferous forests and native grasses, are the stronghold of confident buffalos, pronghorn antelopes, and prairie dogs. You can shoot from your car or hike

Long Beach, Pacific Rim National Park, Vancouver Island (below). Wide, sweeping beaches, sunset vantage points, tidepools, wildflowers, marine wildlife and Pacific Coast rain forest top the list of spring attractions on Vancouver Island.

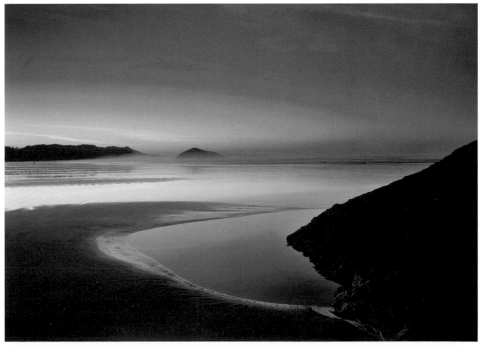

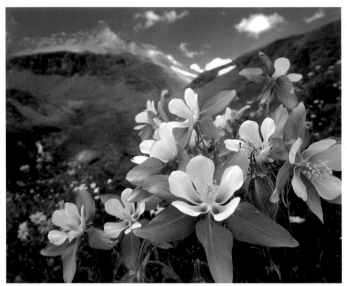

Colorado columbine, Yankee Boy Basin, Colorado (above). This compact basin offers a profuse display of sub-alpine wildflowers together with waterfalls and frothy streams.

Mount Moran from String Lake, Grand Teton National Park, Wyoming (right). In autumn, you can record the change of seasons, elk rut and numerous geologic phenomena in the Yellowstone/Grand Teton area.

Mount Rainier, Mount Rainier National Park, Washington (far right). Lush wildflower meadows and outsized landscape features lure shooters to this destination during July and August.

out into the fields for more intimate views. Major airlines fly into Rapid City, South Dakota, your jump-off spot.

July: San Juan Mountains

The San Juan Mountains of southwest Colorado boast some of the most exhilarating alpine topography on the continent. In July these soaring corridors of granite and sandstone are splashed with wildflowers, prime photographic targets in their own right, as well as exciting foreground features for the processions of snow-clad peaks. The San Juan range is crisscrossed with roadways, many of them built during the mining boom of the last century. A two-wheel drive buggy will trans-

Summer Alternatives

• *Katmai National Park, Alaska: Brown bears fishing for salmon during last half of July, all of August and into September.*

• *Jasper National Park, Alberta: Elk rut begins in September featuring some of the continent's largest bulls. Also fabulous scenery.*

• *St. Paul Island, Alaska: Northern fur seal rookery, denning arctic fox (blue phase), and seabird rookeries including puffins during August/early September.*

port you to plenty of beautiful locations but a four-wheel drive chariot will deliver an authentic high country adventure with access to ghost towns and knee-trembling vistas. Telluride and Ouray are famous tourist destinations with varied accommodations and numerous first-class eateries. Pick up your jeep in Durango.

August: Mount Rainier National Park

The namesake of Mount Rainier National Park is an active, oversized volcano so large that it creates its own weather system. When surrounding areas are basking in sunshine, the park is commonly wreathed in cloud until midday. For many

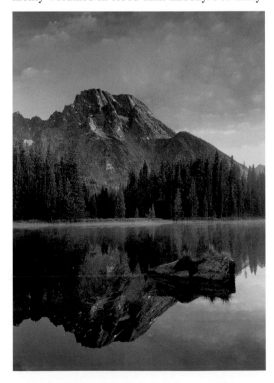

subjects this offers ideal shooting conditions. August is the peak of wildflower season and sub-alpine slopes dance with paintbrushes, daisies, arnicas, and scores of others that the soft light flatters for a good part of the day. There are creeks, rivers, cascades and waterfalls, and even old growth rain forests that are also at their best under overcast skies. When the clouds part and the mountain's snow-crowned peak is revealed, scenic compositions are possible from numerous vantage points, the mirrored view from Reflection Lakes being the most famous. Book your flight to Seattle.

SEPTEMBER: YELLOWSTONE AND THE TETONS

September is the busiest time of year for photographers in Yellowstone and Grand Teton National Parks. The crowds of summer have dissipated, the aspens and cottonwoods glow yellow and orange, morning meadows are hung with frost, and moose and elk are in rut. The latter attraction brings out platoons of photographers armed with 500 and 600mm telephotos. Sturdy Gitzos fence in the willow flats where moose are feeding and corral the open meadows where wapiti bulls lord over harems and bugle their supremacy into the cool atmosphere. Aside from wildlife there are the singular Tetons, the Grand Canyon of the Yellowstone with its stupendous waterfalls, and numerous geyser basins to photograph once you collect enough wildlife trophies. Next door to the

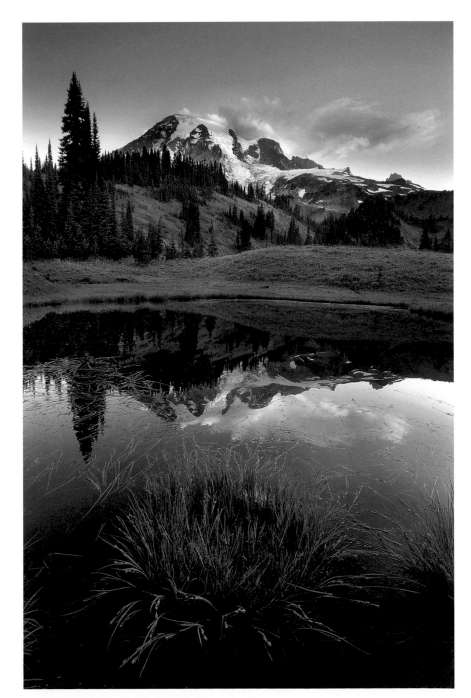

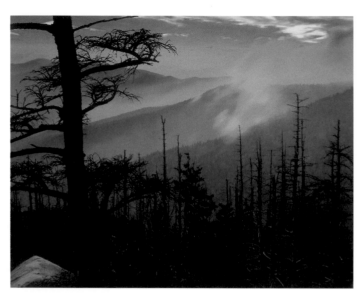

View from Clingman's Dome, Great Smoky Mountains National Park, North Carolina (above). This is the continent's premier autumn color destination with peak displays in late October. Also of interest are brooding, fog-shrouded landscapes and waterfalls and streams.

Sandhill cranes and snow geese, Bosque del Apache National Wildlife Refuge, New Mexico (right). Birds and more birds with the best shooting lasting from November through January. Blinds are not necessary. Best shooting is usually from a car window or pondside.

park, Jackson, Wyoming, is (blessed?) with tourists' every possible need and served by a couple of major airlines.

OCTOBER: GREAT SMOKY MOUNTAINS

We'll head east a few states to Great Smoky Mountains. If you are impressed by the glamorous but admittedly restricted palette of the cottonwoods and aspens of the West, then your motor drive will overheat in Great Smoky Mountains National Park in Tennessee and North Carolina, where giant deciduous forests, some in virginal old growth condition, proliferate. Each of the dozens of tree species sports a distinctive autumn hue, from lemon yellow through flaming red to rusty brown. Forests clothe the mountains and valleys, providing endless composition possibilities. Mix this surfeit of color with any of the many streams and cascades, an early

sprinkle of snow or a writhing fog bank, and you are in Fuji-chrome heaven. Asheville, North Carolina, and Knoxville, Tennessee, are both within easy driving range of the best photo areas. Gatlinburg and Pigeon Forge are both near the park boundary and provide after-the-shoot, country-style sustenance and lodging.

NOVEMBER: BOSQUE DEL APACHE

Bosque del Apache National Wildlife Refuge is a

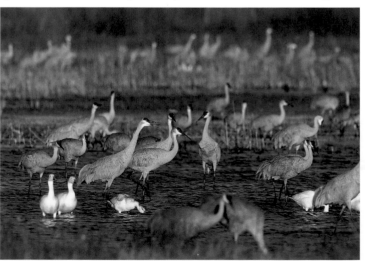

Autumn Alternatives

• *Yoho National Park, British Columbia: Golden larch display among dramatic peaks and alpine tarns at Lake O'Hara in late September/early October.*

• *Acadia National Park, Maine: Peak fall color in mid-October against a backdrop of lakes and stunning coastal scenery.*

• *Churchill, Manitoba: Curious polar bears (including mothers with cubs) wandering the Hudson Bay shoreline from mid-October to mid-November. Be prepared for arctic conditions.*

60,000-acre preserve that stretches along the Rio Grande River in central New Mexico. This collection of marshes, deserts and woodlands, set against the backdrop of the Chupadera Mountains, is a winter haven for migratory birds — 50,000 ducks, 50,000 snow geese and about 18,000 greater sandhill cranes, as well as numerous wading birds, owls, eagles, hawks and falcons. The refuge is the year-round home for mule deer, coyote, wild turkey, roadrunner and others. There are hiking trails, five viewing platforms, and a 15-mile wildlife drive, all of which provide opportunities for photography. Most animals are accustomed to humans and allow a slow approach, making frame-filling telephoto portraits easy. Open from an hour before sunrise to an hour after sunset, the refuge is located twenty miles south of Socorro, New Mexico, about ninety minutes by car from touchdown in Albuquerque.

DECEMBER: MAUI, HAWAII

This is a great place for shooting landscapes, waterfalls and close-ups of plants, but not wildlife

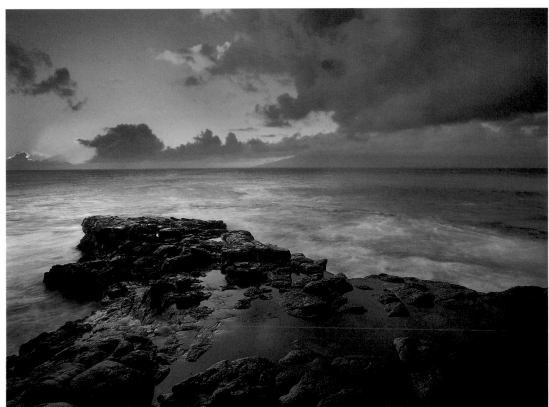

(except for sea turtles which are plentiful in many locales near or on shore). The photography highlight is the Hana Coast of Maui. Here are found the wildest, loneliest beaches with big surf, interesting shoreline rock formations, and lots of tropical vegetation on the fringes. Waterfalls nestled in tropical forest abound all along the Hana Highway. Haleakala National Park's beach region is found here and offers both waterfalls and dramatic beach scenes in a compact area. Aloha and happy shooting!

Little Makena Beach, Maui, Hawaii (above). You can't beat paradise for its combination of pleasant weather and varied natural attractions including humpback whales, idyllic seascapes, silky waterfalls, tropical blossoms and lush rain forests.

Part Two

Essential Skills

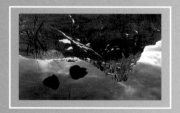

Exposure

Play the odds when practicing the art of exposure

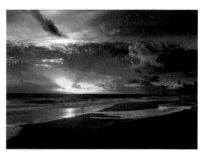

HOW TO PROPERLY EXPOSE FILM is a favorite around-the-tripod discussion topic and the first step in becoming a photographer. Approaches to achieving consistent exposure are numerous although some are not very practical for photographers confronted by the rigors and time constraints inherent in both landscape and wildlife photography. A few traditionalists cling to the efficacy of hand-held meters. These gizmos are great if your camera doesn't have a built-in light meter — a rarity in 35mm SLRs produced in the past three decades. Otherwise you'll find the on-board meter superior in all situations. The multi-patterned TTL meters of today's more sophisticated SLRs offer numerous ways to measure the brightness of a warthog's hairy back — averaging, center-weighted, or spot; partial spot, evaluative, or evaluative 3-D matrix; color matrix, honeycomb, user-selectable multi-pattern, highlight and shadow AE biasing, or spot-linked to

active AF sensor. One of these options is sure to work . . . if only I knew which one. Complicating the consumer-oriented high-tech approach, is the fact that shutter speeds, apertures, film developing, and film speed ratings are imprecise. (What is the ISO of Velvia anyway?) Exposure readings of my Pentax cameras differ by 1/2 stop and my Canon cameras are only slightly more consistent.

THE SUNNY F/16 RULE

Nihilists can forget about falling back on the

John D. MacArthur State Beach, Florida (above). This beautiful scene was high in contrast with significant parts (the sun and its reflection) much brighter than others. By basing my exposure on an average mid-tone and taking four additional frames (two over and two under this setting), I made sure of getting a satisfactory exposure in a tricky situation. When the film was developed, I carefully made my choice of the best frame on the light table.

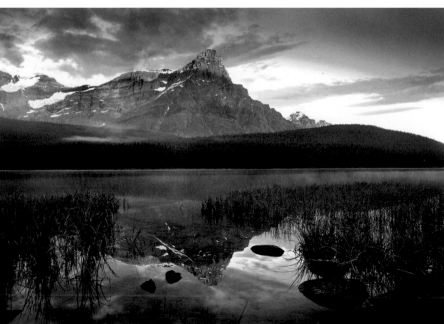

Mount Chephren, Banff National Park, Alberta (left). Recording both shadows and highlights in good detail is exposure's main challenge. Here is I used a one-stop split neutral density filter to darken the sky and sunlit peaks to better fit the luminosity range of the scene to that of the film.

Swift River, White Mountains National Forest, New Hampshire (right). This colorful riverside view represents a typical low contrast scene which can be reliably metered with average, center-weighted, or evaluative/matrix patterns. Soft overcast light provides even illumination of all picture elements with no defined shadows evident. There is an even mix of varied colors and tones. The brightness of the stream froth is balanced by the darkness of the trunks. The scene is framed so that no portion of the bright overcast sky is included. There would be no need to bracket this scene when shooting print film or digital. With transparency film, bracketing by 1/2 stop over and under the base setting would guarantee an exposure that optimized color saturation overall and captured the best detail in both the brightest and darkest parts of the image field.

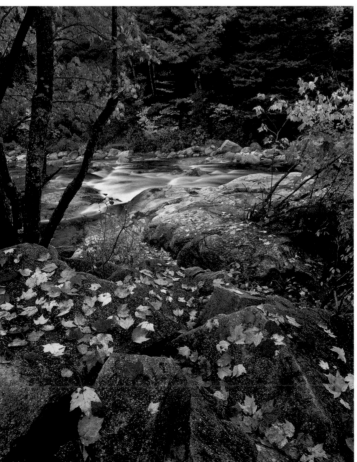

Sunny f/16 rule — the meter-in-your-mind method that has you set the shutter speed to the inverse of the film speed (ISO rating) and the aperture to f/16 when the sky is clear, the subject is mostly front lit, and it's lunchtime. For example, you would expose Fujichrome Velvia (ISO 50) at 1/50 second at f/16 or any equivalent combination of shutter speed and f/stop. The rule works fine except that it only provides an approximate exposure (useful for double-checking your light meter's basic accuracy) and nature photographers usually spend the harshly lit midday period resting, eating lunch, or scouting out new locations rather than actually shooting.

CONSISTENT EXPOSURE BY BRACKETING

Good exposure is a matter of best fitting the luminosity of the subject within the exposure space of the film or CCD (digital). Transparency films, which have little exposure latitude but the best reproduction quality, pose the greatest challenge. For me, consistent exposure is a matter of playing the odds. I try to fine-tune my initial exposure choice but whenever I have the opportunity, especially with a fetching subject, I take extra frames over and under my base exposure (called bracketing) to make sure I've got it right. Bracketing is usually unnecessary when shooting print (negative) film or shooting with a digital camera. However, it's always recommended when using transparency (positive) film, the load of choice for professionals and serious amateurs, which offers little allowance for exposure error. Bracketing is doubly important when the scene is illuminated by high contrast light (shadows are readily visible) or the subject itself is inherently high in contrast (a zebra or puffin, or a moose in the snow). Such situations are not only tricky to meter but several exposures may be acceptable while only one will be preferred. You will want to make this considered determination on the light table after the film is developed. Exposure nuance is critical to a picture's success and cannot be evaluated reliably through the viewfinder, especially while you are simultaneously engaged in the hurly-burly of shooting.

The greater the contrast in the scene, the greater the range of bracketing should be. For a low-contrast image (e.g. a forest or field on an overcast day showing no sky) you need only bracket 1/2 stop. For a high-contrast scene (e.g. a backlit seascape under a clear sky) you should bracket by a full stop, or more, both over and under the base setting.

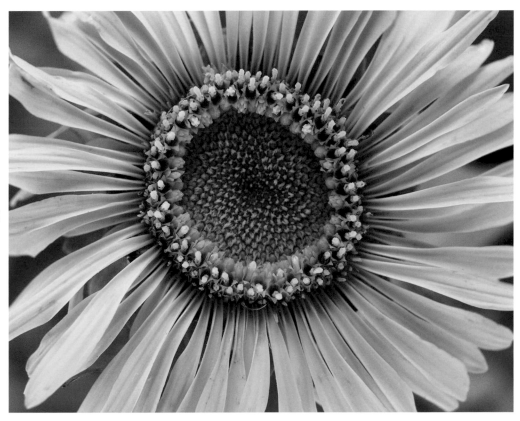

SET EXPOSURE MANUALLY

When using transparency films I prefer to set exposure manually, a method which provides advantages over the too numerous automatic modes of modern 35mm SLR's. Most importantly the physical act of setting shutter speed and aperture cues a psychological link between the settings needed for correct exposure and those which you consider necessary to satisfy the creative requirements of the image. Engaging yourself repeatedly in a physical manner in the shooting process stimulates an immediate and ongoing appreciation of the various parameters working to create the picture. You know, for example, that the image you are working on will have greater blur in the background because you have readjusted aperture. In shutter-priority auto-mode, aperture would be changed for you and though this may be indicated in the viewfinder, it can be easily overlooked due both to the amount of additional technical information visible in

Yellow large-flowered fleabane, Crested Butte, Colorado (above).
By setting exposure manually, I was able to conveniently shoot a single additional insurance frame of this evenly illuminated specimen. I increased exposure time by 1/2 stop over my base setting (taken with a center-weighted pattern) to make sure I had one frame which exhibited both the brilliance and strong color of this delicate, light-tone specimen.

Exposing Slide Films

• **Low-contrast Situations**
(cloudy or hazy skies with no
bright or dark picture components, faint or no shadows,
front-lit subjects). Take a center-
weighted, average, or evaluative
(matrix) reading of the composed
image and bracket by 1/2 stop
over and under (three exposures).

• **High-contrast Situations**
(clear skies with subjects lit from
above, back, or side, well-defined shadows with an even mix
of light and dark picture components. Take a center-weighted,
average, or evaluative (matrix)
reading of the composed image
and bracket by one stop over and
under in 1/2-stop intervals (five
exposures).

• **High-contrast Subjects**
(zebras, puffins, black bears in
snow, frothy waterfalls, compositions dominated by unusually
dark or bright tones, e.g. snow or
sandy beach scenes. Take a
restricted spot or close-up
(zoom-in) meter reading of a
middle tone/average picture
component. Bracket one stop
over and under in 1/2-stop intervals (five exposures).

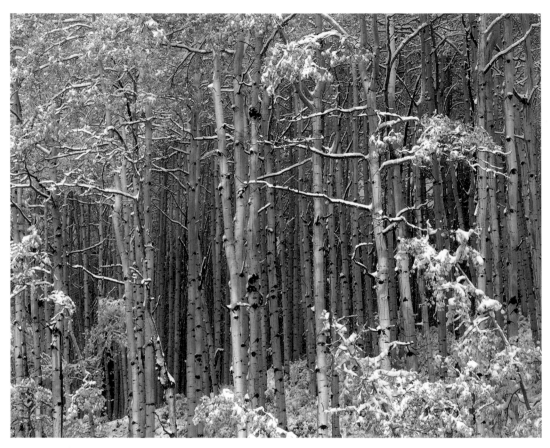

many viewfinders as well as to your necessary
concentration on the subject.

BETTER BRACKETING

Bracketing exposures is more efficient when
done manually. To begin with, you bracket using
the two controls you are most familiar with —
those for adjusting aperture and shutter speed.
You can bracket using either control or a mix of
the two without having to change program modes
as is necessary if you are shooting on automatic.

In many situations, you know that exposure
error will be more tolerable in one direction than
another. Only manual exposure adjustment
permits you to directly modify the bracketing
process in the direction you think advisable. You
can, for example, easily make two bracketed
exposures at 1/2 and one stop *under* the base setting and only one additional exposure at 1/2 stop
over the base setting. There are situations (e.g.
birds in flight) when automatic exposure offers
real benefits over working manually. These and

other departures from standard procedure will be discussed in relevant chapters.

SETTING THE BASE EXPOSURE

Hopefully you're getting the idea that exposure is more art than science and that to be sure of getting the exposure you want, you must bracket when using transparency films. Finding the base or starting point for your exposures is most of the time routine. Use one of the standard metering patterns — center-weighted, full-screen average, or evaluative (matrix). For most scenes, all of these will provide the same, or nearly the same, result. Average scenes are those that do not have significant contiguous areas either much darker or lighter than the overall scene. To get a feeling for this, practice taking spot-meter readings of various parts of a variety of scenes.

FOUR-STOP LATITUDE FOR SLIDE FILM

For all picture elements to register on slide (positive) film in fine detail and color they should fall within a span of about four stops—two stops over and under the base exposure setting. (Negative film and digital capture have a six-stop range.) It's common to encounter subjects and scenes that go beyond these parameters but you needn't despair. It's not essential that all parts of the scene be

exposed in a revealing way to make a great photo. In fact, you can use this characteristic of film to your advantage to emphasize or suppress strategic parts of the composition.

LIGHT METERS ARE JUST AVERAGE

If you keep in mind that a light meter interprets every scene as if it were average (evaluative/matrix metering modes excepted) you will quickly learn to set the base exposure with consistent accuracy. Scenes of normal brilliance (a mixture of colors with no dominance of dark or light hues), illuminated from the front or side, can be read at face value with no need for compensation.

Aspen grove near Gothic, Colorado (far left). This stand of trees was softly illuminated by light bounced in from snow-covered ground and an overcast sky. After my first shot, I opened up 1/2 stop and made one insurance frame to retain the light tones.

Wolves near Driggs, Idaho (below). To retain the dominant whiteness of this landscape, I made a tight spot-meter reading of these mid-toned, born-in-captivity howlers and then reframed the composition.

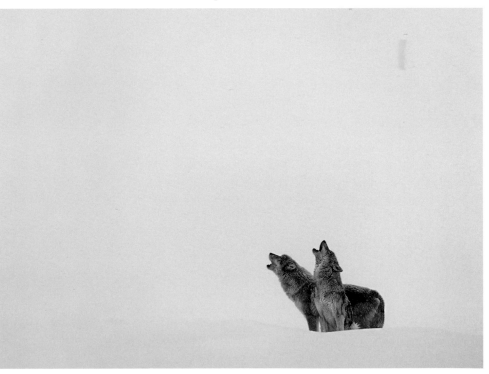

COMMON SENSE COMPENSATION

Scenes of unusual brightness or darkness require a bit of meter-tinkering for best results, although even these normally will surrender a good exposure if you bracket. Keep in mind that a meter can only measure light; it cannot distinguish a snow field from a coal field and it always indicates settings for an average subject. If you were to blindly follow an averaging-meter reading in such instances snow and coal both would turn out gray. By understanding this straightjacket operation of your light meter, you can readily improve the accuracy of the base exposure and ensure that you will end up with a slide you like with a minimum of film waste. To retain the snow's whiteness, give the film more exposure than the meter indicates by increasing exposure time or opening the aperture (usually one stop). For unusually dark subjects taking up most of the picture area, start the exposure series at 1/2 to a full stop under the meter reading.

METERING A MID-TONE

If the scene is contrasty, i.e. a mix of extensive areas or patches of very light and/or dark tones, set the base exposure by taking a restricted reading (switch to spot-metering or fill the frame by moving closer or zooming) of a mid-tone (grass greens, autumn reds, bark grays) that is illuminated similarly to the most important part of

Black bear with salmon, Gunnuk Creek, Alaska. Picture-dominating subjects that are either very dark or light require special exposure compensation to bring out detail in highlight and shadow areas. For a subject like this black bear, a straight exposure based on a restricted reading of a mid-tone, such as the blurred foliage in the background, would not provide enough light to reveal the darkest details of the bear's fur unless you opened up 1/2 stop from the base reading. For a dominant light-toned subject, such as a snowy egret, you would need to close down 1/2 stop to save the brightest highlights. Even with exposure compensation, such subjects can only be recorded in full detail when the sky is overcast. Under sunny conditions subject contrast extends beyond the exposure latitude of slide film. In the snapshot below the red circles indicate good areas to pick a mid-tone spot reading.

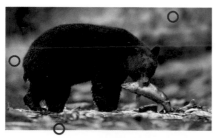

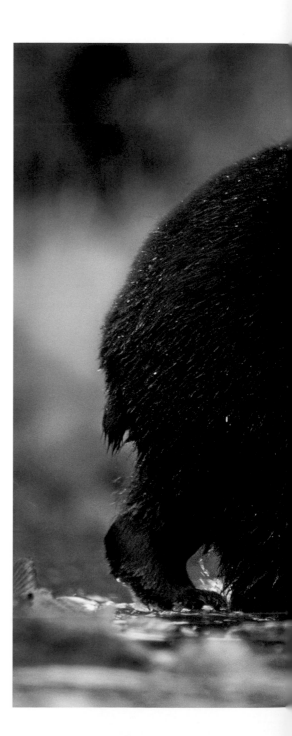

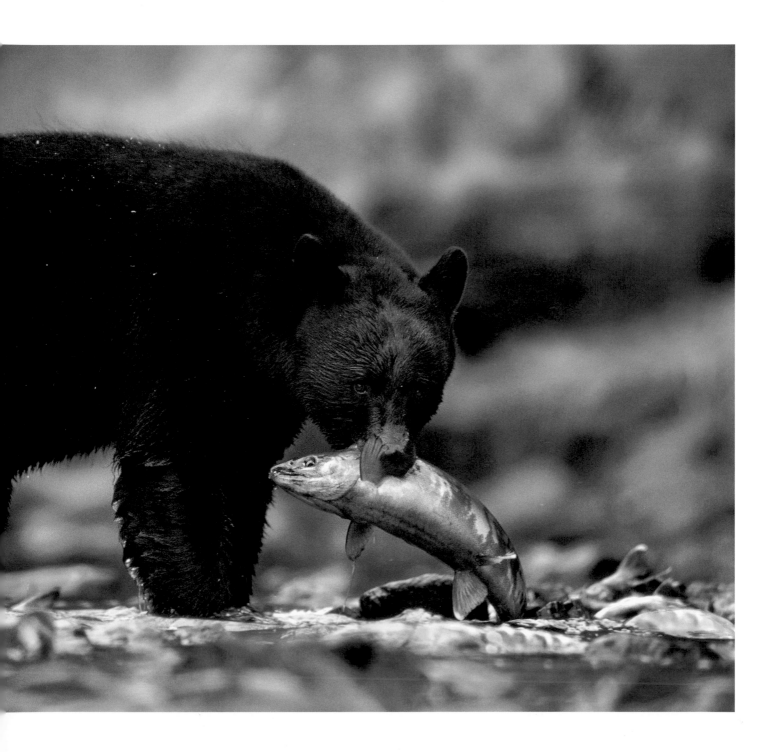

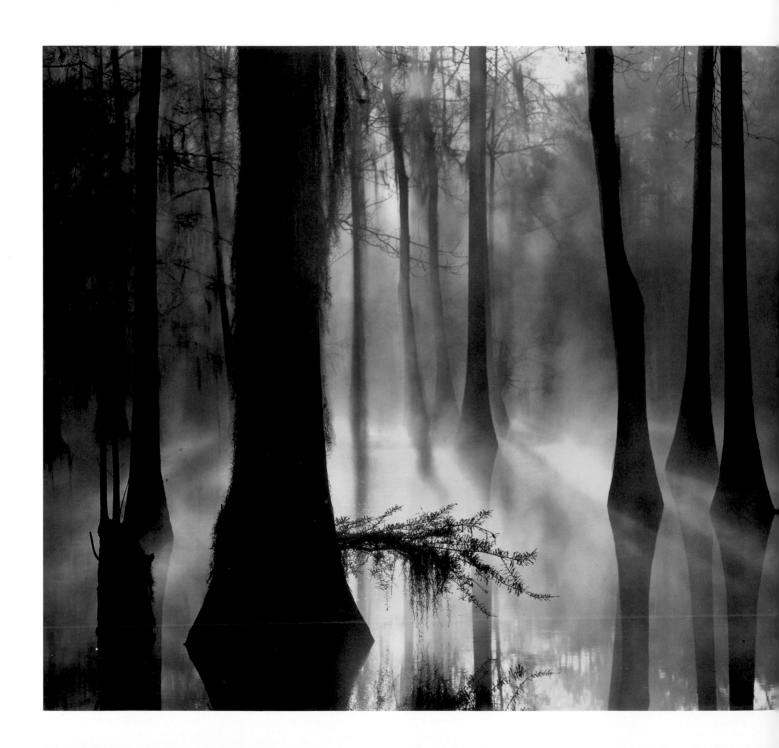

your composition. On a clear day the blue of the northern sky about 45° above the horizon is also a reliable mid-tone target. You also can use the mid-tone method for scenes that are uniformly light or dark, like snowy landscapes and sandy beaches, or when conditions are overcast, or for portraits of darker animals like grizzlies and moose.

WHITE PELICANS AND BLACK BEARS

For subjects that are especially dark (black bears, ravens, spiders) or light (snowy owls, white pelicans, arctic fox) depicted within a larger setting, a seemingly contradictory departure from standard procedure is called for if detail is to be retained in the sub-

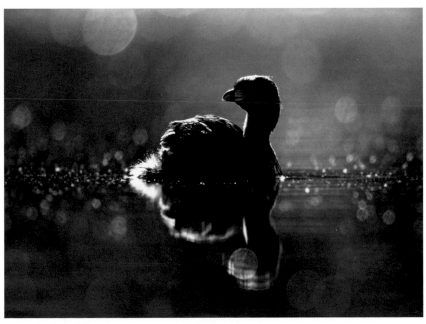

ject — especially under sunny or otherwise high-contrast conditions. Once you have established the base setting by reading a mid-tone in the composition, you need to open up 1/2 stop with very dark/black subjects to reveal shadow detail and close down by the same amount to

hold highlight detail in very light/white subjects. If this seems to go against what has just been said about making compensations for light or dark subjects, keep in mind that in sunny situations the lightest and darkest parts of the scene fall outside the film's exposure latitude. In these areas the film's sensitivity to light no longer decreases or increases steadily as it does for normal values falling within the film's latitude. Rather, it behaves in an accelerated fashion no longer

matched to the straight-line adjustments of shutter speed and aperture. This exposure tweaking is a way of squeezing critical luminance values of your subject back into the tight constraints of transparency film. There will be more said about exposure in subsequent chapters.

Baldcypress silhouettes, Lake Fausse Point, Louisiana (far left). *When the main subject is lit from behind or positioned against a bright background such as the sky, the glimmering surface of a pond, or an expanse of fog, you can throw it into silhouette by taking a close-up or spot meter reading of an average background tone. Such a setting will push the main subject outside the exposure window and render it as featureless black. Silhouetting works most effectively with subjects that have distinctive, linear and well-defined contours. Here I positioned the camera so that the rising sun fell behind a baldcypress trunk to screen the lens from flare and protect the meter from direct rays which will cause inaccurate exposure readings.*

Pied grebe, Burford Lake, New Mexico (left). You can see in this photo that the film was unable to record the great range of tones in this sunny, backlit scene. Nevertheless the picture is effective because the area of over-exposed highlights has been both kept to a minimum and put to good use to halo the bird. Four additional exposures were bracketed around a spot reading in the middle of the mid-toned background.

Reading the Light
How to recognize and use different types of light

Mount Kidd at Wedge Pond, Kananaskis Country, Alberta (below). Getting into the right position and waiting for a dramatic show of light is formula procedure for top landscape photographers. These towering peaks were spot lit due to the scatter of dense, wind-driven clouds above. The spotlighting phenomenon creates great potential for theatrically lit landscape images. Pentax 645, 80–160mm f/4.5 lens, Singh-Ray circular polarizer, one-stop split neutral density filter, Fujichrome Velvia, 1/4 second at f/16.

ONCE YOU'VE PUT the exposure issue to bed (or perhaps just down for a quick nap on the couch), the next exciting step in picture making is learning to record the type of light best suited to your theme, subject and film. In nature's studio, we can't adjust reflector umbrellas or power-up strobe units, we use a get-into-the-right-position-and-wait-for-the-dramatic-moment method of passive control. Tuning into the subtle variations of light and how it is reflected or absorbed by the subject is the key to making exceptional pictures. Light should be considered in terms of its quality (soft or hard), its color and the angle at which it strikes the subject.

STAY OUT OF THE MIDDAY SUN

On cloudless days the light generated by the sun from a couple of hours after sunrise to a couple of hours before sunset casts dense, well-defined shadows and generates brilliant highlights, producing a contrast range that may span a dozen stops or more — several times the range that film or digital can record. In such light much of the subject's detail will be lost to excessive contrast. Being daytime creatures, we are accustomed to high noon lighting and find it commonplace. Shooting during these sunny midday periods is usually a waste of effort and film.

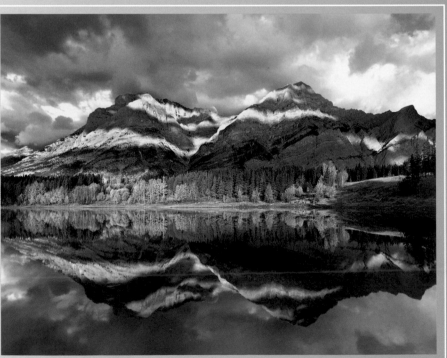

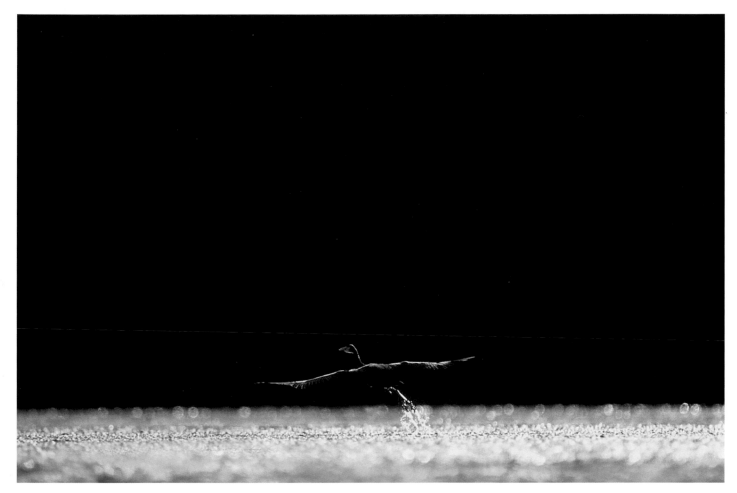

Conditions improve when clouds break up the sky. Although direct overhead sunlight is still the main light source, some of the light is scattered as it passes through clouds and is deflected into shadow areas to lower contrast and improve color saturation. In general, the visual appeal of natural light improves the closer the sun is to the horizon and these are the periods when your shooting will be most productive. Keep this in mind as you read through these descriptions of lighting situations.

Front Light

Shoot with the sun behind you, and you are using frontlight. Due to its direct and even illumination, frontlighting is recommended when you wish to portray saturated color, contrast between different colors, and fine detail in all parts

Great blue heron taking flight, Esquimalt Lagoon, Vancouver Island (above). Although backlighting is the riskiest directional lighting to use, it offers the most potential for exciting imagery. Here I based my meter reading on the shining water and caught the backlit subject against a shaded bluff.

Grand Canyon from Toroweep Overlook, Arizona (below).
Sidelight is the best all-around illumination for most subjects, particularly landscapes. Its oblique angle reveals both surface texture and terrain contour. Pentax 645 NII, 80–160mm f/4.5 lens, Singh-Ray circular polarizer, one-stop split neutral density filter (to darken sky), Fujichrome Velvia, 1/15 second at f/11.

of the scene. It is best for photographing birds and mammals early and late in the day when a definitive picture of the species is desired. Due to the high relative intensity of front light it is normally used when you wish to make stop-action images of animals at brief shutter speeds. Exposure readings are reliable under front light and bracketing can be kept to a minimum.

SIDELIGHT

When the sun illuminates the scene from the side it reveals form and texture. Sidelight produces long, deep shadows that reveal the wrinkles, dimples, ridges and other details of a surface in greatest relief. Because sidelit subjects are a mixture of highlight and shadow, exposure should be based on a mid-tone, and fully bracketed if using slide film. If clouds are present they will deflect and reflect light into shadow areas and serve to reduce contrast. In determining the best exposure, it's better to give priority to highlights and allow shadows to block up if contrast surpasses the film's latitude: It's normal for us to come upon subjects too dimly lit to see clearly, but it rarely happens in reverse.

BACKLIGHT

Like other types of directional lighting, backlighting varies in degree, and is most extreme when the sun is right behind the subject. Backlighting's effect is dramatic on subjects with indistinct, shaggy

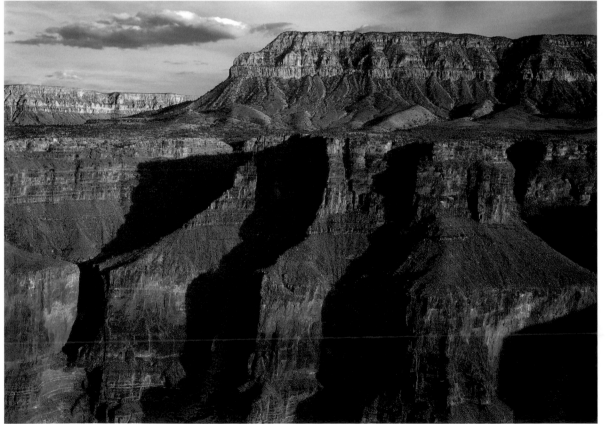

peripheries — furry and feathered animals in particular. When the subject is translucent — plumes of a spoonbill or leaves of an autumn maple, for example — backlight projects through, imparting to such elements a luminosity of their own. Backlighting is the most abstract and dramatic type of illumination. Its inherent high contrast is accentuated by film and produces a novel effect not fully accessible to normal human vision. If the main subject is photographed against a bright background that receives exposure priority, it will be underexposed and appear as a silhouette. If the subject is softly edged, it will be outlined by a halo of golden light. If exposure priority is given to the main subject (take a close-up reading of the shaded side) the background normally will wash out due to overexposure unless you can position the camera to capture a background that is also in shade. Attractive effects are possible anywhere between these two exposure extremes. In backlit situations, it's advisable to bracket extensively and choose the take you like best once the film is processed.

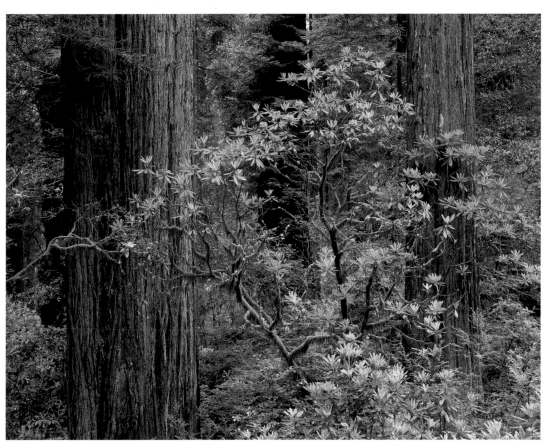

BEWARE OF LENS FLARE

Photographs made in backlight may lose quality due to lens flare. This occurs when the rays of the sun strike the front lens elements directly, resulting in a loss of color saturation, contrast and the appearance of octagonal hotspots caused by light reflecting off the interior diaphragm blades of the lens aperture. Flare can be eliminated or reduced using a lens hood when photographing wildlife. When shooting landscapes, the need to affix and adjust filters to the

Redwoods and rhododendrons, Redwood National Park, California (above). Soft light from an overcast sky is often the best illumination for detailed studies of plants, animals, and tight takes of the landscape where the sky and horizon are excluded. Overcast light creates low contrast and yields fine detail and saturated color throughout the picture area.

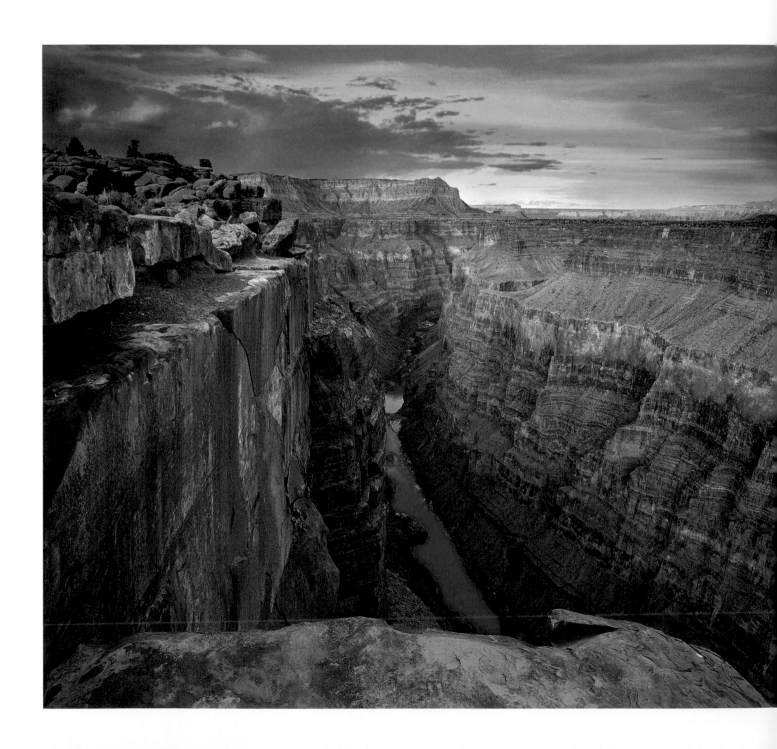

front of the lens makes it more convenient to shade the lens with your hand or hat just prior to making the exposure. You can check for flare by peering through the viewfinder or simply by making an exterior examination of the lens itself to be sure that it is shaded. You can also tame lens flare by taking a camera position so that the sun is not directly in front of you or by using a picture element, including even the subject itself, to block the sun. To ensure that flare has been avoided, check the scene at shooting aperture (use depth-of-field preview) if you have a chance.

TWILIGHT

When the sun is just below the horizon, only the light from the glowing sky overhead illuminates the scene. If clouds are present they will reflect additional warmer, directional light into the scene which will help to give more defined shape to terrain contours. Although twilight calls for long exposures (several seconds to a minute are

common when using fine-grained films), this is one of the premier times for landscape shooting, not only because the scene's contrast range can be comfortably accommodated by transparency film but the light source casts rosy hues onto the terrain. If present, clouds are painted in fiery, rapidly changing tints and add compelling structure and visual interest to the composition.

OVERCAST LIGHT

Overcast skies produce soft light which illuminates the subject evenly without noticeable shadows. Soft light allows even transparency films to record the complete range of tones of most scenes, serving up saturated color and fine

Grand Canyon from Toroweep Overlook, Arizona (far left). The soft, rosy illumination of twilight is superb for landscape shooting especially when there are clouds above the subject to absorb and reflect the rays of the sun coming from below the horizon. As with all scenic work, a tripod is essential as exposure times may be extended to a minute or longer. Pentax 645, 45–80mm f/4.5 lens, Singh-Ray circular polarizer, one-stop split neutral density filter (to darken sky), Fujichrome Velvia, 1/15 second at f/11.

Tricolored heron, Ding-Darling National Wildlife Refuge, Florida (left). Frontlighting is preferred when a detailed, color-saturated rendering of wildlife in action is desired. The high intensity of front light permits the use of brief, action-stopping exposure times and its lack of shadows makes exposure determination reliable with little need for bracketing.

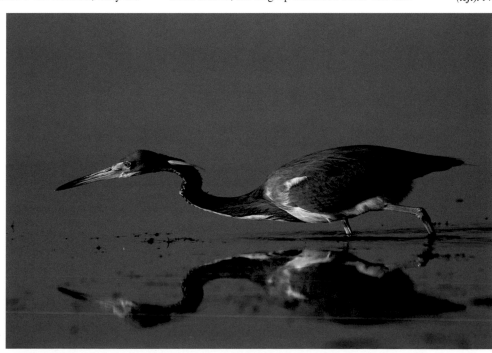

detail in both the brightest and darkest parts of the picture area. Exposure is easy to determine and changes little regardless of where you point the camera. For close-ups of animals and plants and tight shots of the landscape where neither the horizon nor the sky is included in the composition, overcast light is hard to beat.

SPOTLIGHTING WITH CLOUDS

One of my favorite effects depends on a sky full of broken, distinctively shaped, fast-moving clouds and a low sun. The wind-propelled cumulous clouds throw dappled patterns of sun and shade onto the scene. Because the sunlight is diffused by clouds, shadows are lighter than usual and do not block-up. For wide views of the landscape, including those featuring wildlife, take a position on high ground if possible and bide your time until a distinctive patch of terrain or interesting wildlife subject is picked up in the spotlight. Then with all speed, make a series of bracketed exposures before the drama fades. A zoom lens is the ideal tool for working out these compositions quickly.

SUNSET FLASHES

One of the most seductive types of landscape illumination is also the most brief. These heavenly moments occur when the sun is bisected by the horizon (either on the way up or the way down) and its energy arrives in refracted form — colorful and breathtakingly soft. This light has enough definition to model topographies and plenty of warmth to paint clouds in delicious tints of mauve, crimson and peach. The duration of the show is a matter of seconds so you have to be ready and then shoot as quickly as possible if you're going to bracket and swap filters.

ELECTRONIC FLASH

For me the use of artificial light (i.e. electronic flash) to depict wild subjects often disrupts and contaminates the beauty of the natural theme. I'm not fond of photos where long-range project-a-flash is used in combination with a super-telephoto lens to beam a sheet of garish fill-light into the shadow side of a bird or strike a phony highlight in its eye, or when multiple strobes are used to paint-up hummingbirds

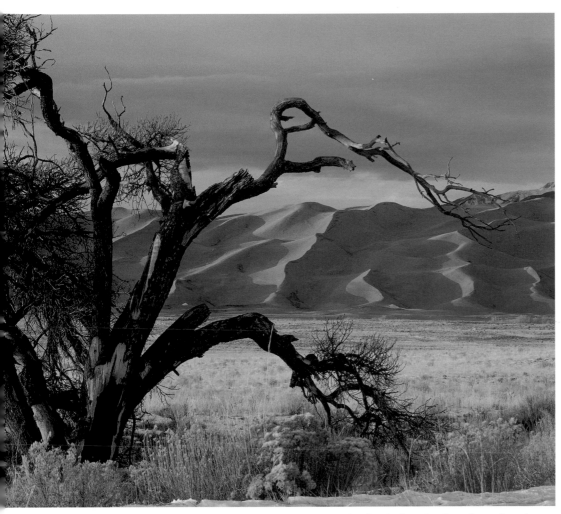

so they look like pastries on display at the Donut King. I like spiders, butterflies, and bumblebees to be illuminated by the real sunlight of their natural setting.

Electronic flash makes it possible, however, to shoot small creatures with lots of depth of field at stop-action exposure times when a scientific record is needed. I also like it for shooting

nocturnal animals (bats, owls and tree frogs) when light fall-off from the strobe yields a black, "night-timey" background. Otherwise, electronic flash announces, with its furniture store lighting, the presence of the photographer and his gangle of equipment. In the next chapter you'll learn how to control light in natural ways that will help you avoid the use of flash.

Great Sand Dunes National Monument, Colorado. Sidelight created an eye-catching pattern of sand ridges. I accentuated the most attractive pattern by framing it with the branches of the foreground tree. Landscape photographers must work quickly to catch such momentary displays of nature's beauty. Not only must you be adept at setting and brack-eting exposures but you have a good idea of your tripod position and framing before the decisive shooting period begins. Pentax 645 N11, 45–80mm f/4.5 lens, Singh-Ray circular polarizer, one-stop split neutral density filter (to darken sky), Fujichrome Velvia, 1/2 second at f/22.

Lioness, Amboseli National Park, Kenya (far left). Backlighting (see page 74) is ideal for wildlife species with shaggy fur or feathers which are transformed into dra-matic trans- illuminated halos outlining the subject. The main precaution with backlight is to use a lens hood and adjust camera position to avoid flare. Color satu-ration, subject detail and contrast will all be compromised if the sun's rays are allowed to strike the front lens elements. Canon A2, Canon 500mm f/4.5 L lens, Fujichrome Provia RDP 111,1/250 second at f/5.6.

Depth of Field

How to control and use in-focus picture areas for dramatic effect

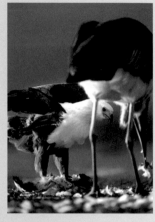

Western grebe, Stone Lake, New Mexico (below). By shooting at maximum aperture to limit depth of field and focusing on the eye, I was able to make this graceful subject stand out from its tangled, bulrush habitat. Canon EOS 3, 500mm f/4 IS Canon lens, Fujichrome Provia 100F, 1/500 second at f/4.

WHILE THE MARABOU STORK and fish eagle squabbled over the dead flamingo, I grew anxious about getting the camera into the right position. I struggled through the tropical ooze, shoving the floating blind along with dangling feet. From my close-up, beach-level vantage point, the marabou's legs rose like posts through a viewfinder filled mostly with fish eagle crouched over prey, its dark wings hooding a

bloody little pile of twiggy bones and tattered feathers.

The weakness of the early morning light called for maximum aperture and, combined with the high magnification of the telephoto lens, there was little depth of field to work with. To record both eagle and stork as sharply as possible, I needed to position the camera an equal distance from both birds. And so I squirmed through the mud while the birds sparred, my presence disguised by the camouflage fabric and fresh marsh vegetation that was draped over my low-slung blind. Every few feet, I checked my progress in the viewfinder until the shooting angle was right and the fierce eyes of my two subjects snapped with equal sharpness from the softness of the distant background — a dreamy wash of pink flamingo flocks against the acacia-spattered walls of the Great Rift Valley. I managed a few exposures before the eagle took wing, leaving the soiled remains to the marabou.

The problem of establishing appropriate

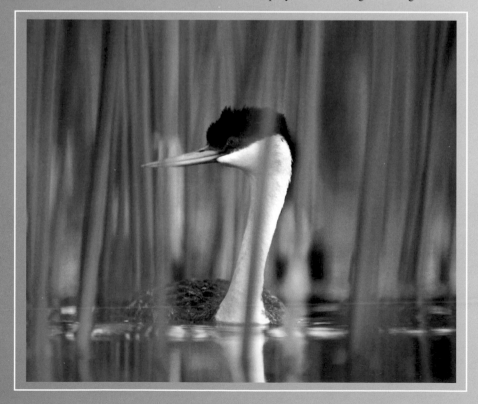

sharpness in a composition is often vexing for nature photographers. Whether you are shooting an encounter between two avian predators, a bouquet of wind-jostled daisies, a red-eyed tree frog, or a stretch of hardwood forest, the twin issues of point of focus and depth of field require careful consideration.

A Depth-of-Field Primer

For those who may be unsure, depth of field is that part of the image that is rendered in sharp detail. The best way to evaluate it is to use the camera's depth-of-field preview feature. This mechanism closes the aperture to the f/stop that you have set for actual exposure, allowing you to see what is sharp and what is not. Otherwise, the lens diaphragm stays open and the viewfinder remains bright to make focusing and composition easier.

From Here to Eternity

When shooting landscapes, setting depth of field generally guides other camera adjustments, like exposure and point of focus. Landscape images are conceptual composites, that is, they are judged by how the various elements of the scene relate to one another, particularly in terms of color, light and perspective. To reveal these rela-

tionships effectively, it is usually advantageous to record as much detail as possible from foreground to horizon. And so the attainment of total depth of field is the starting point for setting up a landscape shot, even insofar as what you choose to include or exclude from the composition.

In a nutshell, depth of field exhibits two characteristics critical to the composition. Firstly, its extent is dependent on magnification of the subject and aperture size in this way: the greater the magnification (regardless of lens focal length), the less the depth of field; the smaller the aperture, the greater the depth of field. Secondly,

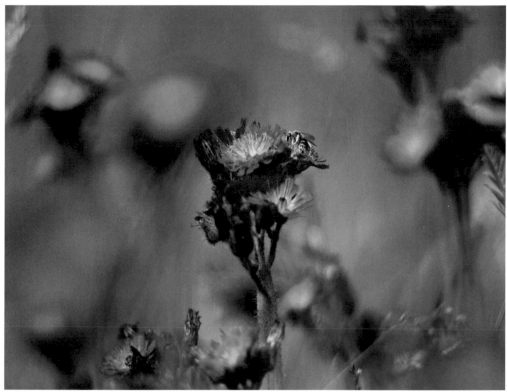

Devil's paintbrush and honeybee, Grand Manan Island, New Brunswick (above). The placement and extent of the depth-of-field zone is critical to the success of an image. Here I focused on the bee and shot at wide-open aperture to blur the remainder of the picture. A careful positioning of the camera allowed me to surround this central picture element with blurred swatches of harmonious color for a painterly effect. Canon F1, 500mm f/4.5 L lens, Fujichrome Velvia, 1/350 second at f/4.5.

its position in the scene is dependent on the point of focus with about one-third falling in front of the focus point and two-thirds falling behind. Armed with these two facts you can adjust the camera to attain total field sharpness at an appropriate shutter speed. Setting the lens' *hyperfocal distance* is the term photographers use for this procedure.

SETTING HYPERFOCAL DISTANCE

I set hyperfocal distance by viewing the scene at shooting aperture (by activating the depth-of-field preview mechanism) and focusing to and fro until both the horizon/infinity and the nearest picture elements are sharp. With the lens stopped down, the viewfinder can be dim and difficult to evaluate and you must give your eyes time to adjust. A floppy, full-brim hat that shields your eyes and the viewfinder from stray daylight will facilitate this process. If the depth of field is too limited to span both near and far elements, you have two options: either close the aperture further or decrease magnification of the foreground by backing up. Every adjustment calls for an artistic decision on your part.

SHARPENING A HERON'S BEAK

If a landscape photograph is generally an expression of *theme*, then a wildlife portrait is an expression of *thing*, with its composition drawing structure from the main subject. You hope to reveal the

Cathedral Rock from Red Rock Crossing near Sedona, Arizona (below). To emphasize the diagonal relationship between the rock monuments on the horizon and the large boulder in the stream, I set depth of field to include both picture elements. Pentax 645, 45–85mm f/4.5 lens, one-stop split neutral density filter (to darken sky), Fujichrome Velvia, two seconds at f/22.

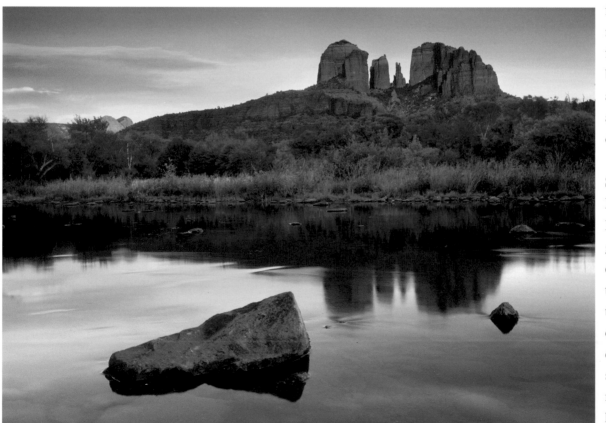

nature of the beast by emphasizing its unique and appealing characteristics and playing down other elements. Priority shifts from a consideration of depth of field to setting the point of focus.

The point of focus for frame-filling wildlife subjects, from spiders to giraffes, is almost invariably the creature's eyes. (Whales photographed breaching, etc., are an exception. For these subjects, almost any body part will do, with the tail flukes, flippers and blow-holes being primary among focus targets.) The reason that eyes are so important, even for such creatures as bears and elephants, for whom their sense of sight ranks second to that of smell, is simple. Humans, not animals, will be looking at your photographs and when we communicate with each other, we transmit most nonverbal information through our eyes. When we view a wildlife photograph we do not feel satisfied with the visual impression until we have examined the creature's eyes. For many wildlife portraits, however, the eyes alone are not sufficient. To these must be added, if possible, sharpness of nose or beak. In fact, what the viewer really wants to see is the entire face in high detail, although this is easier said than recorded on film. With active subjects, the most practical approach is to work for sharp focus on the eyes and hope for the best on the rest. If there is

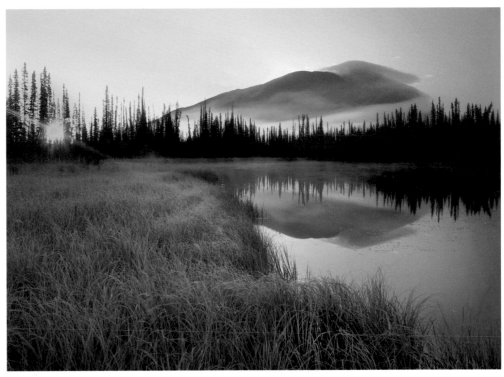

Nisling Range, Yukon (above).
To ensure sharpness over the entire picture field and highest magnification of the foreground sedges, I set the lens at its smallest aperture (f/32) and focused at the hyper-focal distance. For the latter I examined the scene at shooting aperture while adjusting focus to the nearest point that held the mountain in sharp detail and then positioned the camera as close to the sedges as I could without causing them to blur. Pentax 645 45–85mm f/4.5 lens, one-stop split neutral density filter, Fujichrome Velvia, two seconds at f/32.

Maximizing Depth of Field for Landscapes

• Shoot at the smallest or next-to-smallest aperture.
• Focus on the closest foreground element, then refocus a little beyond this point deeper into the picture space.
• Stop down the lens to shooting aperture and allow sufficient time for your eyes to adjust to the reduced brightness of the viewfinder. (Shield the viewfinder from stray light.)
• Make sure the most distant and closest elements in the scene are sharp. If not, focus further into the scene and check again.
• If you are not able to bring both foreground and background into the depth-of-field zone, you are too close to the foreground elements. Adjust camera position and try again.

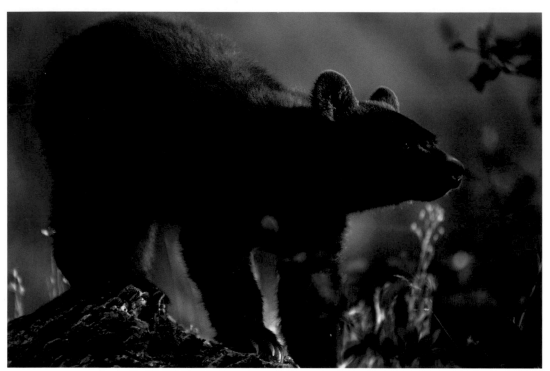

Black bear cub, Waterton Lakes National Park, Alberta (above). When making medium to close-up shots of wildlife, you usually want to shoot at, or near, maximum aperture to minimize depth of field. This will surround your subject with blurred color and emphasize its sharpness. The point of focus rarely should be anywhere except on the eyes. In this portrait the eyes are not only the sharpest part of the image, but I was lucky enough to catch them spotlit by a shaft of sunlight.

you are shooting wildlife near sunrise or sunset with slower films such as Fujichrome Velvia or Provia, you will find that there is seldom enough light to easily accomplish your pictorial goals. Much of the time you will be forced to shoot at maximum aperture to achieve a shutter speed of sufficient brevity. So you select maximum aperture and let the camera set the correct shutter speed. If I am working on a tripod and finger-tripping the shutter then I am fairly confident of sharpness at 1/125 second at any focal length up to 600 or 700mm. However, I will not begin to close down the lens to benefit from the extra depth of field until the shutter speed exceeds 1/250 second. Furthermore, I seldom close down the lens more than one full stop because I do not want either background or foreground elements to lose the smooth blur which contrasts so dramatically with the sharply rendered center of interest. In fact, these areas of blur are highly desirable design elements if they can be placed appropriately in the scene. Moving them around is not easy when shooting wildlife as either the subject or camera position must be altered. I like these blurs to fall

more than enough light to use a shutter speed brief enough to stop the movement of the animal and arrest camera shake during exposure, then use the extra luminance to move to an aperture smaller than maximum to take advantage of the additional depth of field.

DEPTH OF FIELD AND HIGH-TECH OPTIONS

In wildlife photography, where super-telephoto lens work is the norm and high shutter speeds are necessary to freeze action and reduce camera vibrations, most professionals work in the aperture priority, auto-exposure mode. This offers a number of advantages. In the many instances when

in the bottom or side of the frame when the creature is tightly cropped so that the viewers attention does not follow the animal's extremities out of the picture area. Peripheral blur contains and strengthens the central picture area and accentuates elements that are rendered sharply.

If your camera has a safety shift option (often a custom function), then shutter priority exposure works better than aperture priority. If using this option, I set the shutter speed at 1/250 second and allow the camera to select both the correct aperture (maximum) and shutter speed (whatever works) during low light. Once it becomes bright enough for the shutter speed to automatically reach 1/250, the camera begins to close down the aperture and to give the selected shutter speed priority. Then I monitor the effect of aperture size (by previewing depth of field) to make sure that it doesn't become too small to sharpen backgrounds and foregrounds to distraction.

For those who use older manual-exposure cameras, the theory is the same while the procedure is somewhat simpler and more direct under stable lighting conditions. These recommendations are starting points for a photographer's creative journeys. Happy travels!

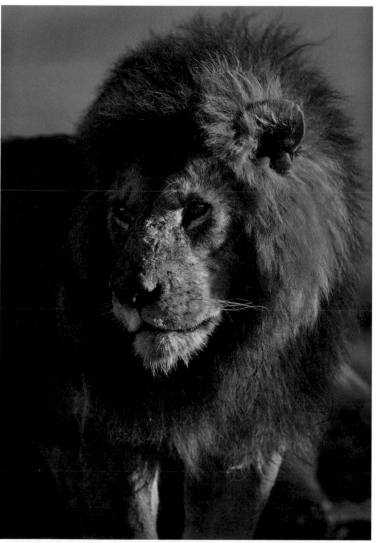

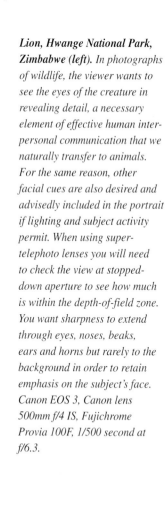

Lion, Hwange National Park, Zimbabwe (left). In photographs of wildlife, the viewer wants to see the eyes of the creature in revealing detail, a necessary element of effective human interpersonal communication that we naturally transfer to animals. For the same reason, other facial cues are also desired and advisedly included in the portrait if lighting and subject activity permit. When using super-telephoto lenses you will need to check the view at stopped-down aperture to see how much is within the depth-of-field zone. You want sharpness to extend through eyes, noses, beaks, ears and horns but rarely to the background in order to retain emphasis on the subject's face. Canon EOS 3, Canon lens 500mm f/4 IS, Fujichrome Provia 100F, 1/500 second at f/6.3.

Motion Effects

Using shutter speed and camera movement to control the effect of motion

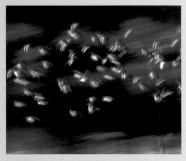

THE DURATION OF EXPOSURE, or shutter speed, affects the photograph in two ways. In concert with aperture, it is used to control the amount of light that reaches the film. Of artistic importance is its effect on motion, that of the subject, or the camera, or both simultaneously.

SHUTTER SPEED'S RULE OF THUMB

It is general practice for nature photographers to use a tripod, due to its numerous benefits to image making and in particular for its ability to arrest camera shake and vibration during exposure. But, whether or not it is necessary, or desirable, to use one is directly linked to artistic concerns and how shutter speeds affect motion. There are infrequent but regular instances when handholding the camera is equally beneficial. To avoid blur due to handheld camera shake, you should shoot from a comfortable, well-balanced position and set the shutter speed no slower than the inverse of the lens focal length (e.g. 1/200 second for a 200mm lens). If using image stabilizer type lenses you can extend exposure times by an additional two to three stops (consult the lens manual).

A photograph can interpret motion in many ways. At one

Short-billed dowitchers, Birch Bay, Washington (below). To make this abstraction, I used a shutter speed slow enough to blur the subjects and panned the camera to match the movement of the flock. This kept the birds in recognizable focus while creating attractive speed streaks in the background. Another version is shown at right.

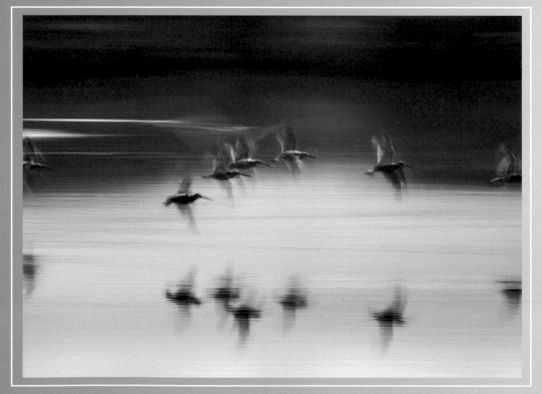

extreme, all action is frozen by the use of a brief shutter speed. At the other extreme, a slower shutter speed allows the motion of the subject to be registered as a blur on the film surface.

FROZEN MOTION

Whenever you are photographing a moving subject, it is necessary to consider the movement relative to the film surface during exposure, rather than what the subject is actually doing. Suppose a small flock of sandpipers is winging *toward* the camera at top speed. By observing the scene in the viewfinder (i.e. as it affects the film surface) you would notice that the animals, though moving swiftly, appear to be relatively stationary and growing slowly larger. A moderate shutter speed of 1/125 second would likely be brief enough to arrest much of the flock's motion (wings excepted).

On the other hand, if you were to photograph the flock moving *laterally* to your field of view, the film surface would perceive the subject entering stage left and exiting stage right (or vice versa) in a flash of time. A much faster shutter speed, dependent on how much the flock is magnified, would be needed to arrest motion — varying anywhere from 1/250 second for a long shot to 1/2000 second or faster for a tight frame-filler.

The selection of an action-stopping shutter speed is then dependent on the magnification of the subject, the speed of the subject, and the

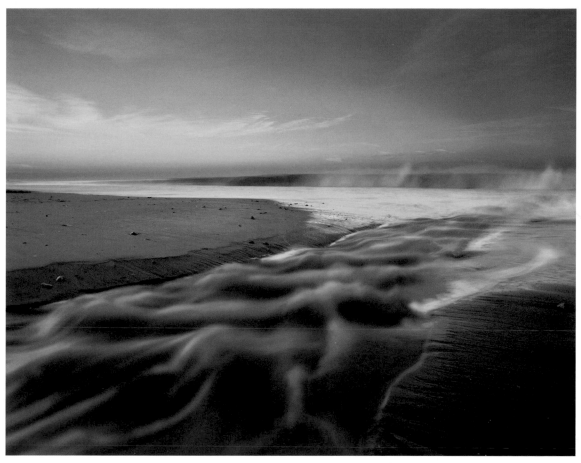

Zuma Beach, Malibu, California (above). Here I immobilized the camera on a tripod and and chose an exposure time of about four seconds to blur this tidal stream rushing into the ocean. When framing moving water, base the design on frothy parts of the flow. These will be interpreted by the film as milky, curving forms that usually are the most eye-catching elements of the composition.

direction of the subject's movement relative to the film surface. All of these factors are interrelated. Different parts of the subject also move at different speeds. With sandpipers, for example, their bodies move with a certain velocity while their wings move not only at a different speed but in a different direction.

PEAK ACTION SHOOTING

There are several ways that you can improve the action-stopping property of any given shutter speed. One way is to coordinate the moment of

Action-stopping Shutter Speed Primer *(for frame-filling subjects)*	
• hummingbird (including wings)	1/3000 sec
• hummingbird (body only)	1/250 sec
• mallard duck in flight (with panning)	1/750 sec
• great blue heron in flight (with panning)	1/350 sec
• snow goose in flight (with panning)	1/500 sec
• tundra swan in flight (with panning)	1/500 sec
• running deer (with panning)	1/250 sec
• running giraffe (with panning)	1/125 sec
• walking grizzly (with panning)	1/125 sec
• 15-foot waterfall	1/250 sec

exposure with a break in the movement of the subject — the apex of an impala's leap or the moment just before an eagle lands with wings spread and toes extended. You catch the subject when it is stopped or slowed, however briefly, and thus project an impression of stop-action. Such situations normally happen in a fraction of a second and are difficult to time precisely. For best results, study the behavior of your subject in order to better anticipate its movements. Also shoot with your motor drive at top speed and be persistent.

Choosing the slowest shutter speed that will stop the action of your subject is usually an educated guess. The slowest setting is desirable as it affords the smallest aperture, hence the greatest depth of field and the most tolerance for focus error — an advantage when working with active

Yellow-billed stork, Lake Magadi, Kenya (below). This stork's flapping wings were captured as they changed direction and were nearly still. A relatively slow shutter speed was all that was needed to achieve an impression of frozen action. Canon EOS A2, Canon lens 400mm f/2.8 L, 1.4x teleconverter, Fujichrome 100, 1/250 second at f/5.6.

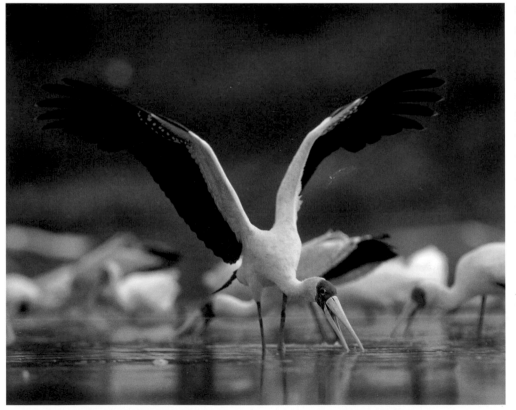

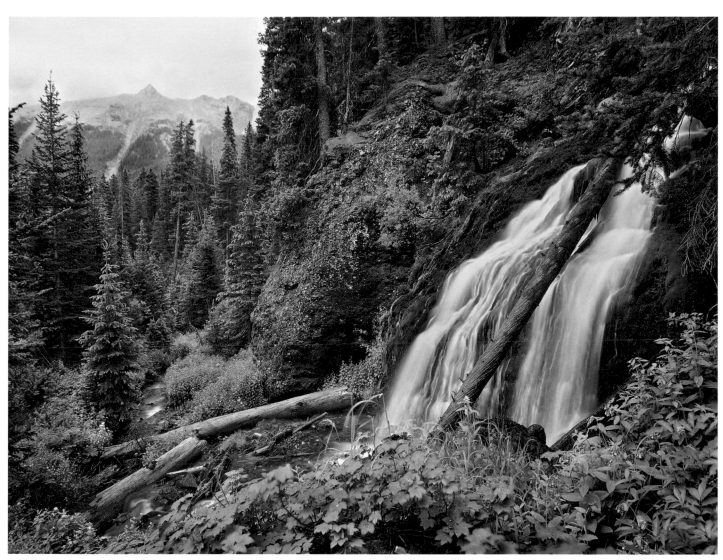

subjects. The chart above provides some basic starting points.

PANNING THE CAMERA

Another way to reduce blurring is to track the subject as it moves, trying to keep its position in the viewfinder stationary. Of course this will not help much to slow the movement of wings or legs but it will reduce blur of the gross subject. Panning is most effective if you keep the camera moving smoothly through the shot, both before and after exposure. The tendency is to stop

Fall Creek Falls near Yankee Boy Basin, Colorado (above).
For best results when making blurred motion shots of water-falls, include sharply rendered comparison elements to contrast with the blur of the water.

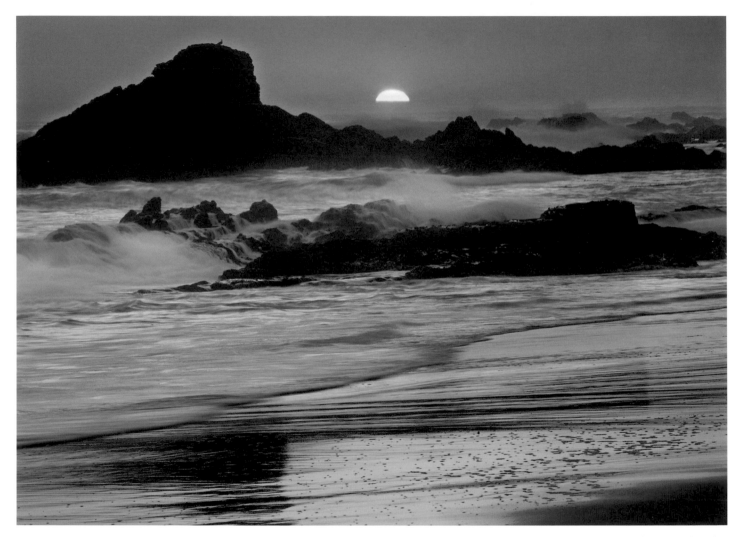

Sunset at Point Piedras Blancas, Big Sur Coast, California (above). *From the silky impression of water cascading over shore reefs to the glisten of surf draining from wet sand, water moving at different speeds creates a variety of effects during this 1/2-second exposure.*

panning as soon as you hit the trigger which can disrupt the process at its most critical moment due to the mechanical delay between actually pushing the button and the release of the shutter curtain. Panning is most smoothly done from a tripod-mounted camera with the controls loosened using a ballhead or even better, a gimbal head. Panning helps reduce blur in the main subject while stationary elements in the scene will become streaked (often beautifully) due to the camera movement. This streaking of the background infuses the picture with a compelling impression of motion. (More specialized tips on stop-action shooting is provided in the chapter

Animals in Action beginning on page 126.)

BLURRING FOR EFFECT

Choosing an exposure time that produces obvious blur in a moving subject is an exercise full of potential for producing beautiful abstract imagery whose precise formulation is normally difficult to predict. It is most commonly used when photographing streams, rivers, or waterfalls to enhance the sensuous movements of water. You will be pleased with such attempts at any exposure time of 1/4 second or longer for scenic-size magnifications. When framing is tighter, faster shutter speeds are possible. The intentional blurring of moving elements in the composition creates a powerful visual impact primarily because this sensation is unavailable to

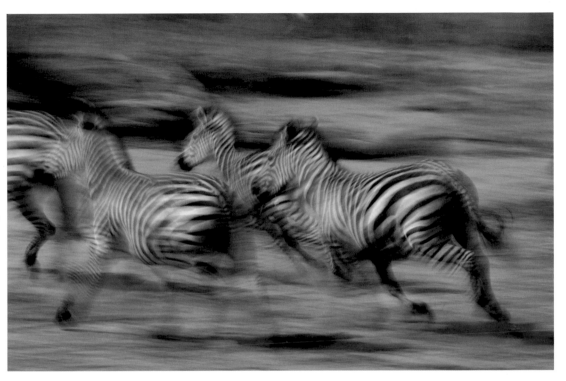

normal vision; it cannot be frozen for detailed examination by the naked eye as it can in a photograph. In addition to water you can use blurring techniques for practically any subject in nature — falling snow, a zooming hummingbird, galloping zebras, breaking surf, stars in the night sky, or a merganser eating its dinner. The key considerations are exposure duration and relative speed of the various moving components — camera, main subject, and secondary subjects. Exploring motion with a still camera is a fascinating endeavor with unlimited possibilities and many surprises.

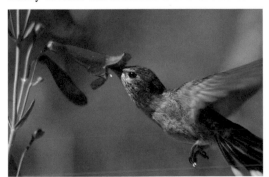

Zebras, Hwange National Park, Zimbabwe (above). A blur of confusing stripes is thought to be a zebra herd's defence against the charge of a lion. This effect was captured with a handheld camera panned to match the motion of the running herd at a shutter speed of 1/15 second.

Broad-tailed hummingbird, near Santa Fe, New Mexico (left). A shutter speed of 1/350 second arrested the motion of this thirsty hummer, caught hovering at a scarlet gilia bloom.

Modifying Natural Light

Using filters and reflectors for better results with the best films for nature subjects

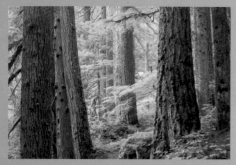

Grove of the Patriarchs, Mount Rainier National Park, Washington (above/below). *Shooting when the forest was wet and using Fujichrome Velvia produced saturated color in both photos. In the lower picture, reflections from leaves were removed with a polarizing filter.*

IN NATURE PHOTOGRAPHY a faithful record of the wild scene is normally desired. Filters are used primarily to reduce subject contrast and enhance color. The relatively small selection of filters described here is about all you need to develop a full, professional portfolio. Filters are mostly used in photographing the landscape and other still life subjects such as trees and wildflowers. They are rarely used for wildlife, insects and other invertebrates. There are many different brands of filter and most are similar in quality and effect. Except for color-enhancing filters, prestige brands provide little if any improvement in quality over less expensive types. For professional applications in particular, however, high end filters offer more variety of types and sizes as well as extra-thin filters for use with wide-angle lenses to prevent vignetting.

ONE SIZE FITS ALL

When developing a filter system, it's best if all filters fit your largest diameter lens(es). Appropriately sized step-up rings can be permanently attached to your smaller lenses to accommodate the larger filters thus eliminating the need for carrying a variety of sizes. Extra filters are not burdensome, but rather difficult to keep track of and organize during high-paced shooting.

POLARIZING FILTERS

I keep polarizing filters attached to my lenses most of the time. They produce greater color saturation by

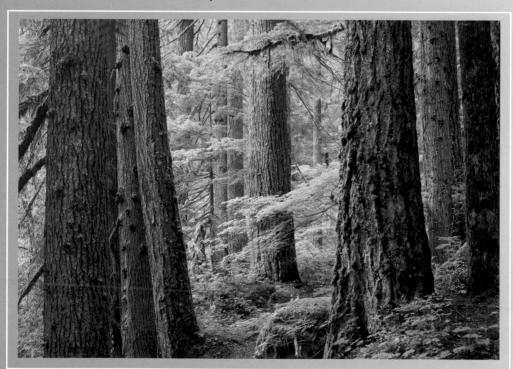

reducing or eliminating reflected glare from nonmetallic surfaces like leaves, grass and water. They also add color density to blue skies when photographed at a right angle to the sun. These filters reduce scene brightness by one to two stops. They are thick and may cut off part of the view in the corners of the frame (vignetting) especially when used with ultrawide-angle lenses. Before you buy, attach the filter and view a bright light source with the lens stopped down to minimum aperture. Darkening in the corners of the viewfinder indicates vignetting and it will be even more apparent on film. When shooting with a wide-angle lens at right angles to the sun, be aware that the lens takes in so much sky that the darker polarized area in the center will be

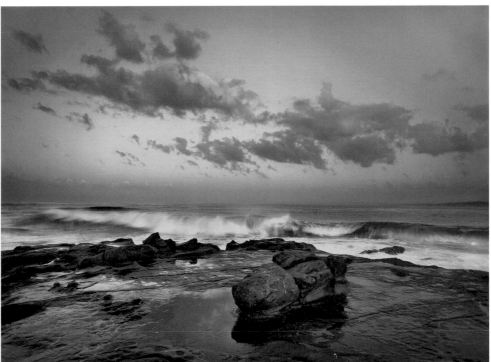

flanked unnaturally by areas of brighter sky. It's better in such circumstances to put aside the polarizing filter and increase sky density with a split ND filter. Most modern cameras require circular (rather than standard) polarizing filters for accurate operation of the light meter and autofocus system. Your camera manual should provide this information. You can modify the amount of polarization simply by turning an adjustable ring on the filter. The effects can be monitored in the viewfinder.

SPLIT NEUTRAL DENSITY FILTERS

Along with the tripod and Fujichrome Velvia, the

Rock shelf at La Jolla Cove, California (above). To retain the rich color of the sky and also capture the detail in the darker foreground rocks, I used a one-stop split neutral density filter (see illustration at left) to reduce contrast in the scene to a level within the latitude range of the film. Pentax 645, 45–85mm f/4.5 lens, one-stop split neutral density filter, Fujichrome Velvia, one second at f/22.

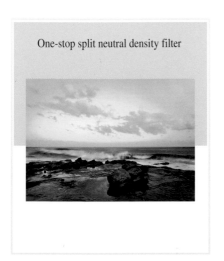

One-stop split neutral density filter

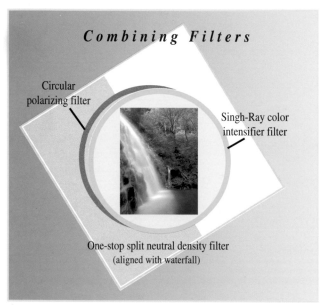

Combining Filters

Circular polarizing filter

Singh-Ray color intensifier filter

One-stop split neutral density filter
(aligned with waterfall)

Crabtree Falls, Shenandoah National Park, North Carolina (right). Three types of filtration were combined to make this image (see illustration above). A Singh-Ray circular polarizer with color intensifier filter was used to saturate color and remove reflections from the water. A one-stop split neutral density filter was placed over the milky falls to reduce brightness and hold detail. I prefer to attach my split neutral density filters using duct or gaffer tape rather than a filter holder (see right) to avoid vignetting when several filters are used.

neutral density (ND) type of filter is one of the landscape photographer's best friends. Half of this square (or rectangular) filter is clear and the other half is neutral density (gray) which darkens the part of the scene over which it is placed to a degree dependent on the strength of the filter. These plastic resin filters are used mostly in high contrast landscape situations when the sky is brighter than the terrain. The filter is mounted in a special holder so that it can be moved up and down and/or tilted to fit the design of the scene. Cokin filter holders are the standard holders used for many brands. Filters and holders are offered in two sizes — a small amateur size (A) and a larger professional size (P). Serious photographers will want to invest in the P series which will accommodate both small and large diameter lenses. I don't use filter holders; instead, I attach the filters directly to the lens using duct or gaffer tape. This eliminates the vignetting problem altogether and allows greater versatility when using more than one filter at a time (see illustration on this page).

The dark part of the filter is positioned over the bright part (usually the sky) of the image by examining the effect in the viewfinder. Study the scene at stopped-down aperture to be sure of placing the filter precisely. Each aperture will

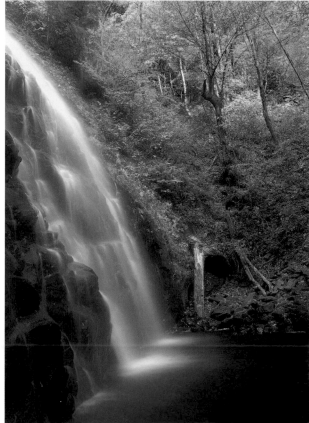

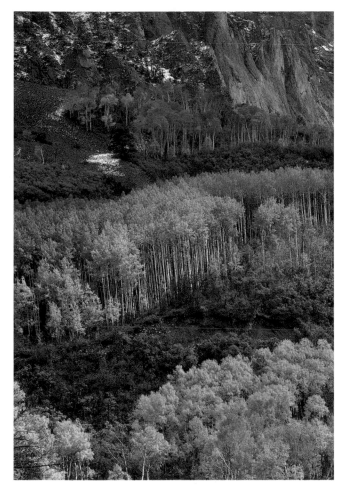

with an abrupt border between clear and dark halves) are more useful than soft-edge types.

GRADUATED NEUTRAL DENSITY FILTERS

Often the region where land meets sky does not match the straight border of the split ND filter. The horizon of many topographies is interrupted by trees, cacti, rock pinnacles, mountains, hills or all of the foregoing. Here the only way to lower the density of the sky without leaving a telltale underexposed swath of terrain along the horizon is to use a graduated neutral density filter. With this filter, the transition between clear and dark regions is gradual and spans the length of the filter. Its effect is beneficial but not as defined or dramatic as that achieved with split ND filters.

COLOR-INTENSIFYING FILTERS

Also called color-enhancing filters, these accentuate mainly red and orange parts of the spectrum. Unfortunately some brands introduce unnatural color shifts that detract from the beauty of the scene rather than enhance it. I use the Singh-Ray color intensifier which gives a

show a different effect as depth of field changes. Avoid overlapping the gray area onto the land (snow-capped peaks excepted) as this will darken the edge of the land unacceptably. Leaving too much space will generate a strange, bright margin along the horizon. Meter the scene in the normal way with the filters in place. One-stop and two-stop filters are suitable for ninety percent of landscape work. Hard-edge filters (those

Aspens near Marcellina Mountain, Colorado (below and left). *The color intensifier filter made by Singh-Ray provides a subtle boost to color without introducing a significant color cast as happens with many other brands. It's expensive but hard to beat for adding extra zip to subject color subdued by soft light. The picture below was taken without the filter while the picture at left shows the result when the filter is in place.*

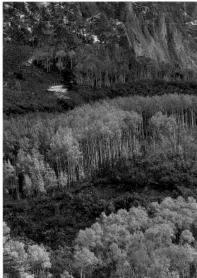

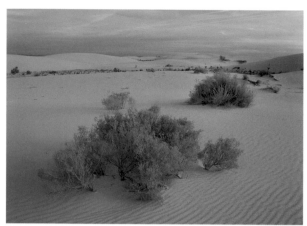

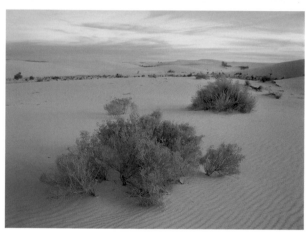

White Sands National Monument, New Mexico (above).

These two frames were made using a blue/gold polarizing filter. The top picture is made with the filter adjusted for maximim blue filtration and the bottom to maximum gold. Although both effects are pleasing, this filter needs to be used with restraint.

subtle, even boost to all colors except yellow. It's great for accentuating fresh greens, autumn reds, and blue skies but you should probably keep it in the bag when shooting aspens in the fall or other predominantly gold/yellow motifs. Other brands of color-intensifying filters you might want to try are Lee and Tiffen. Digital shooters have no need for these filters as color intensity and cast can be precisely adjusted on the computer.

WARMING FILTERS

These amber filters (for film-shooters only) impart a yellow/orange hue through a scene. They're useful for pumping up the colors of a sunset or warming up subjects that are photographed in the shade. Most photographers use an 81A (least effect) or 81B (moderate effect).

COMBINATION FILTERS

When stacking two or more filters onto the front of the lens, vignetting is likely to occur, especially with wide-angle focal lengths. To skirt this problem manufacturers offer two-in-one combination filters that are as thin as a single filter. The most popular combinations are the circular polarizer/color intensifier filter (Singh-Ray), which you will use often, and the circular polarizing/warming filter made by several manufacturers, which will spend most of its time in your camera bag.

BLUE/GOLD POLARIZING FILTERS

Like other polarizing filters these alter light only from reflected surfaces. They are most effective on sunny days (not effective in overcast conditions) in reducing glare, bumping up color saturation on land and water, and boosting density and chroma of the blue sky. They can be adjusted between gold and blue extremes. Effects vary from tinting reflections a garish metallic blue and washing a sky in ultra-saturated cyan (supernatural) to casting the scene in a soupy-looking mix of gold and green punctuated with metallic/gold and bronze highlights (unnatural) to anywhere in between (most natural). These filters do a good job during midday periods by increasing cloud-blue sky contrast and color saturation of terrain, if you adjust them carefully to avoid outlandish effects. They are most useful to commercial landscape photographers seeking theatrical imagery for advertising purposes.

PORTABLE REFLECTOR

I carry a portable reflector most of the time suspended from a strap on the back of my vest (see page 42). This reflector is a large (diameter 40 inches), circular, fold-up model manufactured by Photoflex. It is double-sided with a soft white surface (most useful) and a high-intensity silver surface. I use the reflector in two ways, though most often for bouncing light into the shadows of close-up subjects (usually wildflowers) to enhance color saturation. I normally use the soft, white side and keep the reflector far enough away to avoid any artificial effects (i.e., disappearance of natural shadows or elimination of tone modulation). Less frequently, I also use this reflector for landscapes to throw more light onto foreground elements that are shaded or illuminated by harsh sidelight. In such situations, I use

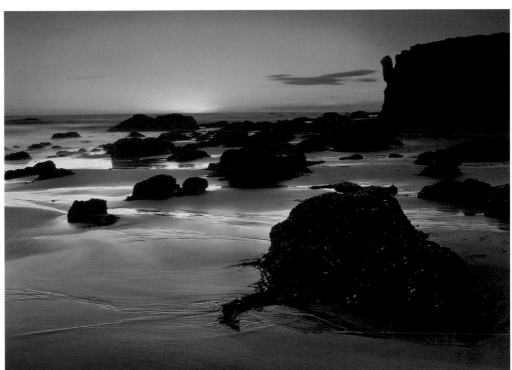

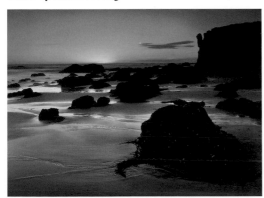

the silver side of the reflector for greater intensity as the target elements may be several yards or more away. When working in this way, I release the shutter with the camera's self-timer to keep two hands free for precise angling of the floppy reflector.

FILL-IN FLASH

You can use fill-in flash for much the same purpose as a portable reflector — as a light source auxiliary to the natural illumination to help brighten shadow areas. Unless you are shooting digital, however, you can only guess at the results until you get the film developed. Cameras

El Matador Beach, Malibu, California (above and left). A large (forty-inch diameter) silver reflector was used to bounce light onto the mussel-encrusted boulder in the foreground to better display the details and improve foreground interest. I held the reflector with both hands and tripped the shutter using the self-timer (ten-second delay). The take at left shows the unadulterated version.

Badwater, Death Valley National Park, California (below). I combined two one-stop split neutral density filters to modify this high contrast situation (see illustraion at right). One filter was angled to darken all of the scene except the foreground shrubs in order to bring out the detail and color of this element. The second filter was positioned higher to further darken the blue sky and snow-topped peaks. When working with more than one ND filter, attaching them with tape permits more versatility in positioning them than do standard holders.

with onboard pop-up flash normally provide automated settings for fill-in flash allowing you to choose the intensity of the fill. Normally a setting between minus one and two stops works best. Regardless of the type of flash used, be it built-in, off-camera TTL automatic, off-camera automatic, or off-camera manual, you need to adjust the camera for a normal exposure and then set the flash for an exposure that is one to two stops less. A simple way to do this, in the absence of an automated fill-in feature, is to set the flash ISO speed at double (one stop less) to quadruple (two stops less) the actual speed of the film in use.

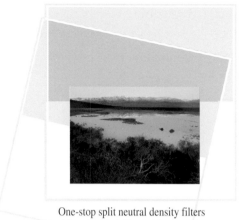

One-stop split neutral density filters
(aligned with skyline and foreground)

BEST FILMS FOR NATURE

Color transparency (slide) films are the most popular with nature photographers. These yield more brilliant color than print (negative) films. Transparencies can also be projected for an audience and they are preferred by the publication industry for reproduction, should you wish to see your pictures in print. There are many films that will produce beautiful, professional results but only a few that are the consistent mainstay for serious amateurs and professionals. These films are chosen for their fine detail and accurate but saturated color (especially green). The slower films are used primarily for landscape work where capturing subject movement at fast shutter speeds is less important

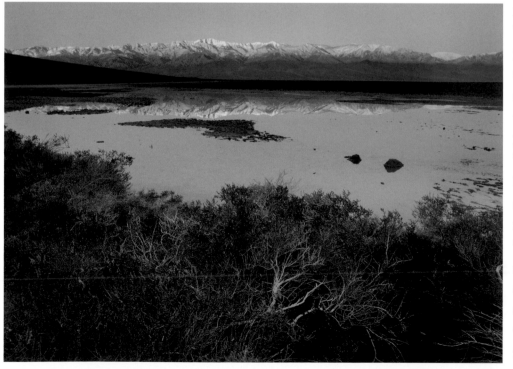

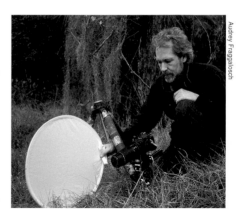

Audrey Fraggalosch

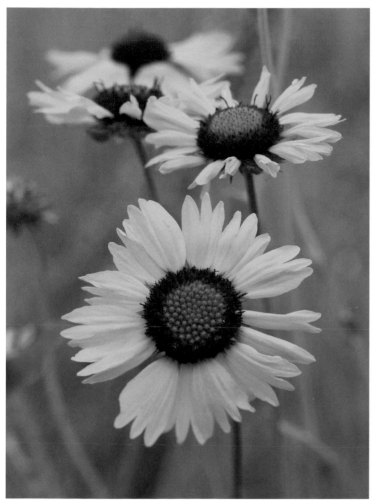

• **Fujichrome Velvia (ISO 50).** Ultra-fine grain, saturated color, vivid natural green, high contrast, the pre-eminent film for nature professionals. Superb for scenic work and wildlife under bright conditions. Can be pushed one stop (to ISO 100) when extra speed is needed.

• **Fujichrome Provia 100F (ISO 100).** Natural color (not as saturated as Fujichrome Velvia), ultra-fine grain, best film for shooting wildlife, can be pushed one stop without discernible increase in grain, also excellent when pushed two stops to ISO 400.

The remaining films are excellent but less popular among professionals.

• **Fujichrome Sensia 100 (ISO 100).** Fine grain, good color saturation, contrasty.

• **Ektachrome E100G (ISO 100).** Ultra-fine grain, compares very favorably to Provia 100F.

• **Kodak Elite Chrome 100 (ISO 100).** Fine grain, bold colors, moderate contrast.

Great shooting and stay out of the noonday sun!

Gaillardia clump, Badlands National Park, South Dakota (left). I used a small handheld reflector (see illustration above) to brighten the shadows of this spring bouquet. You need to evaluate carefully how much light is falling onto the subject to avoid a studio look. Keep in mind that the film will provide added contrast that your eyes will not see. All that is needed is a subtle boost of illumination to heighten color and detail. The effect of a matt white reflector is subtle and easy to modify. You control its intensity by changing the distance of the reflector to the subject.

than recording fine detail. Medium- to high-speed films are used mostly for wildlife subjects where action-stopping shutter speeds are used commonly. For best quality, you will want to use the slowest (lowest ISO speed) film possible. The films below provide the best quality results of any transparency films and are the only ones you need to consider for nature work.

Designing the Picture Space

How to manage image features to achieve clarity of expression

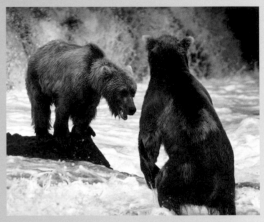

Giraffes, Masai Mara National Reserve, Kenya (below). *The brightest, clearly defined feature in a composition is almost always the most attractive. If such an element does not represent the center of interest, it should be eliminated or subdued by changing camera angle, focus point, aperture size, etc. Here the sun is the strongest visual element; timing the exposure to link it to the passing giraffe silhouette preserved the unity of the composition.*

IT IS NECESSARY TO master the principles of picture design, or composition, to effectively express yourself through photography. A knowledge of picture design lets you clearly communicate experiences in the natural world that you see and feel.

Composition is the way you arrange the elements of a picture, that jumble of lines, shapes, and textures that appears in the viewfinder. By giving order to these elements you are able to relate a clear message. Composition is the key that unlocks the emotions of the viewer. It is a universal language that reveals the photographer's message to anyone who can see.

DOMINANCE

Learning to use the language of composition is hardly more difficult than learning to make a correct exposure. All design is based on the premise that some elements are visually dominant, catching the eye more than others. The systematic use of this principle of dominance will help you decide how to manage the graphic features of a scene.

Many compositions are organized around a single, striking element (a visual center of interest). More complex compositions are based on a number of elements working together to create a theme or visual impression.

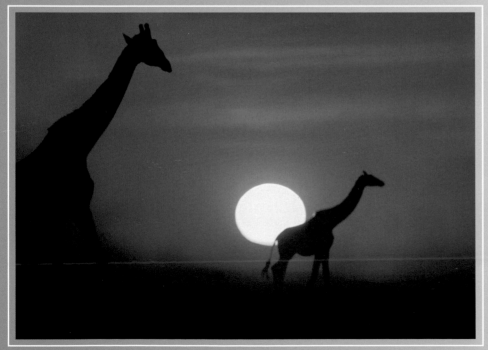

Establishing visual priorities for picture elements is based on an intuitive sense that renders these kinds of conclusions: red is more attractive than yellow; large draws more attention than small; difference draws more attention than conformity; jagged lines are more striking than curved ones; diagonal lines are more attractive than vertical ones; sharpness is more attractive than blur; and, most significant for photographers, light is more attractive than dark. This list is only a sample of the myriad elements that can be compared and objectively evaluated.

The view that confronts you at the edge of a lake is not as simple as the examples on this list. The complexity of visual elements more often requires you to compare a curved red line with a jagged yellow one; a gray diagonal, rough texture with one that is chartreuse, vertical and smooth. These visual comparatives seem difficult to evaluate when described in words, but our eyes intuitively make such assessments with

speed and accuracy. This evaluation process starts unconsciously as soon as you look in the viewfinder and begin manipulating picture elements by asking your subject to smile or to move a little closer to the camera.

Newcomers to photographic composition evaluate the elements they see in the viewfinder based on the intellectual or emotional identity of these features rather than their graphic import. When photographing a moose, an inexperienced photographer understandably fails to notice a

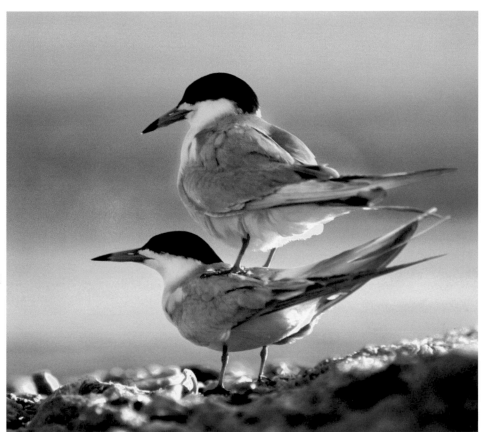

Common terns, near Rockport, Texas (above). This composition has no center of interest but uses the repetition of graphic features to emphasize the concepts of harmony and togetherness over subject matter. Canon EOS 3, Canon 400mm f/2.8 L lens, 1.4X teleconverter, Fujichrome Provia 100F, 1/250 second at f/5.6.

Brown (grizzly) bears, McNeil River Falls, Alaska (far left, top). Precise timing and selective focus give a tight, dramatic structure to this encounter between two bears vying for the same fishing spot.

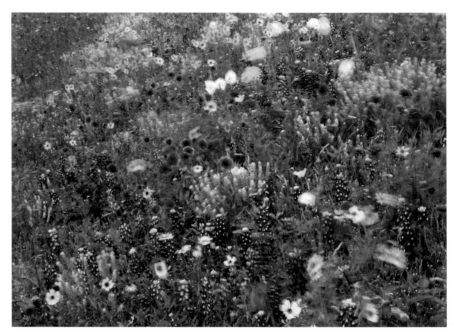

Wildflower meadow near Llano, Texas (right and below). This photograph displays under soft light a full spectrum of saturated primary hues, red being the most attractive. The composition is structured on the diagonal sweep of red gaillardia blooms that stretches from the right foreground to the left background. These pictures were taken from the roof of my motor home with a telephoto zoom lens which afforded a variety of magnifications even though my movements were restricted. The detailed version was shot at a shutter speed of 1/125 second and the wind-tossed rendition at 1/2 second.

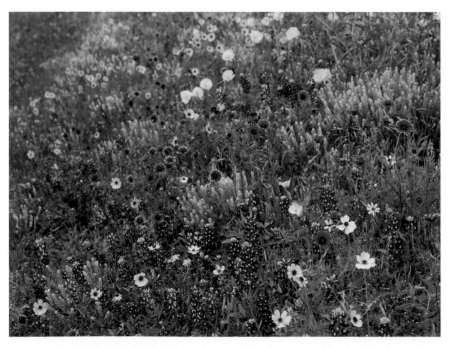

hotspot or telephone pole that mars the background. Such elements go unnoticed until the full sensory experience of the field is transferred to film and placed on the light table for unhurried scrutiny, with vision the sole frame of reference and plenty of time to analyze the scene. The moose is a still, brown, shape hardly discernible from the surrounding vegetation while the out of focus highlight is a brilliant pool that attracts immediate attention.

To avoid these oversights, photographers wisely train themselves to ignore the identity of elements in a scene and perceive only in graphic terms. The photographer sees his center of interest — the moose — as a furry, brown shape rather than the planet's largest deer. Before making the exposure, he adjusts the camera to eliminate the bright highlight, adjusts aperture to reduce depth of field and blur the surrounding vegetation, and waits to catch a highlight in the subject's eye.

COLOR

Color evokes the greatest emotional reaction of any graphic element. Its presence significantly influences every design. More often than not, it is this aspect of a scene that induces a nature photographer to stop and set up the camera. Color not only projects a visual force all its own but it is also an integral part of other picture elements — shapes, lines, textures — that we find in a photograph. Our reaction to color is spontaneous and instinctive. Color control is achieved primarily through subject selection, framing, and camera angle, particularly as it is applied to the relationship of differing hues and tones.

Each portion of the color spectrum evokes a distinct emotional response. The most attractive, but not necessarily the most appealing color, is red. Being the color of blood and fire, it is simultaneously a signal of food and warmth, danger and death. It is rare for red to be used effectively in a photograph unless it represents or supports the center of interest. Red, yellow and orange, the warm colors, have more visual power than cool colors — the blues and greens. The appeal of a particular hue is specific to each viewer depending on his or her experience, mood and inherent tendency. We can be subjective in the use of color in our designs so long as it is premised on the universally distinctive qualities of warm and cool hues.

In assessing the relative strength of color you also need to consider its purity. A color is most powerful when it has not been diluted by either white or black. Color purity is inherent in the

Lichen-encrusted rock, Rocky Mountain National Park, Colorado (below). *This composition is a study in warm color harmonies and texture. The scene was framed to capture the rock strata flowing through the frame in a diagonal, unifom pattern.*

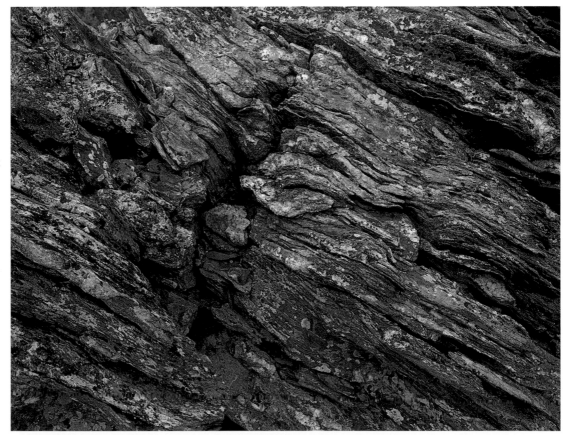

The Bonfires of Autumn

North America's deciduous forests present the planet's most spectacular show of seasonal color. These recommendations will help you record this luxury palette in clean, saturated hues with zippy contrast full of detail in highlights and shadows.
• Shoot digitally or with Fujichrome Velvia. This film is far and away the scenic emulsion of choice of both professional and top amateur nature photographers. Colors are rich and saturated, pushing the envelope of credibility without bursting the seams.
• Use a polarizing filter to eliminate reflections from wet or waxy surfaces of leaves. These shiny highlights mask the true pigmentation of the vegetation and reduce color saturation.
• Bracket exposures in 1/2- or 1/3-stop intervals by

a full stop or more above and below your base exposure. (Even with a lot of experience, exposure is unpredictable with a narrow-latitude transparency film like Velvia.) By bracketing you can choose the image with the best color on the light table or CCD after the fact; nothing could be simpler.
• Plan your shoot for the best light. The ideal time for capturing tight forest shots (lots of trees but no sky) is usually on a cloudy day during mid-morning. On sunny days you will achieve the richest color with front-lighting in the early morning and late afternoon. However, be aware that when the sun nears the horizon, light has a warm color temperature which corrupts clean greens and blues and lights up reds and oranges with an unworldly neon brilliance.
• Shoot when the vegetation is wet with rain or dew. In combination with a polarizing filter, the soaked look yields the most color saturation.
• Schedule your session to coincide with the peak of color. This is easy to do by consulting an appropriate internet website. You can easily find these sites by doing a search using the name of the place followed by the words "fall color". If I am visiting a faraway location, my preference is to err on arriving late in the season rather than early. This approach increases the chance of encountering a photogenic dusting of snow or frost and there are also more leaves on the ground and in streams and pools which make for interesting still-life shots. With less leaves in the canopy you can show more than just a wall of vegetation; the openings allowing the camera to peer into the forest itself for more varied design possibilities. If you must choose in advance among several destinations, keep in mind that

Aspens, pines, and spruces, White River National Forest, Colorado (below). Mountain locations are always a good bet for exciting fall shooting. Even if your timing is off and you miss the main show, the changes in elevation causes a staggered display of fiery pigment with the earliest color generally appearing on high, north-facing slopes and moving down to the valleys and riversides as the season progresses.

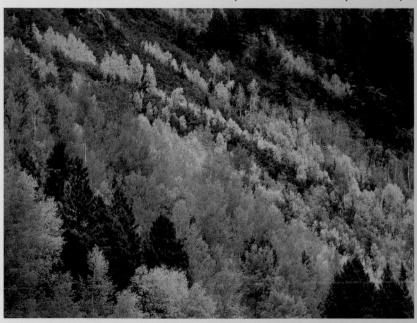

elevation is as important as latitude in kindling autumn bonfires. Mountainous locations are generally your best bet as they offer autumn's spectrum in various stages of readiness, depending on what part of the mountain you're aiming for. Should you, for

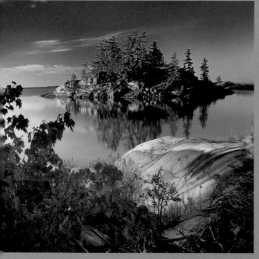

example, arrive too early for attractive color in the valleys and lower slopes, you're sure to find more advanced development higher up, and vice-versa.
• Look for compositions that team autumn's warm hues with their complementaries (opposites) — combinations such as green/rose (white pines/sugar maples), or blue/red (clear skies/hardwood forests). By bringing complementaries together, each color appears by contrast to be more intense. Due to the absence of color, black (silhouetted trunks and branches) and white (snow and frost) strengthen the apparent intensity of adjacent color elements.

subject matter, but it can also be affected by the intensity and the angle of illumination. Colors in shadow areas have more black and are less brilliant; in highlight areas they become washed out. Exposure and filtration can be used in selected parts of the scene to control color saturation and contrast.

The strength of a color is greatly determined by its relationship to other colors in the picture. Colors gain apparent strength when juxtaposed with an opposite or complementary hue (green with orange, red with blue, yellow with purple). Fiery autumn foliage appears more intense if set against a blue sky or when mixed with the green of conifers.

Intense, vibrant colors are more attractive than muted ones but they are not necessarily more desirable. The color scheme of a photograph should support the main theme. A design that incorporates intense, contrasting colors is visually exciting, causing the eye to bounce back and forth between competing hues. A contrasting color

Georgian Bay, Killarney Provincial Park, Ontario (left). Autumn foliage gains intensity if set against a complementary hue, in this case the blue of a polarized sky. A one-stop split neutral density filter allowed for better color saturation in the shaded foreground.

Guadalupe Mountains, Texas (below). In this composition the brightly toned boulders shepherd the eye in an S-curve journey through the picture field toward the spotlit ramparts of El Capitan on the horizon. The selection of camera position generated this winding arrangement of boulders and a one-stop split neutral density filter held back the sky and distant mountains to emphasize the pattern.

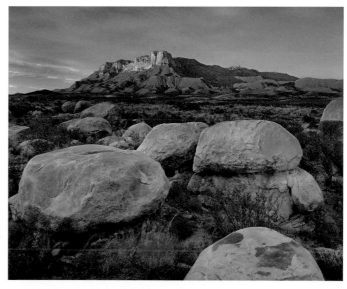

Dragonfly, Lake Newell, Alberta (right). Simplicity is often the key to effective design. Because of the soft background and strong leading lines, I was able to place the center of interest (dragonfly) high in the frame to emphasize its seemingly precarious perch atop the bulrush stem.

Cloud bank over Chama, New Mexico (below). Although these color hues are subdued, the image is attractive due to the ironic marriage of modulated textures with the instinctive significance of the clouds as indicators of stormy weather.

scheme suits dynamic picture themes that express action, conflict, joy, anger or celebration; it is not usually suitable for portraying passive, introspective themes.

Harmonious color schemes are those composed of one or two similar hues, such as blue and turquoise or brown and maroon. They may be made up of contrasting colors like red and blue if an intermediate hue (purple) is included to create a smooth transition. A picture structured on color harmony produces a coherent visual effect. Color harmony suits

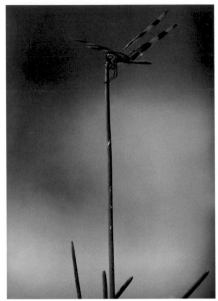

images with peaceful themes and those incorporating horizontal lines and smooth shapes.

The effect of color on the image is pervasive. It helps to distinguish and identify the subject of a composition, it communicates mood and emotion, and in many pictures its sensory appeal is strong enough to act as the central theme. Color is an integral part of our perceptive process, our dreams, our memories and our personalities. It will work best in your photographs if you approach it intuitively, using it in a way that feels right to you. An openness to new color experiences will keep you in touch with your color instincts.

THE CENTER OF INTEREST

Most photographs have a visual center of interest — one element that dominates the composition. In its most simple application, it is a picture of something — a cheetah, a maple leaf, an otter, a canyon. The center of interest orchestrates the design: It determines the nature and arrangement of all other picture elements.

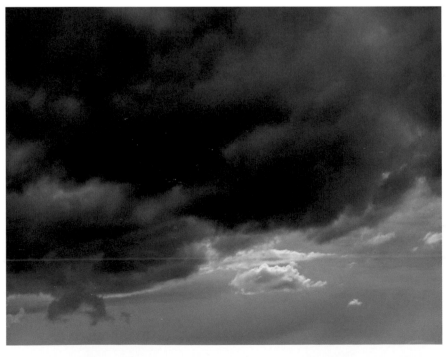

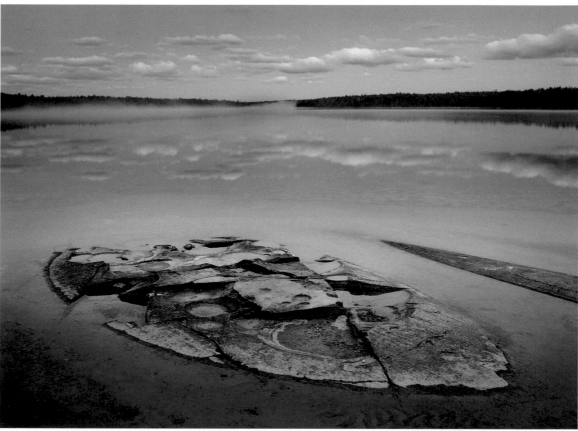

In wildlife photography the composition process is primarily one of elimination. You frame and focus on the center of interest and then examine the rest of the scene for elements that may detract from it. This includes anything that is brighter or of a more interesting shape. These elements can be eliminated or subdued in a variety of ways, such as changing the camera angle or moving in closer to the subject. Less often you may incorporate new elements in the scene that reinforce or support the center of interest. In the case of a portrait of a speeding roadrunner, it might be a cactus (to show habitat) or a streaked background (to show movement).

PLACING THE CENTER OF INTEREST

Where to locate the center of interest within the frame can only be determined in the context of the other design factors. The prime real estate of any picture is the center. This is where the eye is most likely to begin its exploration of the image. If you place the center of interest in this position it creates a static design — an effect that is rarely desirable. The eye settles on the center of interest, scrutinizes it periodically and then scans the remainder of the frame for anything else of interest. As it has already found your most compelling element, it soon returns for another look, grows bored, and asks you to turn the page or move along to another exhibit.

Suppose you leave the most valuable area of the frame empty and place the center of interest

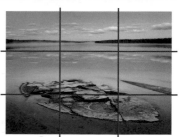

Twilight at Cypress Lake, Bruce Peninsula National Park, Ontario (above). Color harmonies and the rule of thirds work to create this peaceful, dreamy impression.

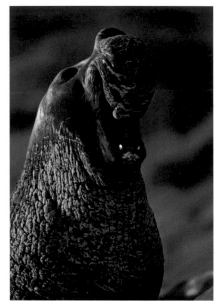

Elephant seal bull, Point Piedras Blancas, California (above). The eye is the center of interest in this portrait and is placed according to the rule of thirds. Open space is left in front of the seal to hold the energy of its threatening roar. Although all of the scene is washed in the same earthy hues, the center of interest is graphically dominant due to sharp focus and glinting highlights.

Heerman's gulls, Isla Isabel, Nayarit, Mexico (right). One of numerous frames made of this group of active subjects, this take captures a moment when supporting elements (red bills) direct the viewer's attention to the center of interest, sharply rendered in the upper third of the frame.

elsewhere. The eye enters in the middle, finds nothing of interest, and begins to scan the frame. Sooner or later it finds the center of interest but on the way it has come across other attractive elements. When all is seen, the eye gravitates back to the center of the frame, but again it finds nothing and begins the search anew, perhaps this time taking a different path to the main subject. The dynamism of this process excites our visual sense and sustains viewer interest.

The visual power of the main subject determines how far from the center it can be placed. If there are other equally powerful visual elements, then it can become dominant only by occupying the central area of the frame. A main subject that has strong visual properties can be placed almost anywhere and it will be discovered by the eye. However, if it is kept too near one edge and the remainder of the composition has

little to sustain visual interest, the composition becomes unbalanced.

RULE OF THIRDS

If you priorize the features of a scene based on their visual dominance, you can be pretty sure of a strong composition if you follow the well known rule of thirds (see page 107). This guide calls for the center of interest to be placed one-third of the way from the top or bottom of the frame and one-third of the way from either side.

THEMATIC CENTERS OF INTEREST

The organization of many images, particularly landscapes, is based on theme rather than a single dominant subject. Such pictures attempt to

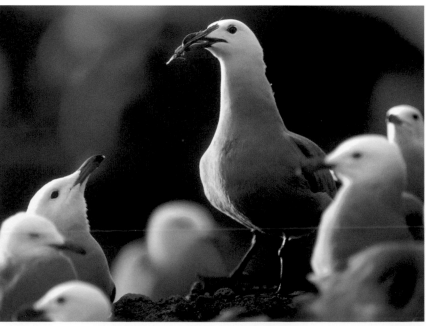

project an idea, relationship or concept through the collective impact of diverse picture elements. The success of a theme such as "peace" might be expressed by flowing shapes, pastel colors, horizontal lines, fair skies and calm pools. Some themes are purely visual, finding full expression as provocative patterns, expressive colors, stimulating textures, or abstractions of line and form. Some compositions incorporate a visual center of interest as a component of a

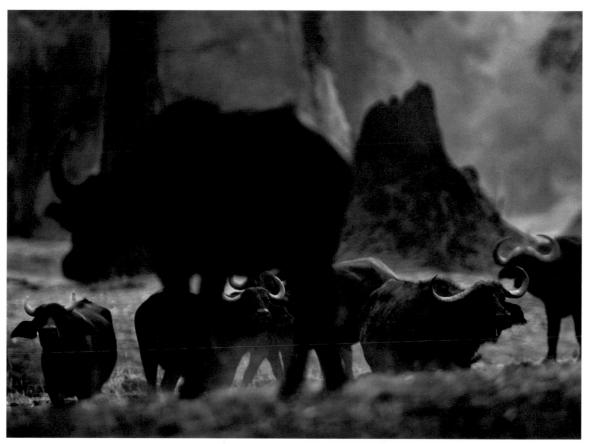

thematically organized design. This twofold method of shaping the viewer's examination and feelings can be especially compelling.

There are many ways of controlling, modifying, emphasizing and locating the features of a scene in the development of a composition.

• Select a subject that expresses your intent.
• Choose the precise season, time of day and moment of exposure.
• Set the camera-to-subject distance.
• Adjust for an appropriate angle on the subject.

• Use filters and reflectors to modify lighting.
• Select focal length to control magnification and perspective.
• Set depth of field by adjusting aperture.
• Control motion, sharpness and blur by setting shutter speed.

Learning how to put the principles of design to work in your photography will help you make the most of photo opportunities you encounter in the field and allow you to more clearly express your feelings about nature.

African buffalo near the Zambezi River, Zimbabwe (above). This is a complex composition with many elements competing for attention. Placing the main subject near the center of the frame and timing exposure to catch it framed by another buffalo provides critical emphasis and subsequent structure to the design.

Photographs as Impressions

Some easy departures from realism toward subjective imagery

Basswood leaves frozen in a stream (below). That this is a subjective study of pattern, texture and color rather than a literal representaion of leaves is signaled by the camera angle (from directly above) and tight cropping (to obscure identity).

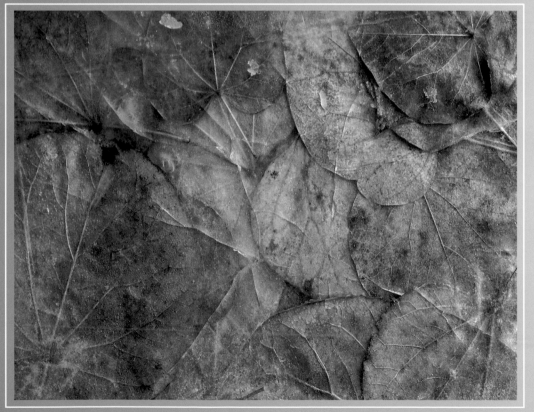

NORMALLY, PHOTOGRAPHERS strive to make an accurate visual record of the natural world. But there is just as much truth to photographing in a way that expresses your feelings about nature as there is in operating your camera as if it were a photocopier of wilderness. One way presents a generally objective reality, the other a subjective one. Realism provides as much insight into the sentiments and philosophy of a photographer as more subjective approaches, especially when a body of work, rather than a single image is considered. But a subjective approach speaks more immediately; it's a voice that offers commentary about the photographer's feeling on an image-by-image basis. We know this because each picture offers unmistakable graphic cues that signal a departure from objective visual convention. In this chapter I'll describe some of the ways you can announce your intentions to express what you feel rather than what you see. These graphic techniques are the tools for making impressionistic imagery. Using them won't make you any more of an artist than you already are, although their novelty might provide enjoyable short-term diversion. If art is in one sense a search for truth, these techniques may provide stepping stones for your journey.

The techniques that follow are methods generally for bringing abstraction into your imagery.

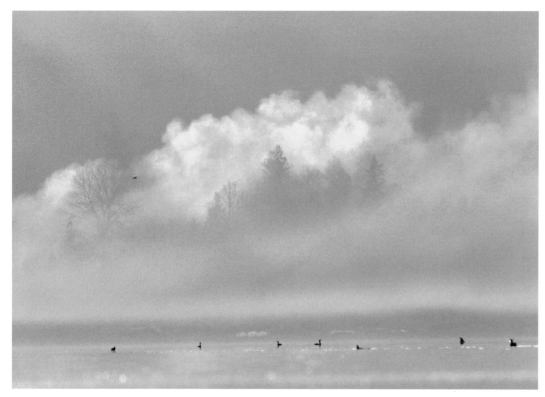

Esquimalt Lagoon on a foggy morning, Vancouver Island, British Columbia (left). *Fog obscures the shoreline as well as the horizon making it appear that the seabirds are suspended in time and space. By isolating this patch of ill-defined, mist-shrouded seashore, I was able to say that mood and atmosphere were more important than recording a clearly defined set-ting. I used a zoom lens to crop out features that would have provided more literal informa-tion about the scene.*

Twilight at El Matador State Beach, Malibu, California (below). *A blur of birds and rol-ling surf signal that this image is intended to show the feeling and atmosphere of the seashore rather than to define its visual parameters.*

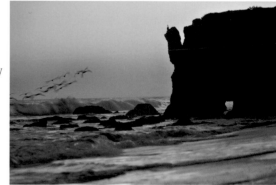

They are ways to reduce or eliminate the links between the visual reality of a scene and the graphic features of your composition. Any tech-nique that moves away from conventional procedures (normal exposure density, camera po-sition at eye-level, main subject centered in the frame, sharp focus on the main subject, etc.) is a move toward impressionism.

COMPUTER-GENERATED EFFECTS

Subjective impressionistic effects can be gener-ated on the computer using image manipulation software like Photoshop. With a little experience you can duplicate (often with greater ease and control) some of the in-camera techniques described below. However, you'll find that the experience of making these effects in-camera provides a valuable and often essential inspirational basis for imagery you may later create on the computer.

SUBDUE REALITY CUES

Generally you can exclude or mask cues from the composition which signal

Autumn dreams (below). I shot two slightly offset frames of this forest, one sharply focused from front to back and the other blurred. Each frame was over-exposed by one stop and then sandwiched together to achieve normal density but with almost surreal color.

time and space, such as the horizon, clouds and direct sunlight. Fog is great for blurring details and spatial references of the environment.

ALTER THE ANGLE

Any view that shows the scene from an angle different from our normal vantage point five or six feet above the ground reflects the photographer's subjective bias. The most abstract angle is usually from directly above but any framing that establishes a vantage point unlikely to be visited by the viewer in normal circumstances works.

ZERO IN

Frame the details of a subject rather than including features that signal its identity. Shoot the textures evident in the bark of a tree rather than showing the contours of the trunk or even the entire tree. In this way the viewer sees the photograph as an expression of sensation rather than a presentation of fact.

SELECTIVE FOCUS

This simple technique uses sharp focus and shallow depth of field (set the lens aperture at or near its maximum size) to cast a focus spotlight on restricted areas of a scene. This constitutes a personal announcement of what the photographer thinks is important. This is an easy and obvious way to express your feelings about any scene.

ISOLATE A PATTERN

An integral component of many

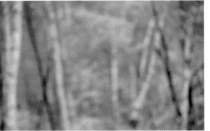
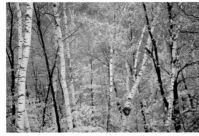

natural phenomena, patterns comprise one of the most alluring features of the environment — the cadence of a galloping pony, the petals of a sunflower, the momentum of ocean surf, the trumpeting of an elephant. A pattern is generated by a rhythmic repetition of accent and interval, varying from a single uniform accent repeated at regular intervals (sand grains on a beach) to those more complex such as repetitions of accelerating sequences (flight of a jackrabbit). Visual rhythms occur everywhere in infinite variety and they are readily incorporated into realistic imagery. Impressionistic effects result when the pattern is isolated and refined to the extent that subject identity is either lost or assumes only secondary importance and viewer attention is focused on visual melodies and the sensations generated by colors, shapes, and textures. When setting camera angle and magnification, try to capture only the most telling and refined visual rhythms in the pattern by selective focus and framing.

Set the Camera in Motion

As realistic imagery is normally rooted in showing detail, you can create subjective effects by recording the scene indistinctly. One way to do this is to move the camera during

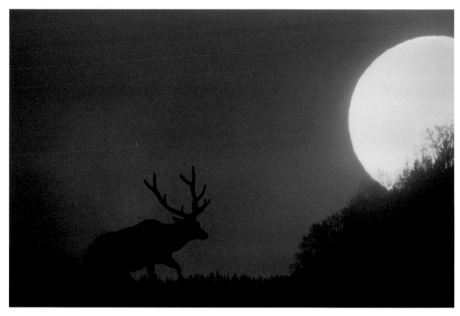

exposure either by swinging the camera on a tripod, handheld movements, or zooming during exposure. You can't easily tell what the results will be so it's advisable to vary movements over several attempts. Keep in mind that blur increases as the scene is magnified, as exposure time increases, and as speed and the extent of camera movement, including zooming, increases.

Shoot A Photo Montage

If you are shooting slide film, interesting effects can be created by sandwiching two slides together. This procedure Is commonly used to create

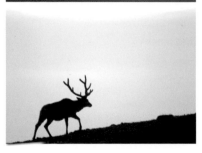

Bull elk at sunset (above). *This image exhibits many of the hallmarks of realism — sharpness, spatial cues, natural color and normal tonalities. However, perspective has been compressed and the principle features (sun and elk) are out of scale which gives the scene a surreal, other-worldly feeling. Although assembling the components of this montage required more skill, experience and field time than the picture on the opposite page, the photograph's melodramatic theme and graphic emphasis on subject places it more in the category of commercial illustration than art.*

Suspensions of flight (below).
The lack of defined environmental cues in this image, resulting from non-directional lighting, tight cropping and a camera position directly above the scene leads us to consider the interpretive presentation of color and pattern rather than more objective qualities of subject, location and circumstance. This flock of lesser flamingos was photographed over Lake Magadi, Kenya from an ultralight plane with a Canon EOS A2 and Canon lens 70–200mm f/2.8 lens.

realistic sunset/wildlife composites or other in-scale silhouetting motifs. For impressionistic effects, you can combine two or more images that are unconnected in time, place, size and/or perspective. These combinations are based on abstract and subjective qualities of color, texture and/or theme. If you manipulate images on the computer, you can easily combine any of the photos you have already taken. Otherwise, transparencies must usually be overexposed by about

one stop (for a two-slide sandwich) so that their combined densities will show normal exposure and then carefully framed to match up key areas of overlapping.

MAKE MULTIPLE EXPOSURES

Exposing a single frame of film more than once is another way of announcing your departure from literal interpretation. Your first consideration will be attaining normal density in the final

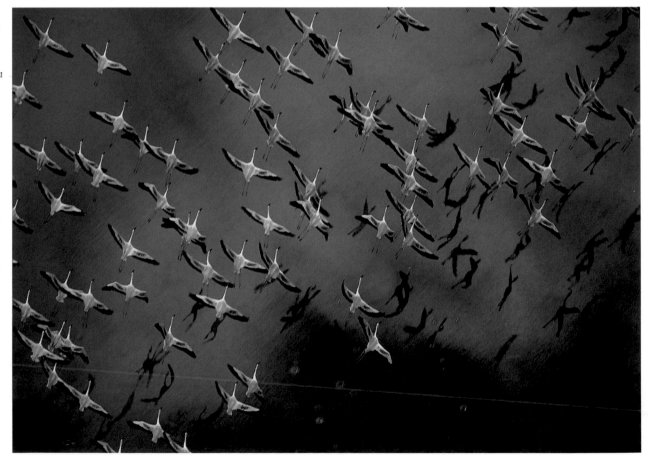

image. For double exposures, you need to reduce the amount of light reaching the film for each take by one-half for each exposure. This is easily done by decreasing shutter speed or aperture by one full stop. For three or more exposures for which you wish to keep aperture constant, make sure that total exposure time remains the same as for one exposure (e.g. four 1/8-second exposures can replace one 1/2-second exposure). If you want to keep shutter speed constant, reduce aperture size by the square root of the number of exposures

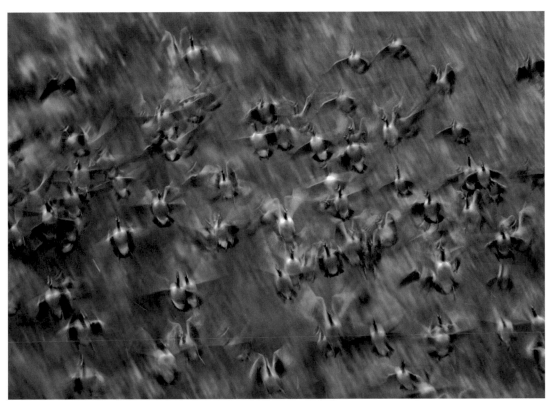

(e.g. two stops for four exposures, four stops for 16 exposures, etc.)

Making multiple exposures is at best a process of educated guesswork. Most of the subjective decisions will by necessity be made over the light table rather than behind a camera. Be sure to take several versions of a scene varying settings and procedures for each image to capture a variety of similar effects. For double exposures, the results are similar to making a montage (slide sandwich). For three or more exposures, it's often best to restrict the composition to a single subject or scene and vary the framing only

slightly with each take. This produces appealing, rhythmic results with lots of movement and pattern. If the re-framing process is too divergent, complementary colors and/or forms are sure to overlay one another causing a loss of definition, contrast and color purity.

Nature photography is as much about how you feel as it is about what you see. Savor the sensations and thoughts that are stimulated by a walk in the woods. Allow your instincts to bring these feelings to the attention of your photographic self. Happy hiking!

Canada Geese landing, near Long Sault, Ontario (above).
Impressionist effects can be generated by extended shutter speeds to produce blurred motion effects. Although we can only perceive movement as a blur of color and form, nevertheless, we do not readily accept it as objective reality because we know that the details are missing. This image is further abstracted by the elimination of picture elements (horizon, sky, terrain) which would help set the scale of the scene.

Part Three

Adventures with Wildlife

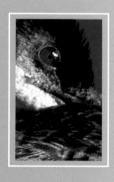

Getting Close

Techniques to draw within camera range of wild subjects

I'M SITTING COMFORTABLY on a ledge far up the mountainside in Oh-be-joyful Pass in the Raggeds Wilderness of central Colorado. In front of me is one of Canon's 500mm IS lenses supplemented by a 1.4X converter. My vest pockets are bulging with Fujichrome Provia 100F. The dramatic peaks, the morning sun and the rustle of aspen leaves confirm my sense of well-being. I feel certain I'm going to get some good photos. I've done my homework.

Flashes of fur appear between the loose, clattery rocks of the slope and descend toward the stream. The dab of fur hippity-hops across the water and disappears into a clump of paintbrushes, daisies and other flowers. The arrangement trembles and a fireweed blossom topples and disappears. The fur ball comes back into view (fireweed attached), hippity-hops across the stream and addresses the

slope. In a few minutes the animal materializes (as I thought it would) about five yards away. It's a pika, a high-mountain relative of the rabbit about the shape and size of a furry softball. While I quietly study the pika through the viewfinder, its mouth opens to sound a nasal bleat that echoes through the jumble of boulders. My motordrive chatters and a handful of frames

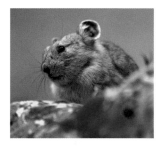

Pika, Raggeds Wilderness, Colorado (above). By researching information about the behavior of this species, I discovered several facts about its behavior and habitat that were essential to making this photograph. Canon EOS 3, Canon lens 500mm f/4 IS, 25mm extension tube, Fujichrome Provia 100F, 1/500 second at f/5.6.

Western grebe, Stone Lake, New Mexico (left). This intimate view was recorded from a distance of about 15 feet. Although uneasy by my closeness, the subject is still in a natural snoozing posture due to the concealment of my presence in a floating blind. The aim of most wildlife photography is to capture typical behavior that reveals the natural history of the subject. Canon EOS 3, Canon lens 500mm f/4 IS, 1.4X teleconverter, Fujichrome Provia 100F, 1/250 second at f/5.6.

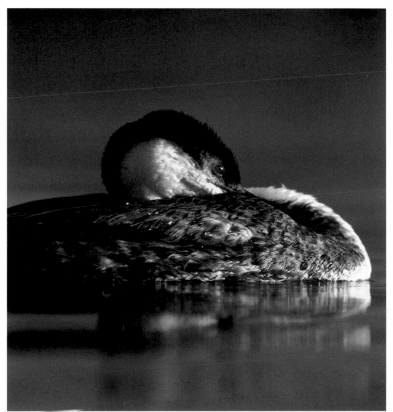

Lions, Hwange National Park,
Zimbabwe (below). In national
parks, many subjects are not
alarmed by the approach of a
vehicle. With the photographer
inside the car, the subject is able
to remain calm and carry on its
normal activities. It's difficult to
predict when the best opportunities
will arise but one thing is sure —
patience and persistence pay off in
better pictures. This photo was
taken from a small jeep with the
camera on a tripod set up over the
passenger seat. Canon EOS 3,
Canon lens 500mm f/4 IS, Fuji-
chrome Provia 100F.

streaks from the cassette. Over the next hour, I take pika portraits, pika vocalizing, and pika munching on vegetation.

Getting close enough to record a pika in detail is easy if you know where and how to look. As with most wildlife species, there are no magic formulas, just common sense procedures and techniques that can be easily mastered by anyone who regularly sets foot afield.

WILDLIFE RULES

As a rule, you can photograph at close range only at the subject's forbearance. Except for the photography of birds from blinds, the senses of wild animals are too keen for you to shoot undetected

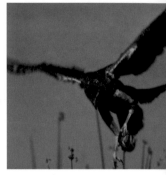

for more than a few seconds. Generally you must seek out animals that don't mind being near you. These critters fall into two groups. The first includes those that have no instinctive fear of humans, either because we don't find them appetizing (marmots, pikas, chickadees, hummingbirds) and leave them alone, or because they evolved in environments where there were few humans to deal with (small sea islands, polar regions). In the other category are animals that have learned that in certain settings (wildlife parks and preserves) humans are mostly harmless .

Not only do you need to get close to the subject, but you also need to remain there for more than a few seconds. It's by being around an animal for hours or even days (not necessarily continuous) that you will come up with exceptional images. Regardless of the circumstances, most wildlife retain some apprehension of humans that must be overcome before you can rack up a series of trophy photos.

DO YOUR HOMEWORK

We need to study the natural history of the animals we wish to photograph. There are

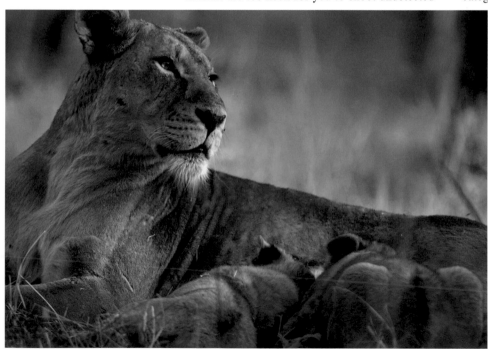

many publications on wildlife. My favorite easy-chair reference for North American mammals is *The Mammals of Canada* (A.W.F. Banfield, University of Toronto Press, 1992) which covers the habits of most species in great detail. A concise reference for toting on field trips is *A Field Guide to the Mammals* (William H. Burt and Richard P. Grossenheider, The Peterson Field Guide Series, Houghton Mifflin Co., Boston, 1998). For a quick reference on individual species, search the internet using the name of the animal. Academic diligence will help you recognize your subjects, locate their favorite hangouts, and interpret and predict their behavior. From such references I learned that the pika inhabits only mountainsides covered with loose rocks (talus slopes), that its presence is nearly certain if there are caches of hay (gathered by the pika for winter food) scattered over the slope, and that you'll hear its calls long before you spot the creature itself. Armed with such facts, you will know where, when and how to set up a camera.

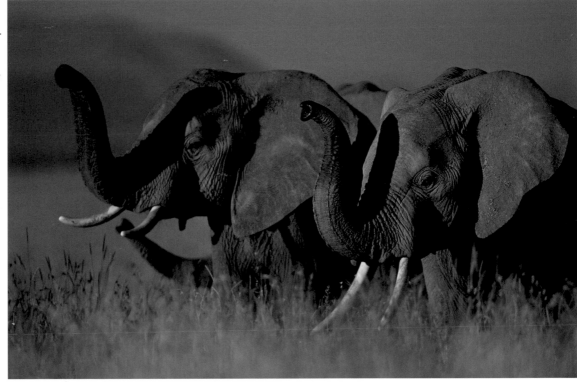

ANIMALS ARE PEOPLE, TOO

I once attempted to photograph marsh hawks at the nest. In succession I found three nests on the ground hidden in stands of bulrush, set up a blind, and retreated to observe the hawks' reactions through binoculars. With the first two nests, the hawks dove repeatedly at the camouflaged structure, forcing me to abandon the attempt. At the third nest, the hawk appeared, vole dangling from its talons, and dropped onto the nest without a glance at the blind. As soon as the bird left I got into the blind and was ready to photograph when it returned. The lesson is that animals are

Elephants, Masai Mara National Reserve, Kenya (above). Shooting from inside a vehicle allowed me to approach this unusually wary herd in safety.

Hovering marsh hawk, Priddis, Alberta (far left, top). This raptor was photographed from a stationary blind, as it returned to its nest. I was lucky to capture some good photos without harming the hawks. There are other ways more enjoyable and just as productive as shooting at nesting sites, a practice that jeopardizes reproductive success, even if blinds are used.

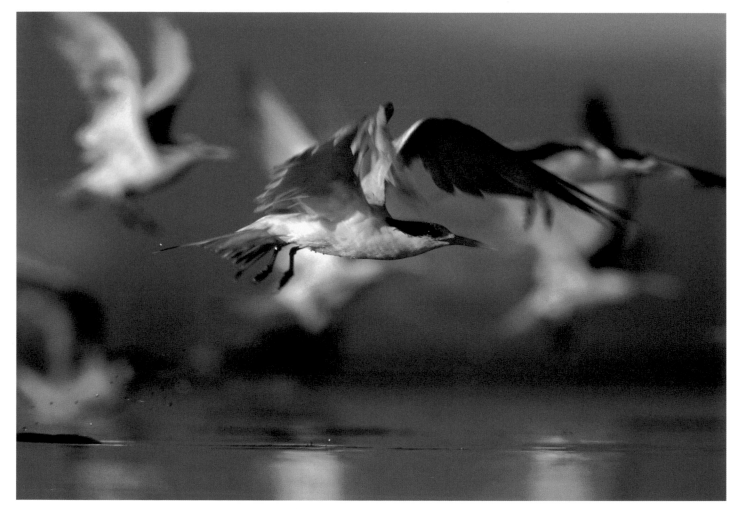

Elegant terns, Morro Bay, California (above). I approached these terns by crawling across packed sand while pushing the camera ahead of me. The terns observed my efforts with detachment, taking flight only when spooked by a dog. I rested the lens on the sand for shooting.

individuals. If one seems to have a distrust of photographers, you are better off finding a subject that is more accepting.

KEEP YOUR DISTANCE

Telephoto lenses work wonders in keeping animals relaxed and the film rolling by letting you shoot at a nonthreatening distance. For serious work, a 500mm lens provides ample power while being easy to carry and set up in the field. Add 2X and 1.4X teleconverters to provide extra reach and framing options. Image stabilizer-type lenses yield sharpness unmatched by standard lenses (including tripod work) when you need to frame and shoot the scene quickly with hands on the camera.

STALKING STRATEGIES

When approaching an animal, stay low and move slowly and quietly while the subject is not looking at you. This is best done by knee-walking while shoving the lowered tripod ahead. Should you attract attention, remain still but relaxed rather than motionless, until the subject resumes its normal activity. Every few steps, rest and sit back on your calves. With this technique you can move at a slow, steady rate, appear small and harmless, and are ready to shoot at any time. Plan your advance over easy, noiseless terrain. Anticipate the lighting conditions at the shooting site and modify your approach vector accordingly. Normally you will want to arrive at the shooting position with the sun at your back. If you are working with dangerous animals (elk, bison, bear), you must always have quick access to an escape route.

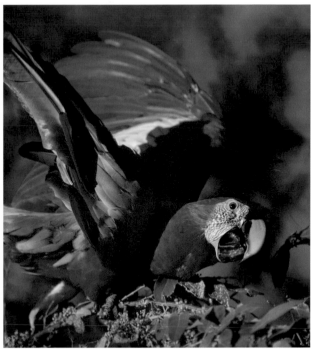

AVOID INTIMIDATION

The most successful stalks usually occur when the animal knows you are coming but isn't particularly worried about it. You can put the subject at ease by taking a circuitous route to the target area (as if you are a grazing Holstein) so that the animal thinks you are preoccupied with other matters. Once the subject is aware of your presence, act relaxed but avoid making loud or abrupt sounds or sudden movements — slowly fiddle with your gear or swivel your head to look at something in another direction.

DON'T FENCE THEM IN

When stalking, avoid a course that will block the animal's escape route as this will make it nervous and precipitate flight prematurely. For example, pelicans, cranes and other large birds

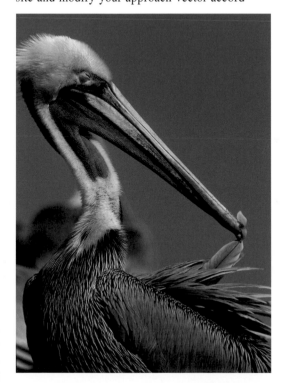

Scarlet macaw, Isla Roatan, Honduras (above). This confiding parrot hung about the lodge where I was staying to munch on fruits offered in the bird feeder. Taking up position near a subject's food source is a reliable way to shoot at close range.

Brown pelican preening, La Jolla Cove, California (left). The cliffs at La Jolla Cove are habitually used as a daytime roost by confiding brown pelicans. Due to high pedestrian traffic in the area these pelicans have lost much of their fear of humans, in the process becoming excellent subjects for the lens.

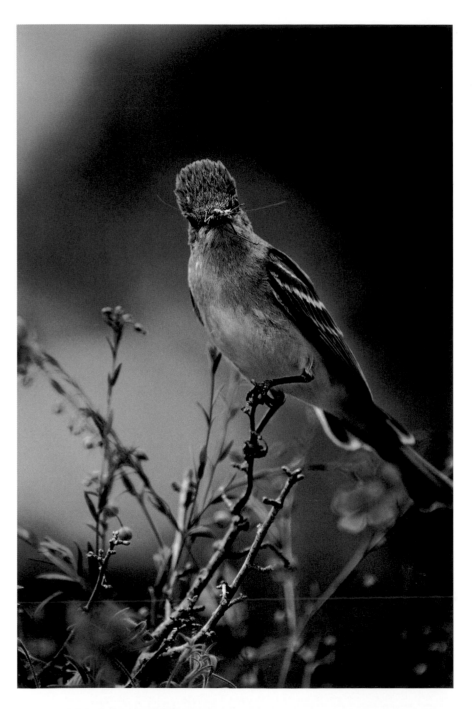

prefer to takeoff into the wind — it gives them more lift. Move in on these creatures with the wind in your face so that they retain this escape advantage. Bighorn sheep flee predators by bounding uphill, so leave them this option by approaching from down-slope. In short, anticipate the movement of the subject. If you know a bison herd is heading toward a water hole, set a leisurely course to meet it there.

GOT WHEELS? YOU GOT A BLIND

A structure that hides your presence from the subject can sometimes allow you to shoot at a range far closer than is possible when working in the open. Blinds are especially effective when photographing birds. I once photographed prairie falcons at the nest from a distance of one yard using a makeshift blind set up in a small grotto on the cliff beside them. Birds have landed on top of my blind (while I was in it) on many occasions. I prefer to use a cheap homemade blind, rather than an expensive commercial model, that can be left in position (a necessity with most subjects) over the course of several days or weeks without worrying unduly about someone walking off with it.

You've see the bumper stickers . . . *My other car is a bird blind*. Well, it's true. One of the most effective blinds of all is sitting in your driveway. Mammals and birds have less fear of a car than of a human on foot. The roadways of national wildlife refuges, national parks and other wild areas are great for cruising and shooting out the window. I set up a tripod over the front passenger seat and anchor it with bungy cords. This way I can stay behind the wheel to position the vehicle just where I want it. Car window mounts can also be utilized although you may find them a little flimsy for heavier optics such as a 500mm lens with teleconverter, the best focal length for this kind of shooting. Also, when these brackets are attached, you can't roll up the window or work the camera controls unobtrusively. Sometimes, I hang a piece of camouflage netting over the passenger-side window to hide my movements. You need to shut off the engine when you are shooting to avoid camera vibration, and have the camera controls set and ready to fire the instant

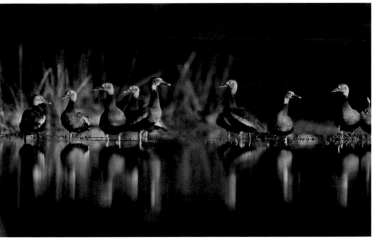

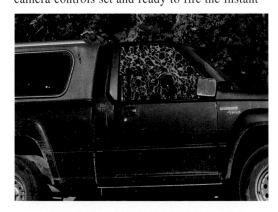

you are in position as your subject will not stay around for long once you stop the engine.

OTHER KINDS OF BLINDS

Blinds that you set up on the ground or in trees can be of practically any configuration or color. Usually they are made of camouflaged fabric stretched over a rigid frame of wood, tent poles, tree limbs, etc. The blind should be large enough to conceal photographer and equipment including a set-up tripod. Here are a few tips for building your own blinds.

• Use inexpensive materials so the blind can be left unattended without worry about theft.

• Make the blind portable so that you can carry it along with your camera equipment. Use lightweight materials — ripstop nylon and stiff, plastic plumbing tubing are easy to assemble.

• Be ready to make new openings in the blind to suit each shooting situation.

Black-bellied whistling ducks near Teacapan, Mexico (above). Recorded with an 800mm focal length lens, this nervous flock would not allow me to approach any closer than the view shown here even though I made a silent, painstakingly cautious approach in a floating blind. Likely the birds had been previously stressed by hunters, which made them especially wary.

Ash-throated flycatcher near Santa Fe, New Mexico (far left). Rather than photograph at the nesting site, which is stressful on the subject, I set up my blind at a less threatening distance to target a perch favored by the flycatcher when going to and from its nest. Such perches are likely to have fewer obstructions, more distant backgrounds (for attractive blurring) and better light than the nest site itself. Canon EOS A2, Canon lens 400mm f/2.8 L, 1.4X teleconverter, Fujichrome Provia 100F, 1/250 second at f/5.6

Vehicle as moving blind (left). Many animals are tolerant of vehicles, some to the extent that you can adjust the vehicle's position after a few frames. Others are more wary and you need to remain still and even screen your movements inside the car with drapery. Camouflage mesh fabric is shown here.

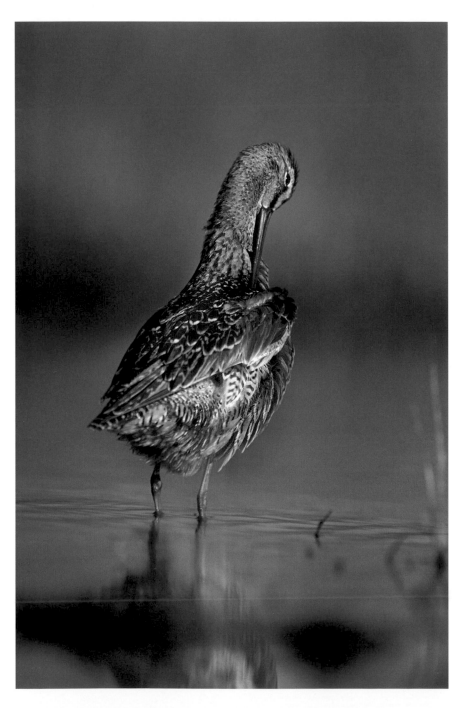

Overhanging limbs, rocks, uneven terrain and other features of the natural setting often force modifications to the standard setup.

• Match the color and pattern of the fabric (camouflage material is best) to the terrain. An inconspicuous blind is less likely to be disturbed or investigated by humans whose presence will frighten your subject and attract predators.

Stationary blinds work best for photographing birds at the nest. They are not very effective for mammals because they can't hide the photographer's scent or sound or be adjusted to suit the often unpredictable movements of the subject. Some animals may be more spooked by a blind (which they have never seen) than a human (which they have encountered often). I have mostly given up photographing birds at the nest because of the danger to the subject. Sometimes just the appearance of a blind causes the bird to desert the nest. More commonly, the scent, sound and view of your activity draws predators (jays, crows, skunks, raccoons, magpies, snakes, chipmunks) to the site for an easy meal of eggs or nestlings. I work usually from mobile blinds (either a vehicle or a self-propelled floating contraption) at sites where wildlife congregates (usually feeding or loafing areas) remote from sensitive nesting or denning locations and locales where other people congregate.

Some photographers carry pocket blinds (bag blinds, Invisiblinds) when on wildlife shooting excursions. Made with camouflaged fabric or netting and patterned after a poncho (see photo below) this blind simply drapes over you and your tripod without any supporting members. It is effective for birds at close range and mammals at greater range where the sound of the motor drive or your scent is not so strong. The only drawback is that your hand and arm movements are not completely hidden because the blind is supported in part by your body.

PEANUT BUTTER INCENTIVES

You needn't always go to the mountain — sometimes it will come to you. I like to use peanut butter to draw subjects toward the camera. This creamy concoction is attractive to birds and mammals of all kinds, from gray jays to bighorn sheep. Often they are not interested in actual consumption but just in taking a good whiff. You can smear peanut butter unobtrusively on a flower, a tree or right on the ground to coax the animal into a photogenic

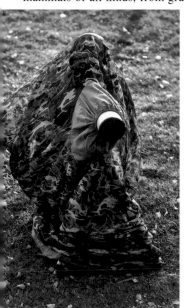

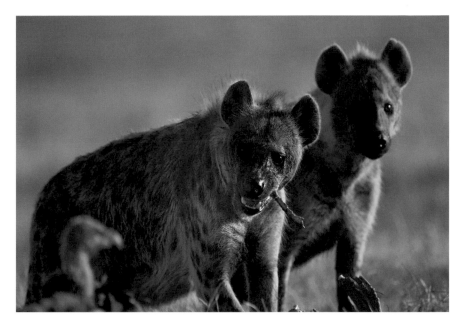

setting. It's not for every situation, but keeping a canister of Skippy in your vest adds one more trick to your bag. Keep in mind that using bait of any kind in national parks is *not* allowed and that in bear country it's not prudent to walk around smelling like a peanut butter sandwich!

PATIENCE AND PERSISTENCE

Making close-up photos of wild animals requires patience and persistence. The planning and preparation phases usually require more time and effort than actual shooting. Learn to enjoy this part of the process — it is just as critical as pressing the shutter and it will keep frustration and disappointment to a minimum.

Spotted hyena, Amboseli National Park, Kenya (above). Natural food sources are magnets for wildlife and great places for photography. Salmon spawning streams (grizzlies), mussel beds (diving ducks), mountain ash berries (waxwings) are but a few examples of such shooting hotspots. These hyenas, though leery of my approach, were too hungry to forgo breakfast — the leftovers of a lion kill. Vultures and jackals took over when the hyenas were finished.

Preening long-billed dowitcher, Lake Newell, Alberta (far left). Preening birds are easy to approach. It feels so good that they just hate to stop.

Animals in Action

Creating a stage and other techniques for recording animals in action

Lesser flamingos, Lake Bogoria, Kenya (below). Wildlife activity recorded as a blur reflects the impression of the moment as accurately as a stop-action approach, both revealing more than can be perceived by the naked eye. This flock was shot with a panning 500mm lens at 1/30 second.

I'M LYING ON A SLAB of styrofoam sandwiched between two sheets of plywood. My camera is mounted on a ballhead screwed to the plywood. Camouflage netting is draped over the whole affair (me included) which is floating in the marshy shallows of Lake Bogoria in Kenya. I'm completely surrounded by flamingos, tens of thousands of them parading steadily past my camera in a pink and crimson stream at a distance of ten to fifteen yards. A freezer baggy bulging with exposed film lays beside me.

I try to capture the swirl of exotic color, panning along with the slow-moving birds, releasing the shutter gently, trying to stay on track as the mirror flips up and the viewfinder blackens for a long 1/15 second, enough to blur and swirl the shapes and colors in the viewfinder. The mirror comes down, the scene reappears and after tweaking focus, I go into the next shot. After the shutter releases, I check exposure and adjust framing; then a few more pictures. I boost shutter speed to 1/30 second and chatter through another dozen frames without pause. So it goes for the next ten minutes until something frightens the flamingos and they move to another section of the lake. I wasn't sure what I had recorded and I wouldn't see the

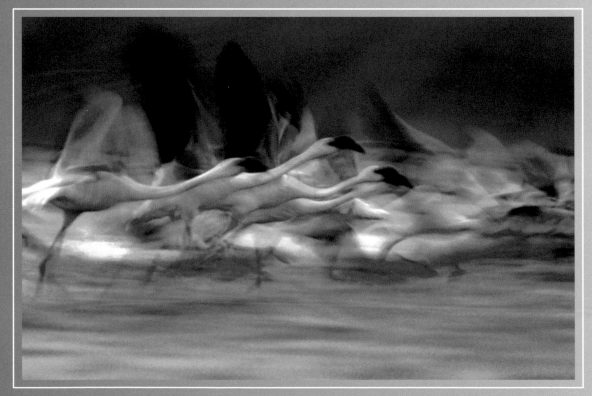

results for another month. But I had exposed enough film to be certain of some great photos.

Birds and mammals provide photographers with exciting action-shot opportunities. They can be recorded vocalizing, yawning, ruffling feathers, scratching, stretching, taking wing, running, fighting, performing courtship displays, bathing, fishing and hunting.

KNOW YOUR HABITATS

But where do you find opportunities for such imagery? The best place to start is at a nearby national park, bird sanctuary or wildlife refuge. There are hundreds of these throughout North America. (To find out about U.S. federal wildlife sanctuaries, consult *Guide to the National Wildlife Refuges* by Laura and William Riley.) In such places, animals are accustomed to photographers, so approaching to within telephoto range is not a problem provided you move slowly and deliberately. Many refuges have driving tours which pass through rich habitats where photography can be done from your vehicle. Becoming familiar with the type of terrain that birds are drawn to within the refuge will make it easy for you to find similar habitats elsewhere with less restric-

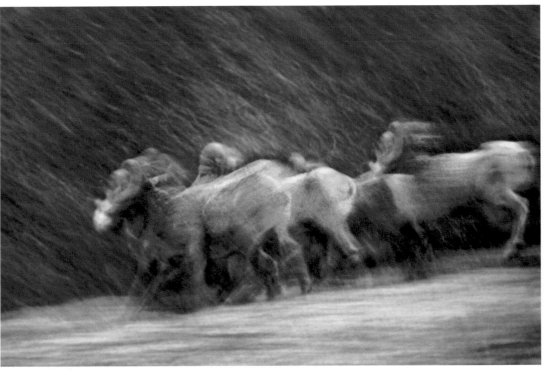

tions and better access. Although such rural areas are being steadily lost to development, they may provide equally good shooting.

Wildlife activity is seasonally dependent. Spring is the best time to photograph reproductive behavior such as courtship and care of young; fall provides opportunities to shoot masses of birds and mammals on the move and rutting moose, deer, and sheep; winter (in the south) is a period of rest and relaxation and provides opportunities to record feeding and socialization, especially of migratory birds. During midsummer, wildlife activity is at its lowest for most species except in alpine habitats, arctic

Bighorn rams, Mount Norquay, Banff National Park, Alberta (above). A great setting for action shooting, open meadows on Mount Norquay are occupied by rutting bighorns in autumn. This group was kept on the move by passing hikers. I timed this shot to catch the sheep passing a dark stand of spruces which formed a contrasting backdrop for the rams and the falling snow. It's pleasing to leave a cushion of space in front of moving subjects to absorb its visual momentum. Canon T90, Canon lens 500mm f/4/5 L, Fujichrome 50, 1/15 second at f/11.

White pelicans and laughing gulls, Rollover Pass, Galveston Island, Texas (below). Shooting birds first thing in the morning usually provides the best results, but there are exceptions. In coastal habitats, the most productive photography occurs at low tide regardless of the time of day. With very dark or light subjects, like these snowy pelicans, overcast light around midday does the best job of reining in contrast and providing plenty of light for brief exposures. For this photo I fashioned a quick stage on the pelicans leaving the top of the frame empty and then waited for the gulls to fly through.

regions and offshore seabird nesting islands, where it is at its highest.

BE ON SITE BEFORE THE SUN RISES

The typical wildlife routine is different than our own and appreciating this fact is crucial to successful photography. A marsh or woodland that is teeming with bird life at sunrise will seem quiet by 9:00 and desolate by noon. With the approach of sunset, animal activity resumes. You will experience the best action-shooting opportunities during the first and last hour of the day when coincidentally the light is at its best.

You may be waiting for a September sunrise at Moraine Park in the Rockies to photograph bull elk in rut, or perhaps the setting is McNeil River Falls in Alaska in August when the river is crowded with fishing brown bears. Whatever the scenario, you've done your research, made your preparations, arrived on site in a timely manner, and now you're ready to set up your equipment and get to work.

LOWER THAT TRIPOD

A tripod is necessary to steady the camera and support the heavy lenses required to keep a long enough distance from your subjects to avoid disturbing their normal activity patterns. I like to sit or kneel on the ground with the camera positioned at eye level. This provides an intimate, eye-to-eye view of the majority of wildlife subjects. The low angle throws the background into soft focus, making the subjects of stop-action photos jump out of the frame dramatically. In this position, your reduced size is less intimidating to animals and less noticeable to curious passersby who might frighten your subjects. When low to the ground, you can move about inconspicuously, shifting the tripod position

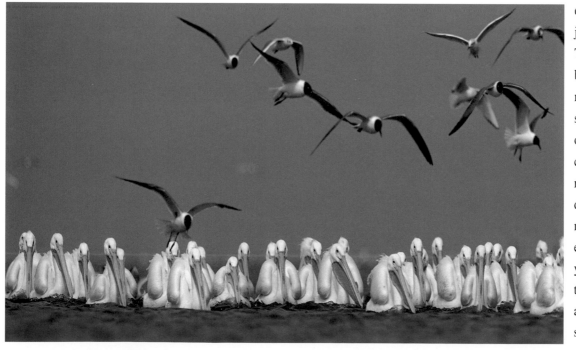

a foot or two at a time to improve composition. A low tripod is also less susceptible to wind disturbance, resulting in sharper pictures. Perhaps most important, the kneeling posture is comfortable for long periods, affording you the patience needed to wait for dramatic action.

To avoid camera shake and maximize sharpness for a stationary subject, tighten all tripod controls once framing is established and trip the shutter with a cable release; for a moving subject, loosen the controls so that you can pan the camera smoothly to follow the action.

The most useful lenses are in the 500–600mm range — enough power to yield a frame-filling photo of a flying eagle at 100 feet. A 300mm lens matched with a 1.4X or 2X teleconverter also provides satisfactory magnification and is best used with a film in the ISO 200 range.

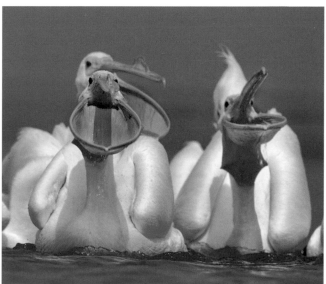

WASTE FILM NOT TIME

Once the subject initiates an activity that you wish to record and you are sharply focused and satisfactorily framed, shoot without delay at a rapid rate. For action sequences so quick that you cannot follow the details readily with the naked eye (flying crane, bounding giraffe, fishing pelican, courting egret) you will only capture one out of twenty or thirty frames that is of publishable quality. If this seems like a poor ratio, keep in mind that things go wrong: heads are obscured, an eye is closed, limbs are foreshortened, wingtips leave the frame, a hot spot looms in the background, critical features are blurred, exposure is off.

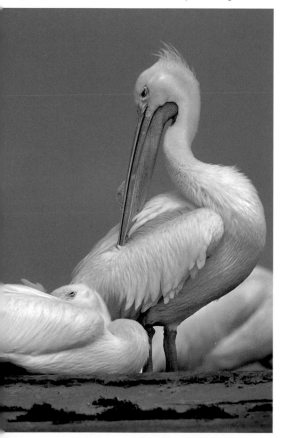

White pelicans fishing, Rollover Pass, Galveston Island, Texas (above). I used the trap focus method to shoot this close-up. Waiting in a floating blind, I set focus a few feet in front of the birds and followed their approach in the viewfinder, releasing the shutter when they appeared sharp. I repeated the process several times firing five or six frames in each sequence. Despite the number of pictures taken, none were without flaw.

White pelicans preening, Rollover Pass, Galveston Island, Texas (left). This composition frames the scene so both the preening and sleeping birds are positioned to divide the picture space into pleasing 1/3–2/3 proportions on both the vertical and horizontal axes.

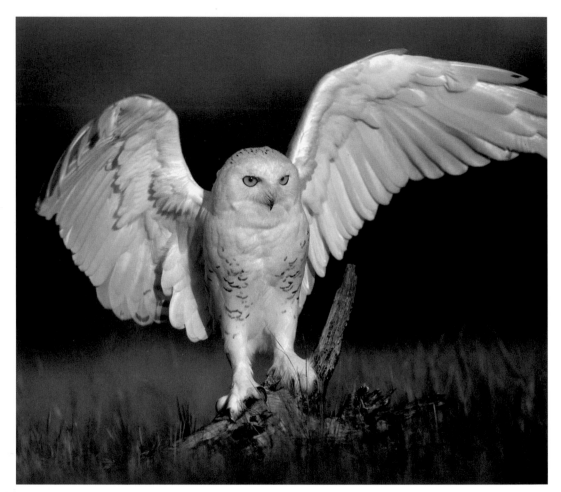

*Snowy owl, British Columbia (**right**). Unable to fly, this owl was photographed at a rehabilitation center for injured raptors. Perched on a wobbly log, the bird raised its wings periodically to regain its balance. I photographed during these moments, in high-speed, motor driven bursts of five or six frames using manual focus and manual exposure settings.*

*Masai giraffes, Masai Mara National Reserve, Kenya (**far right**). For a few minutes I observed this high-energy youngster sprinting about the veldt, returning once in a while to stand at its mother's feet. Using this behavior cue, I formulated a simple stage by framing the mother tightly, setting focus and exposure, and waiting. A few moments later, the calf appeared to complete the composition.*

When the action starts, I shoot with the motor drive at maximum speed, usually in tightly spaced, five- or six-frame bursts, allowing myself a brief peek every few bursts to check framing, focus and exposure. Every three or four bursts, I do a bracket sequence — one burst 1/2-stop over and another 1/2-stop under; then I return to my base settings. All of this I prefer to set manually.

SHARPEN YOUR FOCUSING TECHNIQUE

In many situations it's impractical or impossible to set lens focus in advance, making it necessary to focus on subjects moving unpredictably.

You can use auto-focus for a general fix on the target and then do a manual tune-up so that the subject's eye is razor sharp. On most automatic systems, quickest focusing is achieved when only the central sensor is activated. For close-up magnifications that show detail in the eyes, you will normally have to do a manual fine-tune in order to bring this feature into sharp focus. This is almost always faster than selecting a sensor that falls over the eye, or locking in sharp-eye focus by partially depressing the trigger and then reframing for the best composition. Newer AF lenses have instant-touch, manual override designed for this very purpose. Behavior such as nursing, singing, stretching, squabbling, yawning, mating or preening can be recorded easily with manual techniques provided you have the animal framed and in focus before

the action begins. Sharp focus comes from being prepared and waiting for the right moment.

Focusing is more difficult when you try to capture a crane on the wing or an antelope in full stride. If the subject is moving across the field of view so its distance from the camera is constant, both manual and auto focus are readily achieved because there is more time to lock onto the subject. If the bird is moving obliquely or directly toward the camera, trap-focusing is often the best manual procedure. With this technique, you pre-focus at a magnification that results in comfortable framing of the subject (not too tight for a flying bird or bounding deer). Then watch through the viewfinder as the subject approaches your zone of focus. Trip the shutter just before it arrives to allow for the 1/8- to 1/4-second delay

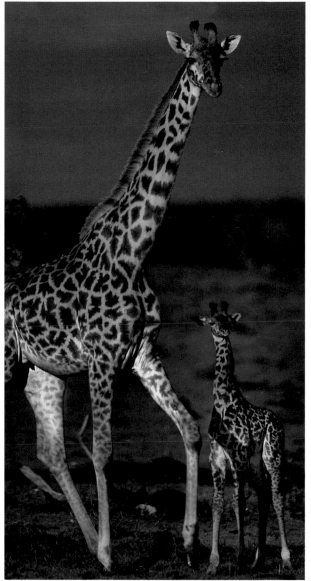

Shooting Tips for Birds in Flight

• Keep the camera on a tripod. Keep your hands on the camera with the tripod controls loosened.
• The smaller the bird, the faster the shutter speed needed to stop its motion.
• Pan along with the bird, squeeze off the shots gently and follow through.
• Don't restrict yourself to stop-action pictures. Experiment by slowing the shutter speed to produce blurring effects.
• The flight path is most easily framed just after take-off. Set camera controls, frame the standing subject, and be ready for the action.
• Study the flight patterns of individual species as well as travel routes to and from nesting sites, roosting areas, or other gathering places.
• Station yourself at right angles to the flight path to gain more focusing time.
• Be aware that birds (especially large species) prefer to take off into the wind.
• Use a high-speed motor drive and (in open terrain) predictive auto-focus with only the central focusing sensor activated. Try to keep the sensor on the flying bird's shoulder.

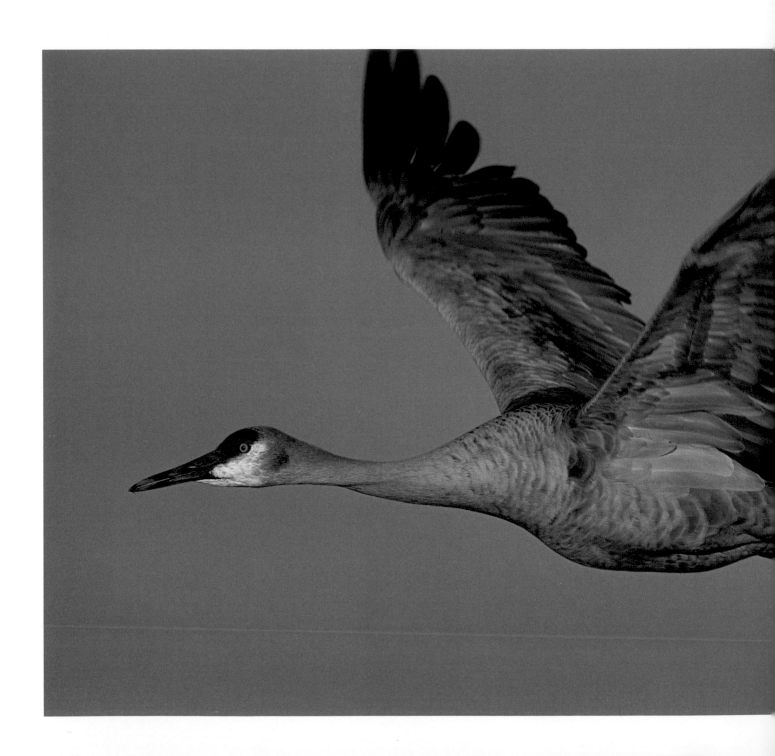

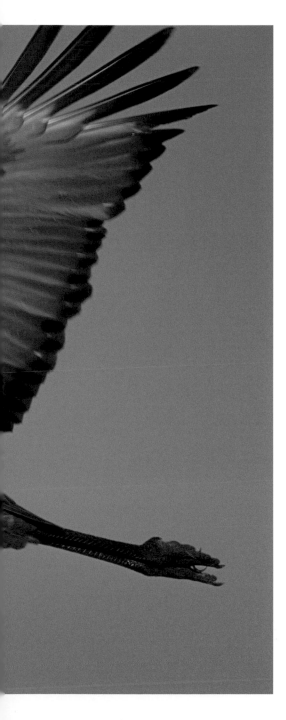

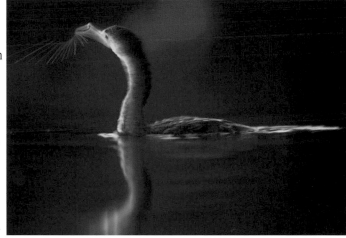

between when you press the release and when the shutter curtains actually open. For auto-focusing, set the camera in predictive focusing mode and keep the active-focusing sensor(s) on the target. Both methods have greater success if you cross your fingers, set the motor drive at its fastest speed, stop the lens down (lighting conditions permitting) so that increased depth-of-field compensates for focusing error, and shoot extra film — mistakes are almost always unavoidable.

BUILD A STAGE TO CAPTURE ACTION

Recording dramatic action shots is among nature photography's greatest challenges and biggest rewards. Three main tasks confront you. First, you must focus accurately on the subject — not easily done on a moving target either manually or automatically. Second, the subject must be comfortably framed and portrayed clearly (no hidden limbs or closed eyes). Third, the setting (background primarily) must be simple and in supportive harmony of the main subject. If you shoot enough film you'll come up with images

Double-crested cormorant, Esquimalt Lagoon, Vancouver Island (above). A shutter speed of 1/30 second creates an evocatively blurred rendering of this seabird landing a squirming fish.

Sandhill crane, Bosque del Apache National Wildlife Refuge, New Mexico (left). Staging techniques were used to record this giant on the wing. I hid among a stand of cattails before dawn, a location and time that would offer front illumination on the subject from the east, the direction the birds would fly to reach their daytime foraging area. As the sun rose one crane after another flew over my position. I tracked the birds using predictive auto-focusing. Despite an ideal set-up and co-operative subjects only a small percentage of frames were satisfactorily framed and focused.

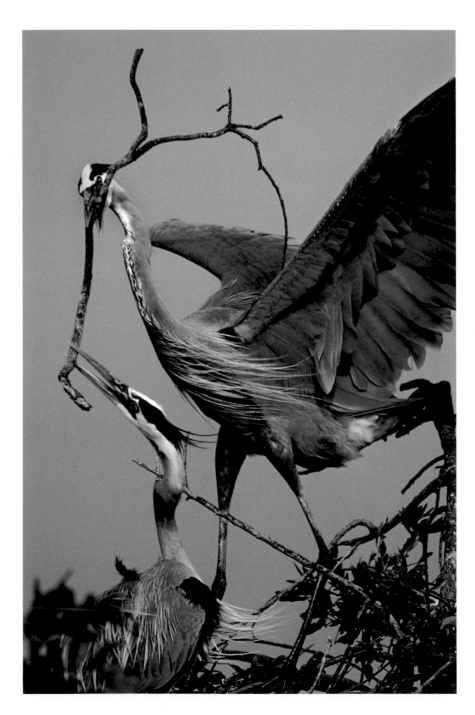

from time to time that satisfy these criteria. However, you can improve your rate of keepers by using staging techniques.

Staging is a process of creating picture environments (stages) that either directly or indirectly control and/or anticipate the animal's behavior in preparation for photography. The staging process normally breaks down into two parts : (1) setting the parameters of the composition in advance of the subject's appearance; and (2) devising ways of controlling or modifying the subject's activity that do not compromise its normal behavior once it arrives on stage. The most successful stages are usually those that already exist in nature and are incorporated into the photographic process by pre-establishing subject magnification, camera angle, lighting angle and precise focus distance.

First, a simple example:
• To photograph a large bird in flight, you can create a stage by choosing a particular lens focal length and a focus distance. This fixes a frame of a specific size (magnification) to hold the subject. The bird is tracked in the viewfinder and the picture taken when the subject moves into the focus zone. The stage can be further defined by choice of camera position — perhaps one that will record the subject against the blue sky or an autumn forest; and taken yet another step by restricting shooting to periods when the subject is illuminated from the front, side, or whatever

suits the photographer's pictorial goals. And next a more contrived example:

• To photograph a ground squirrel amid colorful subalpine blossoms you need to first find a suitable locale (colonial burrows) and then decide on lens focal length and working distance (use an object the same size as the ground squirrel as a stand-in to help you establish subject magnification — in this case a baseball cap would be about right). Next experiment with various camera positions to establish how the wildflowers will frame the subject and fill up the background and foreground.

Finally, you can indirectly control the subject's movement within the set by using bait such as sunflower seeds or peanut butter strategically placed. Lastly you may set up a reflector to improve the lighting within the set. When all is ready sit back and wait impatiently for the action.

STUDY BEHAVIOR

Most animal activity occurs in repeated patterns. By becoming familiar with wildlife habits, your chances of capturing interesting activity greatly increase. A white pelican, for instance, raises its

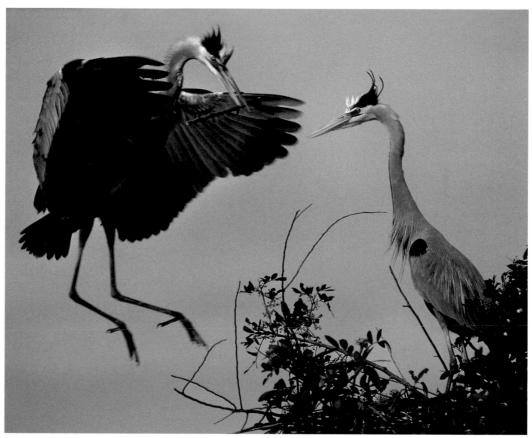

wings slightly a few seconds before takeoff; an American oystercatcher screams and fans its tail when other out-of-territory oystercatchers venture near; a blue-winged teal exercises its wings just as it finishes preening; a great blue heron flips its fish so that the meal can be swallowed head first; snow geese babble excitedly as a buildup to mass takeoffs. Being familiar with such behavioral clues will allow you to prepare the camera and yourself ahead of time so that you are ready to capture the action.

Great blue herons, Venice Rookery, Florida (above and far left).
If you had looked in my viewfinder a second before the frame above was shot, you would have seen an out-of-balance composition — an empty stage in waiting. I timed this shot by watching the approaching bird with my naked eye. At far left, many frames were shot to capture this balanced arrangement of two birds and a giant courting stick.

Wildlife Portraits

Layering the picture space and other techniques for expressive portraiture

Olive baboon, Masai Mara National Reserve, Kenya (below). Telephoto lenses are essential for dramatic portraiture. Their shallow depth of field blurs backgrounds and foregrounds, emphasizing the subject.

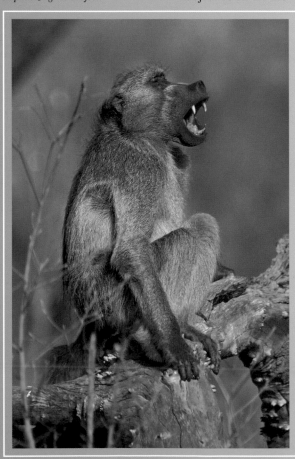

MAKING A COMPELLING portrait of a wild animal is not as simple as it may at first seem. There are numerous factors critical to the picture's outcome, which you need to process efficiently and often in but a fraction of a second should the subject be on the move. Some attempts may be actively pursued by the photographer while just as many must be passively embraced (with the necessary patience) at nature's whim. The suggestions that follow provide a foundation on which you can fashion a personal and expressive imagery. For top results you need a 35mm SLR with a telephoto lens in the 300–600mm range, a 1.4X or 2X teleconverter (or both) for adjusting subject magnification, and a sturdy yet easily portable tripod with a ballhead or gimbal head.

LEAVE WIDE-ANGLE LENSES IN THE BAG

Although some wild animals (particularly those in national parks, arctic regions and deep sea islands) have little fear of humans, close-up wide-angle lens work should be avoided for reasons both practical and artistic. The fisheye-in-the-muzzle approach often has negative consequences for the subject and may set unfortunate precedents for nature photographers generally. Exaggerated perspective cues that signal an abbreviated working distance generate a sensationalist, photocentric effect. By contrast, the telephoto approach records the undistorted dignity of the subject from a non-intrusive distance. Getting too close to large wild animals endangers the photographer and, when it results in injury, may call for the animal to be destroyed or transported out of its home range away from the public. In national parks and other regulated areas conflicts between animals and humans result in the development of policies and rules that limit subsequent viewing and shooting access for everyone. A frame-filling, wide-angle shot may present the subject seemingly unaffected by the photographer's presence, but it does not tell the entire story. Close-range shooting has an impact on the greater picture environment. The photographer's lingering scent, disturbance of vegetation, or actual presence near denning and nesting sites telegraph such locations to predators and usually deter one or both parents from carrying out vital reproductive activities such as bringing nesting material, food for the young, or standing guard.

TELEPHOTO ADVANTAGES

Maintaining a safe, nonthreatening distance by using a telephoto lens allays such problems and provides aesthetic benefits more harmonious to the subject. The telephoto's narrow angle of view allows significant changes in the composition of background and foreground areas with only slight adjustments to camera angle or position. Its relatively shallow depth of field permits ready blurring of distracting elements not crucial to subject development, which accentuates by contrast the sharpness and importance of the center of interest. When not stressed by the close approach of a photographer, the subject will project a relaxed demeanor and be more likely to engage in behavior typical of the species.

BUILD A THREE-LAYER PICTURE SPACE

Conditions permitting, I like to set up the picture space in three planes — foreground, midground, and background — with each fashioned to support the main subject. Foregrounds are usually comprised of out-of-focus grasses, limbs and leaves, wildflowers, or other features of the animal's environment. Three considerations will keep your foregrounds in order. First, take a camera position that places foreground elements well out of the depth-of-field zone. Dreamily blurred foregrounds are unobtrusive and serve to contain the viewer's attention to the

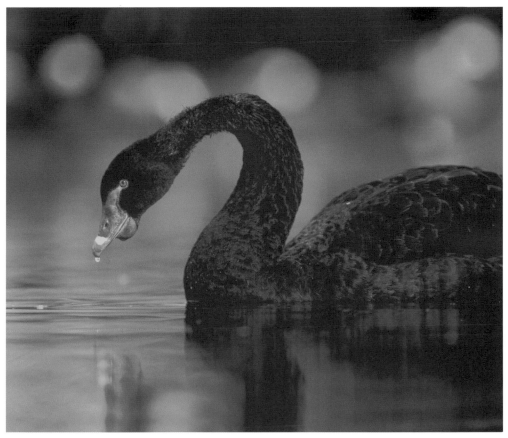

Black swan (introduced), Vancouver, British Columbia, (above). The telephoto lens makes for easy modification of background features. For this portrait I tracked the swan as it glided passed a variety of backgrounds. I chose this one because the dark/ light/circular features harmonized and provided tonal contrast to the main subject. Canon T90, Canon lens 500mm f/4/5 L, Kodachrome 64, 1/125 second at f/5.6.

For example, if you are shooting a bobolink through a patch of yellow daisies, the composition will exhibit greater unity and more pleasing harmonies if daisies are evident in either or both of the other two planes (nirvana if the bird is perched atop one such flower). Third, foreground elements are used most effectively when they fill up the corners of the frame, where their lack of detail absorbs the visual momentum of straight and converging boundaries that lead the viewer's eye out of the picture space.

The picture's midground is of course dominated by the subject (discussed in detail in the next section) which floats buoyantly amid the blurry seas of foreground and background. In order to anchor this most important element to its environment and fix it within the image space, it's beneficial to have a few key components of its habitat in sharp focus — grasses sprouting around the subject's feet, foliage framing its head, or berries being grasped by hungry lips.

Under ideal circumstances the background plane can itself be processed in three sub-layers. Just behind the main subject should appear a few patches of out-of-focus habitat elements,

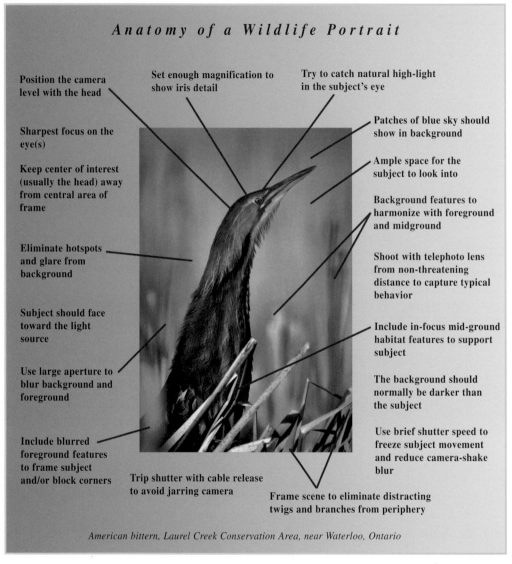

Anatomy of a Wildlife Portrait

Position the camera level with the head

Sharpest focus on the eye(s)

Keep center of interest (usually the head) away from central area of frame

Eliminate hotspots and glare from background

Subject should face toward the light source

Use large aperture to blur background and foreground

Include blurred foreground features to frame subject and/or block corners

Set enough magnification to show iris detail

Trip shutter with cable release to avoid jarring camera

Try to catch natural high-light in the subject's eye

Patches of blue sky should show in background

Ample space for the subject to look into

Background features to harmonize with foreground and midground

Shoot with telephoto lens from non-threatening distance to capture typical behavior

Include in-focus mid-ground habitat features to support subject

The background should normally be darker than the subject

Use brief shutter speed to freeze subject movement and reduce camera-shake blur

Frame scene to eliminate distracting twigs and branches from periphery

American bittern, Laurel Creek Conservation Area, near Waterloo, Ontario

subject, while those just out-of-focus appear distracting and even technically amiss. Second, strive for a camera angle that captures foreground features that are the same as at least some of those in the midground and/or background.

obviously blurred but not to the extent that their identity cannot be matched up with some of the environmental features sharply rendered in the midground area. Next come large swathes of blurred pigment preferably in harmony with the color motifs of other layers. Last to appear are patches of blue emanating from the blur of sky. This most favored of nature's hues enlivens and expands the atmosphere of any wildlife portrait. In practice, you won't encounter it regularly but be prepared to capture the sky's magic by taking a low camera position and shooting at right angles to the sun (for maxing the blue) when possible. For heavenly color saturation together with action-stopping shutter speeds, shoot under sunny conditions with an ISO 400 film and polarizing filter.

SIZING UP THE SUBJECT

With the picture space (theoretically) structured, we can

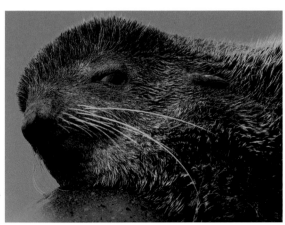

turn our attention to the actual subject. Early in my career, I didn't discriminate between beautiful, robust specimens and those not quite so blessed by nature. But I soon discovered that editors were not too interested in publishing female cardinals in drab plumage or elk with puny antlers no matter how skillfully illuminated and composed. Now I recommend that photographers interested in seeing their work published give priority to those subjects with the most brilliant plumage, the shiniest fur, the longest tusks and the widest rack of antlers.

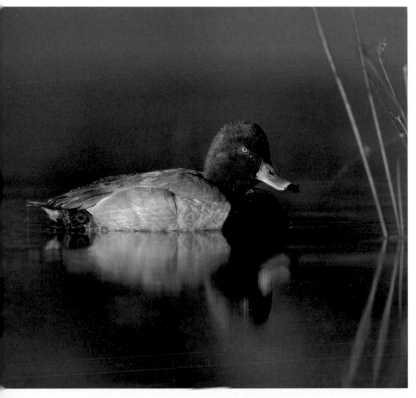

Northern fur seal bull, St. Paul Island, Alaska (above). During breeding season, these bad-tempered bulls will not tolerate humans at close range. Every portrait need not exhibit all the features described in the chart opposite. This portrait's strength derives primarily from the tightly cropped, detailed presentation of the subject's features.

Redhead drake near Moses Lake, Washington (left). A near water-level camera position allowed me to fill part of the background with the alluring tints of the blue sky. It's more pleasing if the sky appears in patches among other background features.

How big should the animal be in the frame? Many factors, including the animal's behavior, affect how you treat this aspect of the photograph. As a rule of thumb, use enough lens power to show detail in the eyes (a clearly defined iris being ideal). Of course, circumstances frequently dictate other priorities. A dramatic display of courtship feathers, a salmon vised in dripping jaws, wildebeest trekking past a rising sun, or the battle-worn trunk of an elephant seal are among a multitude of dynamic factors which may call for a revision to standard magnification and framing practices.

FACIAL FEATURES IN FOCUS

To a human the animal's face represents the most important part of its anatomy and you should make sure that these features are in best focus and well lit. For the most revealing and dramatic interpretation, try to catch the subject looking into the light. The eyes should be wide open, clearly illuminated (see preceding paragraph), and show a small, twinkling, natural catchlight (a contrived catchlight from electronic flash is usually worse than nothing). Ears should be fanned forward in curiosity rather than laid back in fear or tilted askew. The nostrils should be flared and not leaking. Antlers and horns should be angled to show clear

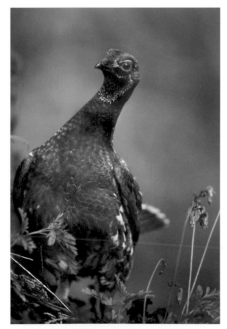

Blue grouse, near Port Coquitlam, British Columbia (below). Dark subjects, like this grouse, are best photographed under overcast skies. Strive for enough magnification to show the eyes with definition in the iris and with a natural highlight.

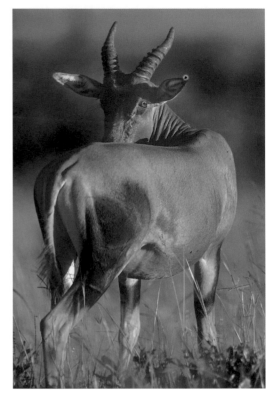

separation of the branches. Presented with a choice, record the head aimed back over the animal's body into the picture frame to generate a circular (rather than linear) flow of visual interest (see photo above). Whiskers should be splayed, in focus, and set up against the blur of background. If showing only a portion of the animal, avoid cropping at joints (knees, ankles, elbows, knuckles) and use blurred foreground features to interrupt the exit of long limbs from the frame. If shooting animals in silhouette, look for opportunities to catch the subject when each of its legs is distinct and separated and its head is presented in profile. This agenda does not work in every situation and rarely can be fully implemented, but by having it at your fingertips you will be able to purposefully apply or discard each of the items depending on the circumstances.

GROUP PORTRAITS

Photographing more than one animal at a time compounds the number of factors you must juggle. The behavior, position and pose of each of the subjects needs to be monitored nearly simultaneously so that the most telling graphic components can be recorded in synchrony. Normally you will achieve the best results by keying the composition to one leading subject, bringing in members of the supporting cast on an *ad hoc* basis when their roles are most powerful and complementary. The strength of the composition is most at risk when shooting two animals, a situation which readily fractures and polarizes the center of interest. To achieve a unified effect, select subjects that are matched in physical appearance; engaged in similar behavior, such as howling or sleeping, relating to one another (fighting, courting); or focusing their attention in the same direction.

LIGHTING

Any type of light can produce an exciting wildlife portrait. The standard and often most productive treatment utilizes front lighting early in the morning or late in the afternoon. You can't go wrong by flipping this switch but there are other options on the console that produce unexpected results frequently more dramatic. Learn to understand and appreciate how light reveals your subject, especially in connection with the suggestions outlined here.

Once you become comfortable working with these procedures in actual field situations, you're ready to abandon the formula and experiment with novel tactics which may flow more spontaneously from your own sense of design and how you experience and perceive the natural world.

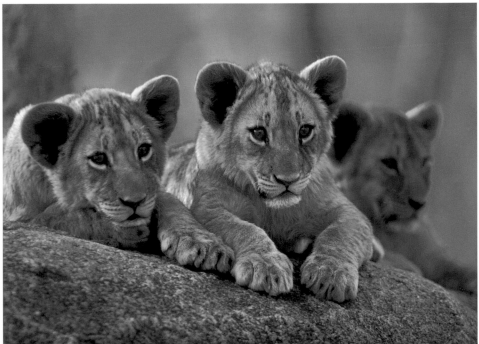

Lion cubs, Hwange National Park, Zombabwe (above). Group portraiture is more difficult to control than mug shots of single animals. Ideally, all subjects should have their attention drawn in the same direction, be in sharp focus, and be similar in form and color — criteria that usually require patience and persistence to attain.

Topi, Masai Mara National Reserve, Kenya (far left, top). Portraits exhibit unity and strong visual flow when the aninal is recorded looking back over its own body.

Part Four

Light on the Land

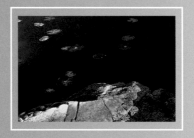

Finding Photogenic Landscapes

Ten clues to evaluating the photographic potential of any landscape setting

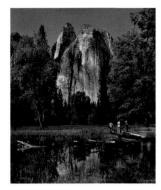

I HAVE BEEN HERE BEFORE to search for clues — to measure the angles and proportions of the view, to take sightings on the looming spires of granite or the ramparts of Navajo sandstone, to gauge the texture of a maple wood or the freshness of a float of water lilies. I have checked the disposition of the stone monuments against my compass and staked a claim that now lies hidden in the darkness, a spot where I will soon set up my camera to capture the first intoxicating light of dawn as it streaks across a cliff or breathes its fire onto tumbling pillows of cloud that I always hope hang above me — a reward for a diligent photographer.

Yosemite National Park (above).
Some landscape venues are unmistakably grand. Nevertheless you need to search for the features and await the conditions described in this chapter in order to present the subject at its most beautiful.

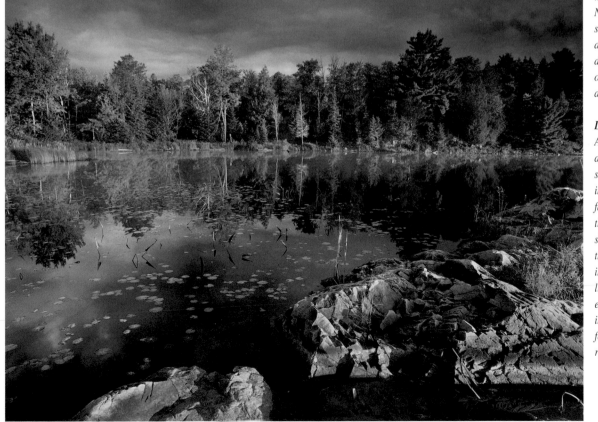

Lang Lake, Ontario (left).
A retiring topography such as this small lake can surrender prize-winning imagery if worked under favorable conditions with the right techniques. This shot was timed to capture the lively colors of autumn in warm, early morning light. Scale and depth were established by framing interesting and detailed features in the foreground reached by wading.

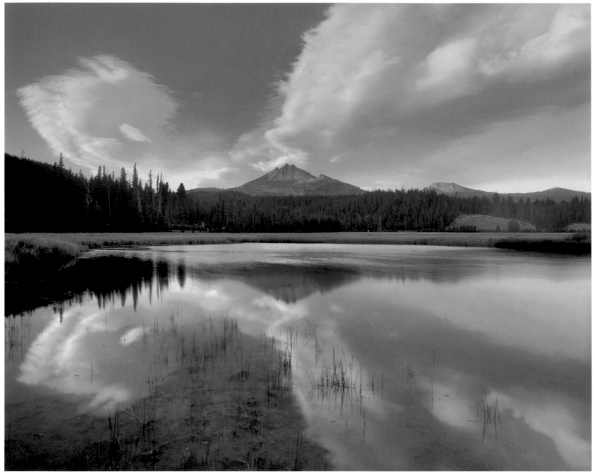

the clues that can lead to great scenic photographs? Following are the ones that I look for. They are relevant whether you are anticipating shooting a sand dune, surf-battered beach, snowcapped peak or slick-rock canyon. I have never found all these clues present in the same site, but I'm still eagerly looking and meanwhile taking photographs whenever I stumble across even a few of them.

COLOR FIRST

The presence of

Broken Top and Sparks Peak, Cascade Range, Oregon (above).

Broken clouds are among the landscape photographer's best friends. They add interest and improved contrast to your pictures at any time. Be especially attuned to their potential late and early in the day. When the sun is below or on a clear horizon, clouds are illuminated in a rainbow of fiery hues.

All has been investigated in advance and now I wait behind the camera, nervous but expectant, to capture this symphony of light and shadow, form and color, texture and line. These I will arrest on film, book into my files of transparencies, and later bring before the judgment of editors, agents and friends.

How can you research a landscape to discover its potential for compelling imagery? What are

strong color is perhaps the best indicator of the landscape's potential for surrendering a great photograph. The most attractive color to humans is red. Find this hue, even in small batches, and chances are you've found a good place to set up your tripod. Wildflowers, lichens, leaves, rocks, even flamingos in rosy hues can be incorporated into the wider scene. Give these color nuggets a lot of attention by placing them prominently in sharp detail in the foreground region of the composition. Entire vistas may be tinted in fiery pigments — the canyon country of the American southwest, the eastern forests in autumn, the arctic tundra in summer. Such clues are impossible to miss and represent well-seasoned clichés of what is beautiful about the North American continent. But more subtle color harmonies can also lead to great pictures, such as those projected by the cool hues of a foggy seascape or the peachy tones of sand dunes in twilight.

Shooting a Waterfall

There are two approaches to photographing waterfalls. One technique is to use a brief exposure (1/125 second or faster) to freeze the movement of the water. The other, usually more appealing method, is to use an extended exposure (1/15 second or slower) so that the water is recorded as a silky blur. To accentuate the effect, try to include features in the scene that are stationary. On calm days, colorful foliage provides a dynamic foil to the milky stream. If it is windy, use rocks or tree trunks to set up the scene. Due to the brightness of the flow, waterfall pictures are normally successful only on cloudy days, when contrast is low and the entire scene is evenly lit. Zoom lenses are helpful because camera positions are usually restricted by both water spray, dense foliage and the stream or river. Most compositions work best when the falls are photographed from below, allowing the viewer's eye to follow the water flow into the picture to the center of interest. Also look for camera angles that capture the flow moving diagonally through the picture frame.

CLOUDS MAKE ALL THE DIFFERENCE

Nothing gets me more excited about an impending landscape shooting session than clouds. My favorites are the cottonball, cumulous variety, but any kind, anywhere in the sky will tickle my trigger finger. Most preferred are formations that are near the horizon and above the target area. At

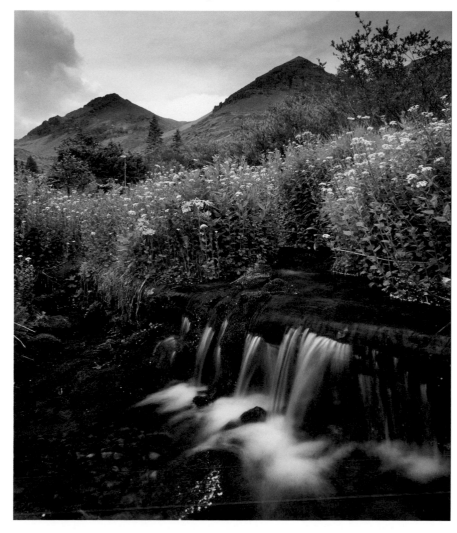

Cascade at Yankee Boy Basin, San Juan Mountains, Colorado, (below). Look for opportunities to bring red into landscape compositions. Being the color of blood (which simultaneously signals food and danger) it is the most attractive hue for humans.

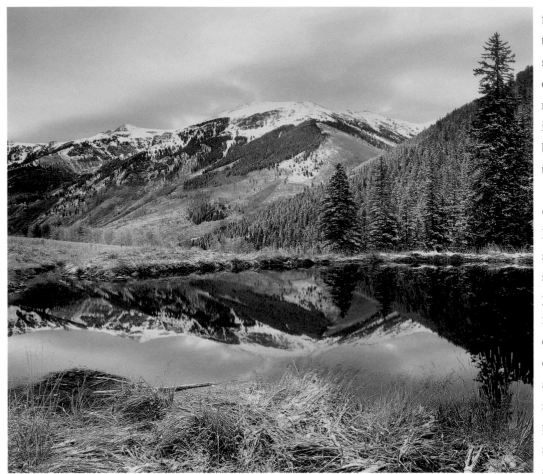

Maroon Bells–Snowmass Wilderness (above). Calm weather greatly improves a scene's potential, allowing you to record foliage detail at slow shutter speeds and small apertures for greater depth of field. The snow's white accents make colors appear more intense.

formations can be used to relieve the starkness of a clear midday sky. Or when passing through clouds, sunlight is diffused and refracted into shadow areas illuminating detail and color and bringing more of the scene within the exposure latitude of the film.

CALM ATMOSPHERE FOR DETAIL

For landscape photographers, a still atmosphere offers added design possibilities. It means that you can shoot with great depth of field subjects that you might otherwise have to edit from the composition because they move about in the wind and cannot be sharply recorded during long exposures. Wildflowers, grasses, shrubs, foliage, pools of water, sand grains (as in sand dunes) and even tree trunks are picture elements affected by wind. Consider the implications of this clue — what is your exposure duration once you have stacked on a few filters, loaded a high resolution/low ISO film, hyper-focaled the scene at f/22 or f/32, adjusted for reciprocity failure, and waited for that last, beautiful, fiery gasp of light over distant peaks? Often it can be in the neighborhood of 15 or 30 seconds. With fingers crossed, I

sundown or sunrise, these clouds can turn many shades of rose, mauve, scarlet and yellow. These powerful picture elements create their own dynamic but complementary center of interest that enlivens the landforms below. Their rich colors are reflected onto the scene to infuse the composition with a distinctive, dramatic, warm color bias. Even when shooting during midday, clouds are beneficial; their interesting

hold my breath in these situations and pray Mother Nature does the same. Your best chance of encountering dead calm conditions occurs about 30 minutes before and after sunrise. Be patient and learn to shoot between zephyrs.

Let it Snow

Fog, mist, haze and falling snow infuse ordinary landscapes with moody energy. Most of us enjoy such meteorological events (as long as TV reception is not affected) and they add novel distinction to scenic photographs. Staying abreast of weather forecasts will help you be on site when the atmospheric effects are working their magic.

North/South Camera Angles

Search for a camera position that is north or preferably south of the target landscape. This camera angle will record landforms (at the preferred times of sunset or sunrise) when they are illuminated by sidelight. Why should you want sidelighting? Two reasons: It allows the most effective use of polarizing filters, giving extra density to sky regions and added color saturation to vegetated landscapes. It also models the terrain, showing contours, shapes and textures more distinctively than any other lighting angle. In North America, a camera view from the south opens the landscape to both strong sidelight and weak front light, resulting in lower contrast and more subject detail.

Check for Open Horizons

When you find a landscape feature that appeals to you, check to see if the east and west horizons

Sofa Mountain, Waterton Lakes National Park, Alberta (below). The eastern or front ranges of the Rocky Mountain chain provide great early shooting due to the open horizon which allows the sun's first and warmest rays (in terms of color temperature) to light up peaks and ramparts theatrically. This photo was taken from prairie foothills to the northeast of the subject at about mid-morning.

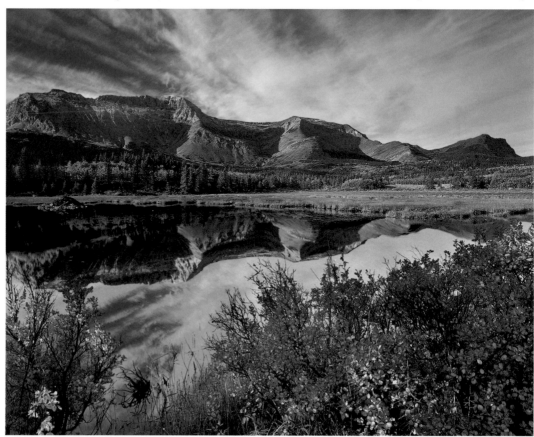

Capturing the Moods of the Shoreline

The shoreline is a reliable source of dramatic landscape imagery — a marriage of soaring skies and open ocean, an unending confrontation between tide and terrain. Following are some of the strategies that I use when working the shoreline.

My first consideration is to be ready for amphibious work. I carry my equipment in a vest (see p. 41) and, depending on the temperature, wear chest-waders or shorts and nonskid river sandals (Chacos). This allows me to move around tide pools, scramble over rocks and shoot even when waves are swirling about me and the tripod. I carry the usual assortment of scenic tools — a couple of zoom lenses covering ultra-wide to moderate telephoto focal lengths, a cable release, polarizing and split neutral density filters, and plenty of Fujichrome Velvia.

The best camera positions (especially when there is surf) are often right where waves break onto the beach, territory hazardous for equipment. I keep handy a cotton cloth to wipe salt spray from camera and lenses and keep an eye on my tripod when it is set up in

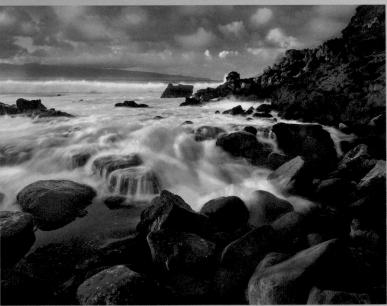

sand that may be shifted by incoming waves. A single wave can quickly undermine the tripod and topple the camera into salt water. I cover up controls on my camera with flaps of duct tape in case I should receive an unexpected splash.

Early morning is the preferred shooting time. Footprints have been erased overnight by the tide and the atmosphere is calm enough to record well-defined reflections in tidal pools. This period is ideal for the Atlantic coast which lays open to the rising sun, but on the Pacific edge, mountains and seaside cliffs leave many beaches in shadow during the best light of early morning. Here, I look for shorelines with low elevation backdrops or

Honolua Bay, West Maui, Hawaii (right). The best place to set up your tripod at most beaches is where the waves break onto the shore. This is a hazardous location for equipment and you need to stay alert for big sneaker waves that may land periodically, splashing or flooding you and your equipment and possibly even placing you in danger. In areas of big surf, spend 30 minutes evaluating wave patterns before descending to the water's edge. Foregrounds and colorful skies form the basis of most compositions. Look for waves breaking over rocks and swirling about in sinuous patterns as they flood the beach. For this photo I used a slow shutter speed (one second) to show the silky, blurred textures of mini-waterfalls and tidal flows of incoming surf.

those on the south-facing beaches of projecting headlands. During periods of low tide, seastars, mussels, kelp and other sea life are exposed to provide added decoration to compositions.

I look for a combination of strong foreground elements and interesting wave action. Once the tripod is set up and the scene is framed, I attach a cable release and observe incoming waves, taking a shot each time I anticipate a dramatic splash or sinuous stream of moving water. On sandy beaches, receding waves leave momentary patterns of glistening sand, rivulets and pools that reflect the color of the sky from a low camera position.

Due to the high-contrast nature of such landscapes, it's essential to use neutral density filters for good detail in both highlights and shadows. Hard-edge (rather than soft-edge) filters are especially desirable, as compositions frequently bring together a clean, uninterrupted union of sky and sea. Beach scenes gain identity and perspective when living elements such as gulls, herons, kelp or seastars are part of the composition. I portray these elements prominently. I may close in on them with a wide-angle lens set for the hyperfocal distance or, using a longer focal length, place them against a clear stretch of sky or sand — any uncluttered picture area where they will stand out.

Photo above by Joy Fitzharris

are clear of light-obstructing landforms — an important consideration no matter what shooting angle you chose. These offensive topographies are most apt to vex you when shooting in mountainous regions. If the site you have chosen to photograph lies close to adjacent peaks, there will be no dramatic color in the sky until after the target landscape is shrouded in deep shade and is bereft of both natural color (especially warm tints), form and texture. If the eastern horizon is open, plan to shoot at dawn; if the western horizon is clear, be on site for sunset. This schedule offers the best chance of combining rich color, dramatic skies and well-modeled landforms.

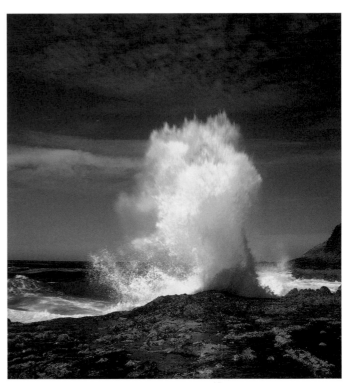

Devil's Churn, Cape Perpetua Scenic Area, Oregon (above).
To accentuate this explosion of snowy surf, I used a polarizing filter to darken the blue sky backdrop. I released the shutter using a cable release while watching the scene with the naked eye. This made it easier to capture the waves at their highest trajectory. Between shots I was quick to cover the camera with a hat to protect it from saltspray carried on strong offshore winds.

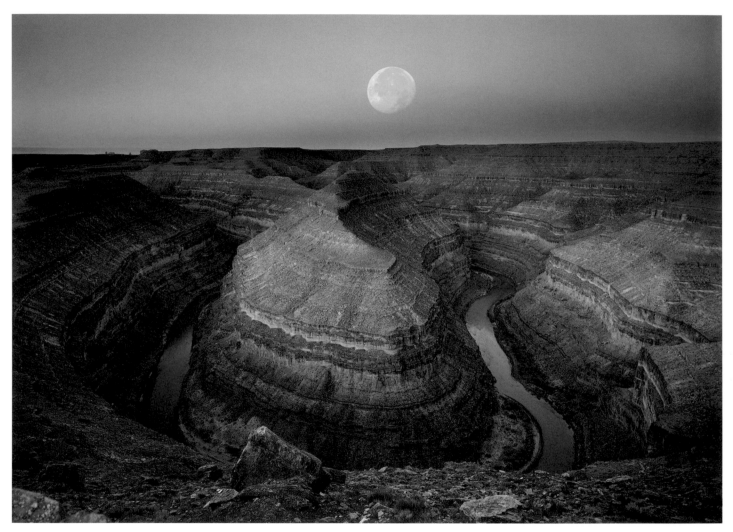

Goosenecks of the San Juan River, Utah (above). *This image was made by double exposure; the land was shot with a 20mm lens, one-stop split neutral density filter for four seconds at f/22; the second exposure of the moon was shot with a 200mm lens for 1/125 second at f/8.*

THE IMPORTANCE OF FOREGROUND DETAILS

The best landscape photographs are made in locales that harbor interesting foreground details. The southwestern deserts have prickly pear and saguaro cacti, the arctic has its bear grass and autumn blueberries, the Eastern Sierra its bowling-alley boulders and sagebrush, the Oregon Coast its sand dunes and sea stacks. These micro features can be used to set up the scale of a scene, establishing important perspective cues that infuse a flat piece of film with a convincing sense of three dimensions. The photographer's choice of appropriate camera angle can use micro features (such as trees and rock formations) to frame and focus viewer attention on a silky waterfall, soaring sandstone arch or brooding snowcapped pinnacle.

Putting the Moon in the Picture

It's easy to include the moon in twilight landscape shots by means of double exposure. A full moon normally gives the best results. To begin, frame the landscape in the normal way, but leaving a section of clear sky (no clouds or tree branches) in which you can subsequently place the moon. (At left I used an ultrawide-angle lens to capture the dramatic perspectives of the river canyon.) Take this picture in the normal way but with the camera set for two exposures (see your camera manual if you don't know how to do this). Then reframe to include the moon in the part of the scene left open for it. Expose the moon at a shutter speed of 1/film speed at f/16 (the sunny f/16 rule) or equivalent.

If you take the landscape portion with a wide-angle or normal lens (as I did here), you may want to change to a telephoto focal length for the moon to make it appear larger (here I used a 300mm lens). All this must be done using a tripod to insure sharpness and accurate framing.

For the moon to look natural, you should try to take an angle on the landscape that is lit from the same, or close to the same, direction as the moon, especially if you are shooting when the sun is above or near the horizon (not so critical in deep twilight). Full moons should be matched with scenes lit from the front, half or crescent moons with landscapes lit from the side (in the latter case the illuminated side of the moon should be faced toward the sun).

Appealing Lunar/Solar Accents

Check your calendar for periods when the moon shows itself in the sky. In rare instances it will appear in your viewfinder over the landscape in just the right place. But usually, you will want to use double exposure techniques to reposition the moon to a site more suited to the composition.

Magic Moments Beside Still Pools

Few landscape elements get me more excited than still water. Beaver ponds, vernal pools, lakes, lagoons, river backwaters and tide pools are all clues to fantastic scenic shooting in the offing. Water bodies, large and small, can be found over most of the continent (including the desert regions of the southwest) with a little diligent searching. With appropriate camera positioning and lighting, they can be used

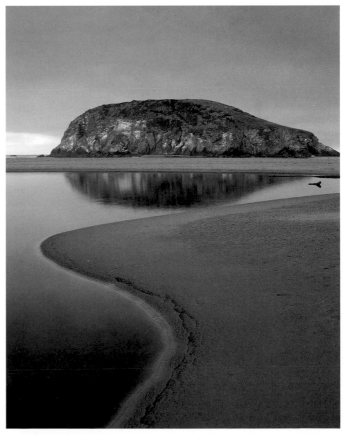

Low tide at Harris Beach, Oregon (below). This calm tidal pool set up the center of interest in reflected symmetry and also provided an alluring S-curve to carry the viewer's eye into the picture. Reflection details in the foreground also add interest to the visual flow.

Wood stork, Anhinga Trail, Florida (below). Although shooting wading birds at the time, I realized the situation was better suited for a landscape view. I switched to a shorter lens and backed up to frame this sunrise moment.

to throw mirrorlike reflections of the landscape, in effect redoubling its beauty and presenting a repeated harmony of picture elements. These reflections become most striking in calm weather during periods of sunrise and sunset when the oblique angle of illumination leaves the pool's substrate in shadow, producing the clearest, most perfect reflections. If you intend to incorporate reflections in a landscape shot, it's best to arrive on the scene prepared to get wet. Sporting hip or chest waders or even shorts and sneakers, you can conduct an uncompromising search for the best camera position (for more suggestions on shooting reflections, see page 162).

Animate with Animals

Opportunities to capture a dramatic landscape that also includes wildlife are rare and to be treasured. Unlike other landscape clues, this one is not reliable and your shooting will generally be more productive if you give priority to devising the compositions based on landscape features alone — but be prepared to make modifications should luck bring an elk, moose or flock of swans into the frame. Better results are to be had by keeping alert for landscape possibilities when shooting wildlife. Should animals, light and landscape features develop the potential for scenic imagery, switch to a wider focal length or retreat to a position that will provide a more expansive view.

No Human Artifacts — The Last Clue

Even in rural areas it becomes increasingly difficult to come upon landscapes that are free of human artifacts — telephone poles, highways, dams and all manner of buildings. Even inside parks and wildlife refuges, the tendency is to build ever bigger visitor centers, commercial facilites and more parking areas rather than using budget resources to either improve or expand natural habitats. And of course there's the increasing intrusion of jet contrails in wilderness skies. All are eerie symbols of a planet's ecosystem out of balance. Of course, many such features can be touched out on a desktop computer once the film is developed and scanned, but this is not as satisfying or authentic as capturing a pristine setting firsthand. For the most peace-

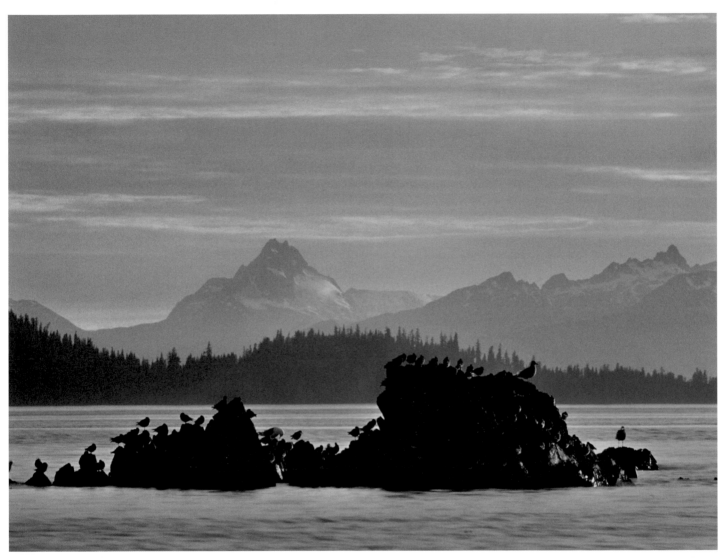

ful, spiritual experience, focus your efforts where nature is protected and human artifacts are largely absent — national parks and forests, designated wilderness areas and sparsely settled territories. And when you are not shooting, pressure your elected representatives to curtail commercial development of all kind, especially in rural areas.

These clues are the fingerprints of beautiful landscapes. Dust carefully for them and you should capture some memorable photographs.

Shorebirds on reef at low tide, Kopreanof Island, Alaska (above). This bird-covered rock adds energy and focus to an otherwise unremarkable stretch of northern coastline under drab skies.

The Power of Perspective

How to infuse your landscape photos with the impression of three dimensions

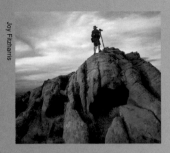

Canyonlands from Grand-view Point, Island in the Sky, Canyonlands National Park, Utah (right). The overlapping sandstone bluffs in this view, normally expressive of deep perspective have been compressed by the use of a telephoto lens to create an impression of visual irony.

Coyote tracks at Totem Pole and Yei Bei Chi, Monument Valley, Arizona/Utah (far right). The feeling of deep perspective evoked by this photograph is the result of converging parallel (or somewhat parallel) lines represented by ripples in the dunes that create the "railroad track" effect. The grains of sand growing smaller as the eye moves up the picture space are also important perspecive cues. Pentax 645, 35mm f/3.5 lens, Singh-Ray circular polarizer, Fujichrome Velvia, 1/15 second at f/32.

IF YOUR PHOTOGRAPHY experience is anything like mine, I suspect you've stood on the edge of a precipice somewhere in the hinterland, lens aimed expectantly at a grand arena of shimmering forest, imperious rock and vaulting sky.

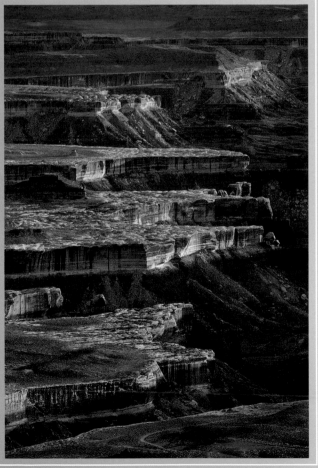

Overcome with beauty, you dreamily ratchet a few frames through the camera then shoulder your tripod, confident, perhaps, that what you have recorded will appear in the next Audubon calendar. But when the processed film is presented for examination, what was initially an exhilarating view of boundless wilderness appears on the light table as a small, flat gasp of photographic frustration. What happened?

Such disappointments are often the result of failing to translate the real world's three dimensions into the two-dimensional vocabulary of film. In many situations the portrayal of depth is the primary attraction of a landscape photograph, more important to the picture's success than subject matter, color or any other pictorial element. To express the third dimension convincingly, we need to capture and arrange the features of a landscape in a way that best projects their spatial qualities, keeping in mind that we see the world quite differently than does a camera. Not only do our two eyes work in stereoscopic view, but we move about, crane our necks and reappraise the scene from different angles, often in but a fraction of a second, to gain a better appreciation of the depth and scale of the visual confrontation. By contrast, the still camera is afforded but a single, frozen view in its generation of a flat photograph. To bridge this optical gap, we need to emphasize and clarify those cues in the landscape that express depth.

SIZE CUES

The relative size of landscape features is one of the most obvious cues in conveying the depth and scale of a scene. Objects that are close to us appear larger than the same objects further away. Utilizing this cue is first a matter of incorporating in your composition familiar features that are similar in size, or at least are perceived to be so by the viewer, and then positioning the camera so that they are presented on film in differing proportions. Such components most commonly include trees, shrubs and wildflowers of the same species. Animals can also be used as size cues — bison, elephant seals, elk, snow geese, sandhill cranes, roseate spoonbills and other gregarious species. The perfect placement of the camera shows such size cues arranged at regular intervals largest to smallest on a diagonal plane or some variation of it (an S-curve for example) which leads to the landscape's most important element — rainbow, setting sun, colorful cloud

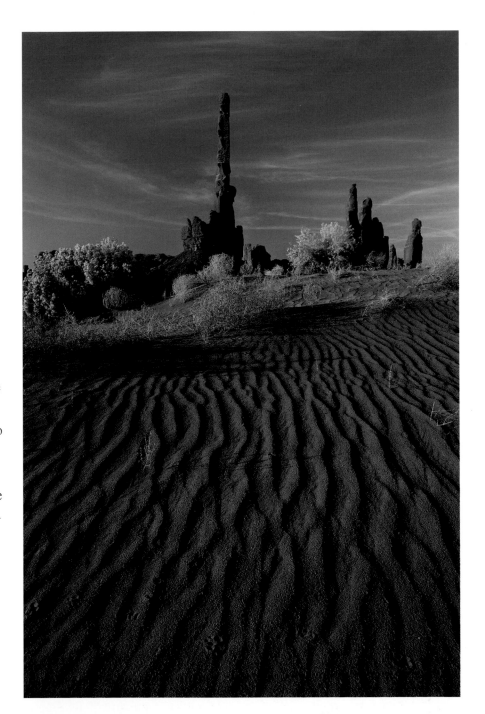

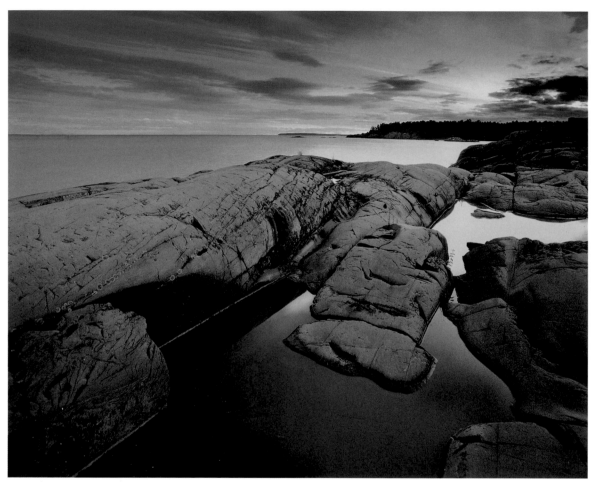

be used to present a uniform pattern of decreasing size cues. From an appropriate camera angle, rivers, streams, sand dune ripples and fallen logs all exhibit the railroad track phenomenon — the convergence of parallel lines toward a vanishing point (actually a variation of the effect of size cues).

ANGLES OF VIEW

When used in conjunction with size cues, lens focal length generates a powerful perspective effect. By emphasizing the dif-

Red Rock Point, Georgian Bay, Ontario (above). In this composition a strong, three-dimensional impression is created by the outline of the large rectangular boulder which displays railroad track phenomenon of converging parallel lines. If possible, arrange size cues in diagonal sweeps as seen here.

bank or a special terrain feature. You may never come across such an idealized circumstance, but it's important to be aware of the potential and work toward it when shooting.

There are other less common but equally powerful size cues to which you should become sensitive. When cumulus clouds dapple the sky, they appear smaller nearer the horizon. Sand ripples, caked mud flats and ocean waves can all

ferences in size cues, wide-angle lenses increase the perceived distance between elements in the composition and promote a feeling of deep space. Telephoto lenses achieve the opposite effect by compressing the distance between elements in the scene. For the most extreme perspective effect you should position the camera as close as possible to the nearest size cue in the composition. You normally will need to shoot at f/22, or smaller, to achieve satisfactory depth of field if you are working for an exceptional effect (i.e. with the closest size cue being near the lens' closest focusing distance). Much of the time, however, you will be working in concert with other design prerogatives at some compromise distance.

LOWS AND HIGHS

Because the eyes of a standing human are some five or six feet above the ground, landscape features that are close to us are usually positioned lower in our field of view than those more distant (clouds excepted). For a maximum three-dimensional effect, I normally set up at about a 45-degree angle (above the horizontal) from the first size cue in the composition regardless of its distance from the camera and using a focal length wide enough to include at least the horizon and a bit of sky. If you place the camera too low, you will lose visual exposure of the spaces between size cues, if you set up too high you

will lose the horizon and the familiar eye-level configuration of the size cue — either angle will result in a flattening of the scene. You also need to position carefully the camera on a horizontal plane so that the number of size cues clearly portrayed is maximized (avoid overlapping of cues). Sometimes this step requires that you move the camera forward or backward as well as sideways. In most situations you should set depth of field to include both the closest size cue and features on the horizon (usually infinity). I don't consult depth-of-field scales or bother to calculate

Sunset at Leo Carillo Beach, Malibu, California (below).
These scattered rocks are ideal size cues — familiar, relatively uniform in appearance and growing steadily smaller as they move up the picture frame. I set the camera at about a 45-degree angle above the horizontal on the closest group of rocks. This position maximizes separation and definition of individual rocks while sustaining the size gradient between the nearest and furthest.

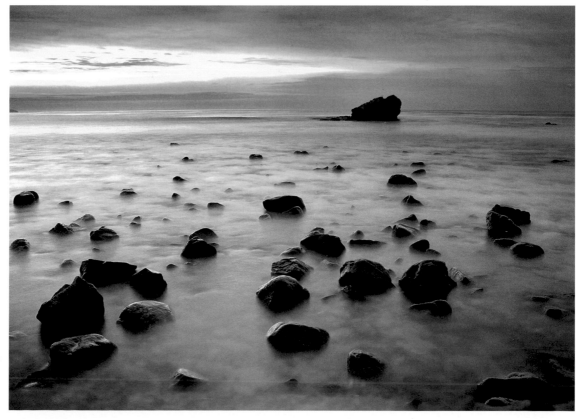

hyperfocal distances. I normally focus on the middle point of the closest cue (rather than the leading edge), dial in f/22 or f/32, have a quick peak at the scene with the lens stopped down, and then hope that the wind stays calm while the shutter is open (exposures are usually in the one second-plus range). In practice, setting camera position is normally a trial-and-error procedure exercised until the most effective design is achieved based on interrelated factors of color,

Composing for Depth in Landscape Photographs

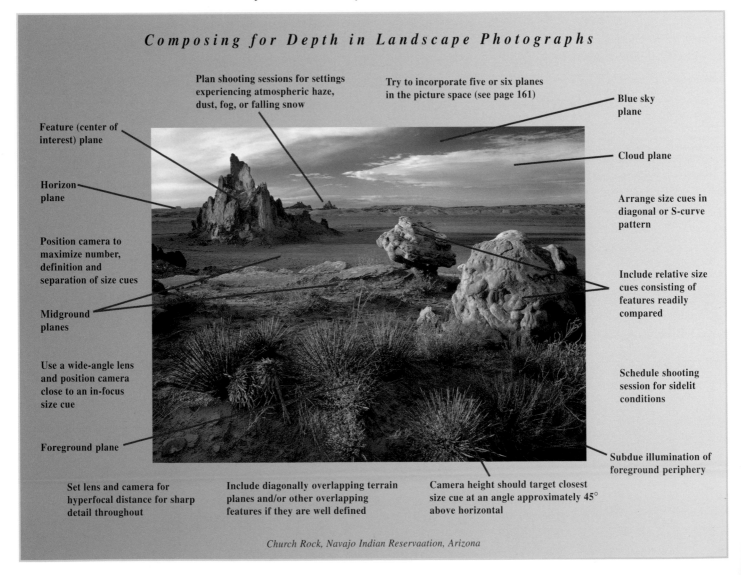

Plan shooting sessions for settings experiencing atmospheric haze, dust, fog, or falling snow

Try to incorporate five or six planes in the picture space (see page 161)

Blue sky plane

Cloud plane

Feature (center of interest) plane

Horizon plane

Arrange size cues in diagonal or S-curve pattern

Position camera to maximize number, definition and separation of size cues

Include relative size cues consisting of features readily compared

Midground planes

Use a wide-angle lens and position camera close to an in-focus size cue

Schedule shooting session for sidelit conditions

Foreground plane

Subdue illumination of foreground periphery

Set lens and camera for hyperfocal distance for sharp detail throughout

Include diagonally overlapping terrain planes and/or other overlapping features if they are well defined

Camera height should target closest size cue at an angle approximately 45° above horizontal

Church Rock, Navajo Indian Reservaation, Arizona

light and subject matter as well as the desired perspective effect. I try not to rush this stage of the picture-taking process.

OVERLAPPING

Another useful perspective tool that needs skilful handling is overlapping. Precise lateral and vertical placement of the camera is usually needed for this strategy to work effectively, especially when utilized with smaller landscape features such as trees or rocks. Such elements are often so similar that when they are recorded in an overlapping arrangement, they may frequently blend together in a muddle not readily distinguished by the viewer. To avoid confusion, try to overlap only simple areas of contrasting color, line direction, brightness or shape (horizontal limbs crossing vertical trunks, for example). The most effective use of overlapping can be done with intersecting landscape

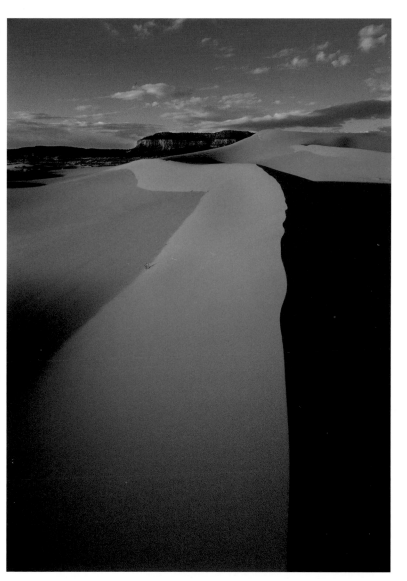

Coral Pink Sand Dunes State Park, Utah (left).
Setting up the camera on top of this weaving dune allowed me to structure the composition on the sidelit ridge which carries the eye from the bottom of the frame directly to the mountains in the distance. Lighting also plays an important part in carrying visual interest from the shaded foreground periphery toward the more strongly lit forms deeper in the picture space. When shooting sand dunes the best locales for photography are normally atop curving dunes illuminated from the side late or early in the day. Look for dunes that run toward interesting landforms or colorful skies. Be careful when searching for a camera position that your foot prints don't accidentally mar the best views. This composition offers six distinct planes which successively capture and hold the eye on its journey through the picture.

planes. Such situations are most frequently encountered in hilly or mountainous terrain. Try to frame areas where there is a confluence of interesting contour outlines running in opposing diagonal directions. Topographies lit from the

Shiprock, near Shiprock, New Mexico (below). The shapes of these massive rock formations are defined by early morning sidelight. Sidelight also helps separate and identify the clumps of grass — important size cues which lead the viewer's eye through the scene toward the distant terrain features.

side or back, or photographed in early morning when mist hangs in low-lying areas, will show the most definition between planes and obvious overlapping.

SIDELIGHT FOR VOLUME

Landscapes illuminated from the side exhibit shapes whose surfaces and contours are well distinguished by areas of highlight and shadow. This makes it easy for the viewer to compare and identify important size cues and other spatial relationships. The overlapping of objects or planes is emphasized and clarified because the shadow portion of one is set against the highlight portion of another. The earlier in the day you shoot, the greater the effect. To flatten perspective, shoot early or late in the day with the sun directly behind you for full frontal illumination.

HAZY DAYS (ATMOSPHERICS)

Due to particles suspended in the atmospheric, close objects appear more detailed than those further away. Known in photo jargon as "aerial perspective," this phenomenon can be used to create three dimensions in landscape photos. It is most commonly encountered in the form of fog, mist, rain, snow, dust and, unfortunately, haze. Few settled regions of North America are free of haze created by fossil-fuel generating stations and other types of industrial pollution. Air quality in the Grand Canyon and Great Smoky Mountains National Parks, for example, has declined to the extent that the panorama photos of ten years ago are rarely possible today because of limited visibility. A little haze goes a long way in creating perspective effects. At present we need less, not more of it, if we are to be able even to see the landforms we wish to record. When shooting in the moody atmosphere of fog, you will encounter varied opportunities on the ragged periphery of a fog bank where you can modulate the effect by waiting for the fog to shift or by changing position yourself. If working in mountainous regions, head for high ground near the ceiling of the fog; in coastal areas head inland toward elevated terrain.

DIMENSIONAL IRONIES

One of the most interesting ways of dealing with perspective is to combine contradictory spatial cues for ironic effect. You can interpret an assembly of haze-rimmed, overlapping foothills by shooting with a space-compressing telephoto or, conversely, use a wide-angle lens to record a featureless stretch of still water punctuated by a single island. The allure of scenic reflection photos is due in part to their inherent perspective contradiction — the reflection at your feet is the same size but usually less distinct and intense that the terrain features it mirrors in the distance.

FIVE PLANES

If you've become overtaxed by this litany of techno-tips, allow me to put one more spin on these important concepts. When scouting for deep-perspective scenics I look for landforms exhibiting five distinct planes. Ordered from near to far, they are as follows: (1) The foreground plane features interesting landscape details that set the scale for the composition; (2) the midground plane contains well-defined size cues that

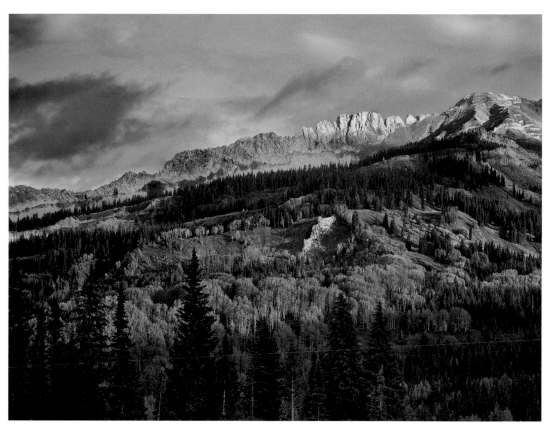

lead the eye into the picture; (3) the feature plane shows the center of interest, usually a dramatic landform; (4) the cloud plane is ideally a puffy collection of cumulus or nimbus; (5) and the sky plane comprises the final backdrop in pure shades of blue, rose, peach or amber, depending on the time of day. Sometimes a sixth plane (the horizon plane) spreads itself behind the feature plane. I try to record each plane clearly and forcefully. Great shooting to you, and may a herd of cloned zebras wander through your next landscape setup.

The Dyke and Ruby Range, Gunnison National Forest, Colorado (above). Interesting visual irony is generated in this composition by the marriage of several expansive perspective cues (size, overlapping, foreground detail, lighting) with the compressive effects of using a telephoto lens. Pentax 645, 300mm f/5.6 lens, Singh-Ray circular polarizer with color intensifier, Fujichrome Velvia, 1/2 second at f/32.

Nature's Mystical Mirrors

How to record dramatic reflections of the landscape

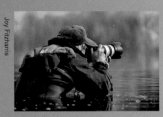

Joy Fitzharris

Avery Peak, Maroon Bells–Snowmass Wilderness, Colorado (below). *Amphibious gear is often essential to accessing the best camera positions. For this angle, I donned chest waders to ford a creek and beaver pond in freezing temperatures.*

A REFLECTION'S GRAPHIC allure emanates from two mingled sources: the strangely inverted repetition of image color and shape and the unlikely marriage of firm ground and liquid illusion. Whatever the dialectic, reflection photos project the most compelling of landscape motifs. How do you capture them on film? In this chapter I've described the techniques I've found most useful.

OUTFITTING

Your normal assortment of gear should provide the basis for a specialized, stripped-down reflection kit. A tripod that doesn't get jammed by water, sand or mud is essential. Zoom lenses are valuable for precise framing when access to the ideal shooting spot is restricted by deep pools, ooze, cattail barriers or slippery rocks. Optical coverage of 20mm to 100mm is ample (35mm format). Be prepared to enter the soup or sit in the mud if perfect composition is important to you. I wear Neoprene chestwaders, which are warm and durable. In summer, shorts and sneakers may suffice if you are young

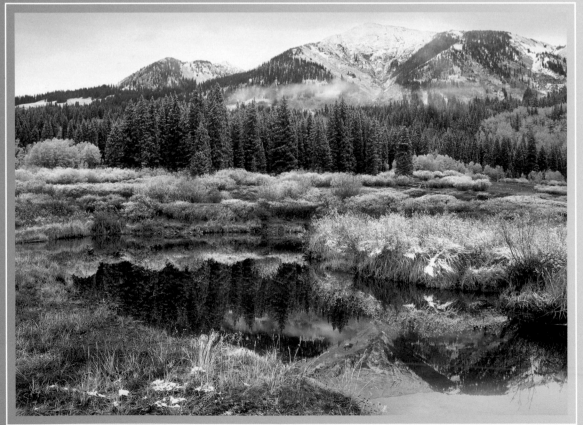

and hardy. This kind of amphibious work calls for a vest big enough to hold (at a minimum) an extra lens, half a dozen filters, your usual film complement, pepper spray if you are shooting in bear country, a cable shutter release, and a small rag for wiping water drops and gunk from lenses and filters. The camera should be carried on your tripod which doubles as walking stick, crutch or depth-finder.

ORIENTATION

Beaver ponds abound in North America's wilderness areas and they are usually ideal places to capture reflections. But anything that throws off an image has equal potential — oceans, lakes, marshes, puddles or even wet sand. The best time to shoot a reflection is just before and after sunrise. To avoid stumbling about in the darkness, you need to scout for tripod spots the day before. It may take a while for you to find a pool that's exactly right. When you are sizing up a location at midday, don't be fooled by the lackluster impression. The light of dawn or dusk will add the necessary magic. I first look for a prominent landscape feature that

is worth a few rolls of film — a mountain, rock prominence or beautiful forest — and then I search for water that might catch its reflection. I look for the best combination of lighting angle (front or sidelighting), subject angle (whatever is most defined and/or distinctive) and foreground elements (simple elements that can be used to interrupt or frame the reflection — logs, rocks or aquatic vegetation.) If it's windy during your reconnaissance, the reflection may be indistinct, but you should still be able to evaluate the

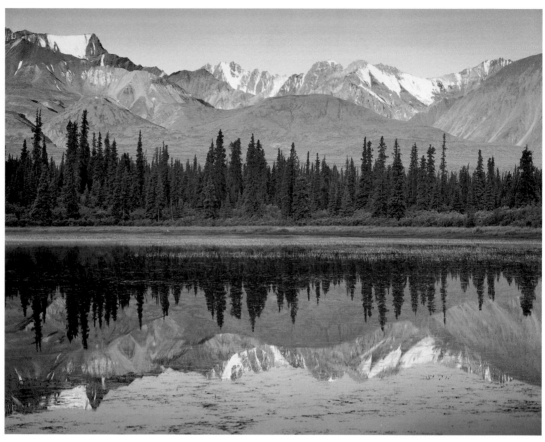

Kluane Range, Yukon Territory (above). This reflection was located among a series of marshes and beaver ponds. I aimed the camera to record a balanced lineup of peaks and give equal importance to the terrain and the still pool. This emphasizes the symmetry generated by the near-perfect reflection. A one-stop split neutral density filter was used to strengthen the intensity of the reflection (see page 165).

North America's Big Four

*These are arguably the most famous re-
flection photo locations on the continent.
Except for the first site, all are well
signed and easy to find.* **Grand Tetons
from Schwabacher Landing** *(Grand
Teton National Park, Wyoming) is a sunrise shoot. I prefer summertime (autumn
is also good) as storms improve the like-
lihood of clouds above these soaring
spires. Ask a ranger to point out
Schwabacher Landing on the park map
(it's not marked). Once at the parking
lot, walk north on the riverside trail 100
yards to just past the beaver dam.*

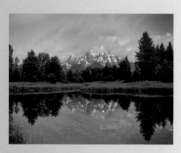

    **Mount Rainier from Reflection
Lakes** *(Mount Rainier National Park,
Washington) is also a morning shot. The
lakes are right beside the highway.
August is best if you want a wildflower
foreground.*

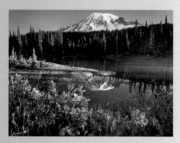

    **Mount Rundle from Vermilion
Lakes** *(Banff National Park, Alberta) is
best at sunset although sunrise is also
good. There are half a dozen nice pools
right beside the road; pick a sheltered
one with your favorite foreground.*

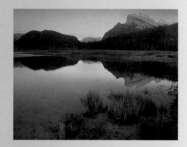

    *A few miles west of Aspen, Colorado,
is the location of a classic alpine landscape,* **Maroon Bells from Maroon
Lake.** *The best time is mid-September
when the aspen-draped lower slopes
flash gold. If you go before Labor Day,
access up to the lake is only by shuttle
bus although private vehicles are
permitted until 8:30 a.m. which is plenty
of time to expose a few rolls.*

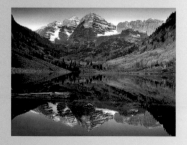

scene's potential and get major features to line
up. All will look much better at sunrise or sunset.

CRYSTAL VISIONS

It's not difficult to capture a perfect, mirrorlike
reflection. No guarantees, of course, but if you
are in the right location at the right time using a
few special techniques, you should emerge from
the underbrush with fine images — even sublime
ones on occasion. Your main task is to avoid or
neutralize the effect of wind on water. Dusk and
especially dawn are likely to be still. If your pool
is rumpled before sunrise, don't be downcast; the
calmest period f requently arrives a few minutes
after dawn. In any case, be patient; allow thirty
minutes or so if the light is holding and the atmosphere is relatively calm. Chances are the surface
will flatten completely for a few seconds —
enough time to collect your prizewinner.

    The best pools are small and sheltered by
large shrubs, trees and boulders out of the line of
fire. Within the pond, look for areas that will be
least affected by breezes — patches of water
protected by floating logs, emergent vegetation,
sandbars or exposed rocks. These buffers can be
incorporated as important design elements in the
composition. As foreground tidbits, they set up
the scale of the scene, create an impression of
three-dimensional space, and where they interrupt the mirrored landforms, reaffirm the ironic
interplay of solid matter and its fragile rebound.

For brilliant reflections in shallow pools, keep the camera position low (I often shoot while kneeling) to prevent the image of the pool's substrate (especially if it's light sand or gravel) from bleeding into the surface reflection.

FILTERS FOR NATURAL RESULTS

Most color-transparency filtering is intended to bring the contrast range of the scene within the more restricted contrast range of the film so that both shadows and highlights show detail. To capture the full drama of a wilderness reflection, you will need a polarizing filter, three to six (or more) square plastic (resin) split neutral density filters and duct or gaffer tape. Because most landscape reflections are shot with wide-angle lenses, large filter sizes (4 x 5 or 6 inches) eliminate vignetting problems. Densities of one, two and three stops (0.3, 0.6 and 0.9) will handle all lighting situations. The transition zone between

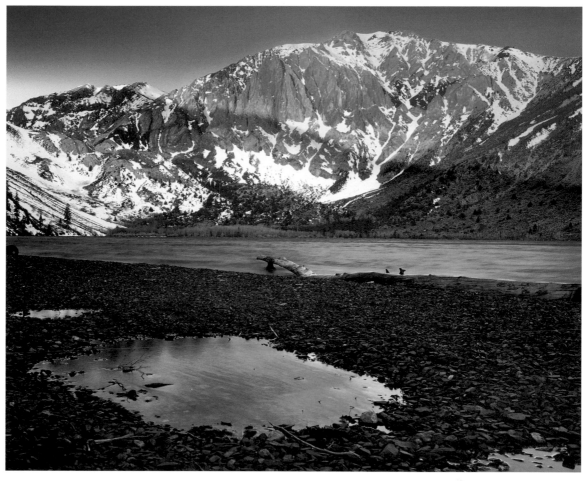

the clear and neutral density areas of the filter can be either abrupt (hard-edge) or gradual (soft-edge). If you don't feel like packing a full set of each, opt for the hard-edged models which are generally more useful and precise. Cokin, Hi-tech, Lee and Singh-Ray offer good selections.

Duct or gaffer tape fixes the filters to the front of the lens. Keep small strips attached to your tripod, camera body and lenses for easy

Laurel Mountains from Convict Lake, California (above). This ephemeral pool was sheltered from winds by surrounding terrain. I used a one-stop, soft-edge split neutral density filter to hold the color in the reflection and a two-stop, hard-edge neutral density filter to prevent the sky from washing out. This resulted in good detail and strong color throughout.

Nisling Range, Yukon (below). For this photo I waded into the marsh to achieve a composition that presented the glowing peak and its reflection framed by clouds above and sedges below. Pentax 645, 45–85mm f/4.5 lens, polarizing and one-stop split neutral density filters, Fujichrome Velvia, 1/2 second at f/22.

access. Why not use a filter holder? Because frequently you will be using two split neutral density filters simultaneously and they need to be set at different angles, one to align with the slope of the landform and the other to align with the slope of its reflection.

Using the filters is easy. Position them by viewing the scene through the viewfinder at small aperture (about f/22). Move the filters around so that bright areas (skies, sunlit land-

forms and reflections) are subdued and shadow regions are unaffected. This will constrain exposure values and provide good detail throughout the frame. With the filters in place, take an average meter reading and then fire away. Bracket by a half-stop or more in both directions.

The eye cannot look at a landscape and its reflection simultaneously. As it shifts back and forth, the pupil adjusts for the differences in brightness with the result that the visual impression of the reflection is brighter (and more exciting) than what film records. This usually can be redressed with filters by giving the reflection (usually a bit darker) about one stop more exposure than the actual landform. In most situations, I attach a polarizer to darken the sky and strengthen color and contrast, and then place a one-stop grad filter over the top half of the scene to bring up the brightness of the reflection in the lower half. With hazy or full sidelight, the

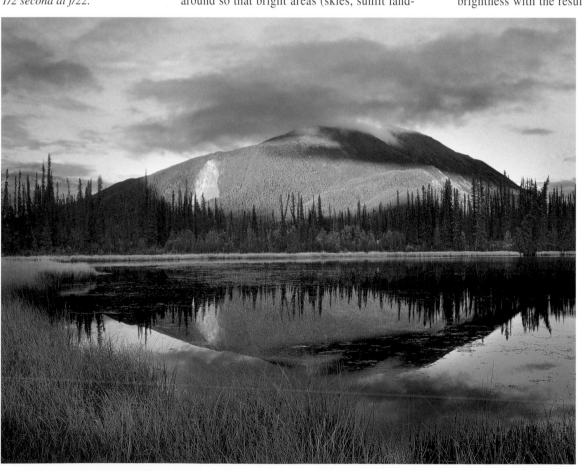

polarizer must be adjusted to avoid weakening the reflection. The brilliance of the reflections should approach but not exceed that of the genuine article.

THE FILTER SQUEEZE

So what are all the other filters for? When shooting at sunrise or sunset, especially in hilly or mountainous regions, you will usually be aiming at a scene that is bright top and bottom (the landform and its reflection) and dark in the middle (areas in shadow). To record detail throughout the scene, you need to squeeze the shadows by placing neutral density filtration over both the landform and its reflection, allowing about a stop more exposure for the land. If the sky is without

Two-stop split neutral density filter

One-stop split neutral density filter

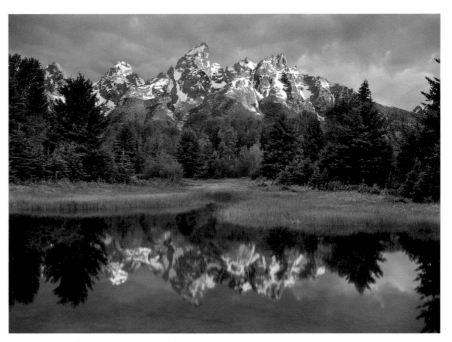

cloud, reach for the three-stop filter to hold back the upper portion of the scene and a two-stop grad to hold back its reflection in the lower area. The shadow areas will then come up into the exposure latitude of the film. Under softer light, you can use a two-stop/one-stop combination. As the border between the sunlit and shadow areas is seldom horizontal, you will need to shift the filters to a diagonal orientation. A sloping skyline would require you to angle the top filter from upper left to lower right and the bottom one from lower left to upper right, for instance. When trying this the first few times, shoot filtered and non-filtered versions so that you can study the results afterward on the light table.

***Grand Tetons from Schwabacher Landing, Grand Teton National Park, Wyoming.** In this dramatic sunrise setting, I used the filter-squeeze — a combination of two filters that constrain subject contrast (see illustration at left) in order to record fine detail and saturated color in both the brightest and darkest parts of a reflection scene. I have photographed the Tetons from this location on seven different occasions in order to capture a variety of lighting and cloud effects.*

Part Five

The Close-up World

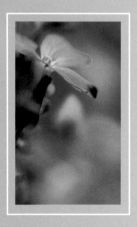

Working at Close Range

How to use the special accessories and lenses of close-up photography

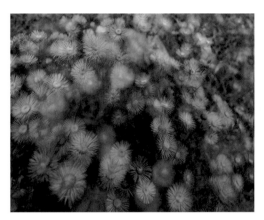

IT'S A WARM SPRING DAY and a bee fly hovers among a patch of wildflowers. It hangs motionless above a blossom and then dives, proboscis foremost, through a fairyland of mauve and mint in quest of another draft of nectar. One of myriad tiny scenes waiting to be discovered by the photographer. Capturing such intimate views requires the use of special close-up equipment. The particular setup required depends on how much you wish to magnify the scene as well as the subject's ability to tolerate your presence at close range.

In close-up photography subject magnification is measured with reference to the size of a single frame of film. If the subject is the same size as its image on film, then it is recorded life-size (or 2X life-size). A frame-filling photo of a bumblebee would be just about life-size, likewise for a human thumb. A frame-filling portrait of a mosquito would be about 10X life-size and the same type of shot of a chipmunk would be 1/4

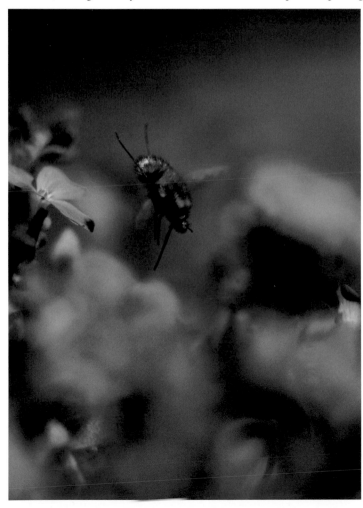

Wind-blown asters near Gothic, Colorado (above). *This image represents the greatest magnification possible with most standard lenses (1/12 life-size).*

Diving bee fly, Vancouver Island, British Columbia (left). *Bee flies are easy insects to capture in flight. They hover like hummingbirds allowing enough time for framing and focusing. They also feed systematically, moving predictably from one blossom to the next. Their fearless nature allows you to work at close range in natural light. This specimen was photographed at about 1/2 life-size with a handheld camera. Canon T90, 100mm macro lens, Kodachrome 64, 1/350 second at f/4.*

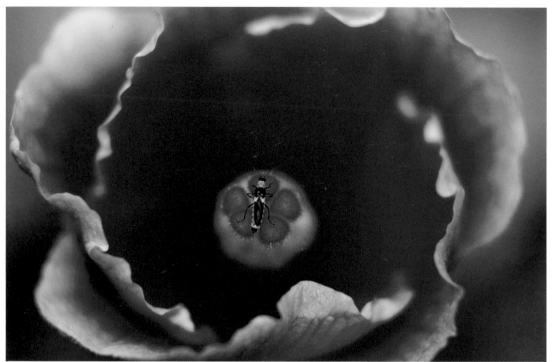

Beetle on hibiscus flower, Belize (above). *I was making a painstaking close-up of this bloom when the insect arrived to feed. After a quick adjustment of focus the shot was easily made. Most beetles are reliably trusting subjects that can be photographed as close as you find necessary. Canon T90, 50mm f/1.8 lens, auto bellows, Fujichrome 50, 1/30 second at f/5.6*

size from the Grand Canyon to a caterpillar. (2) Macro-zoom lenses allow photography in the close-up range but it is not continuous. Usually you simply adjust the focusing ring to a special setting that pulls in a limited range of magnifications.

Accessory devices that modify prime lenses for close-up work — teleconverters, lens extensions (tubes or bellows) and close-up supplementary lenses — may be combined singly or in combination with one another, offering numerous ways of working at close range. How to choose among these options is resolved by the nature of the subject being photographed. For many creatures you need to photograph from a nonthreatening working distance, something that is often difficult to predict in advance. Every animal, even of the same species, exhibits a unique level of tolerance which may vary from hour to hour, day to day and season to season. Butterflies are the most wary of insects, frogs the most wary of amphibians. Turtles are perhaps the most timid of all close-up creatures and bees may be the least. Before approaching a possibly wary subject, try various

life-size. Standard lenses focus only closely enough for a frame-filling portrait of a human head (about 1/8 life-size). For greater magnifications, special close-up lenses or add-on devices are required.

MACRO LENSES

These lenses fall into two categories: (1) A true macro lens is designed and specially corrected for high quality close-up work. It has a focusing range that extends from infinity to a close-up distance that normally yields 1/2 life-size reproduction. Although expensive, this lens can be used without modification for subjects ranging in

lenses and accessories on a life-size dummy subject to find a combination that will allow you to work as close as possible without causing flight.

EXTENSION TUBES AND BELLOWS

These devices permit varied magnification and produce quality images, even at great reproduction. On the negative side, they reduce the amount of light transmitted by the lens, which limits the range of stop-action photography under ambient light and creates problems when you are working in the wind.

Magnification can be estimated by dividing the amount of extension by the focal length of the prime lens. A 50mm lens with a 50mm of extension produces magnification of 50:50 or 1:1; a 100mm lens with 50mm of extension produces magnification of 50:100 or 1/2 life-size.

Most extension tubes couple to all of the camera's automatic functions, except auto-focus (rarely a handicap). All automation is lost when working with bellows except TTL flash. A double cable release can be attached to provide automatic diaphragm operation. Bellows allow the camera to be rotated between vertical and horizontal formats or any angle in between, a convenient feature not possible with

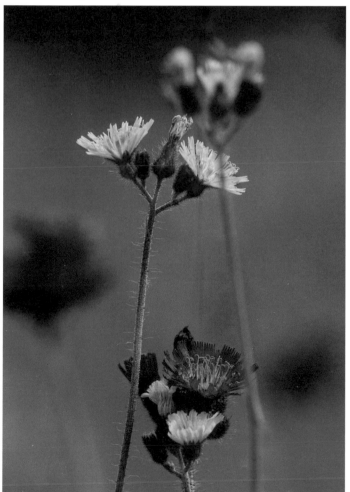

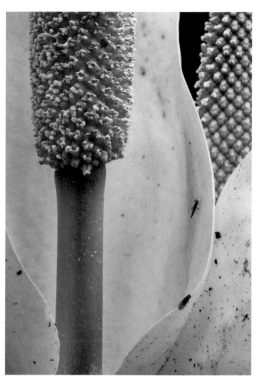

Yellow arum, Vancouver Island, British Columbia (above). To isolate this subject's varied textures, I used a 200mm telephoto lens (with extension tube) set at small aperture to maximize depth of field and flatten perspective.

Hawkweed near Ithaca, New York (left). The camera was positioned to capture an eye-level view and an informal arrangement of blurred blooms in the background. To focus closely I inserted a 25mm extension tube between the 300mm lens and camera body.

Hummingbirds by Natural Light

Broad-tailed hummingbird feeding at scarlet bugler near Santa Fe, New Mexico (below). I purchased these hummingbird flowers at a local nursery that specialized in native plants and used the techniques described at right to make the photograph. Canon EOS A2, 400mm f/2.8 L Canon lens with 1.4X teleconverter and two 25mm extension tubes, Fujichrome Provia 100F rated at ISO 200, 1/750 second at f/5.6.

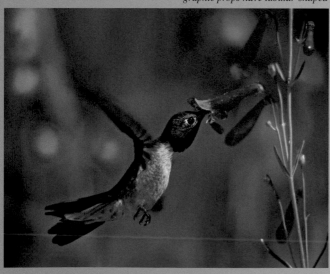

To photograph this tiny bird, you must take advantage of its near constant need to feed. (The hummingbird sips the human equivalent of 20 gallons of nectar each day.) During early morning and late afternoon, a hummingbird forages 15 to 20 times each hour, visiting flower patches within its territory repeatedly, and takes intermittent rest periods in a nearby tree or bush.

To attract the birds, set out hummingbird feeders (widely available). Position them to receive front light in the early morning so that you can shoot at the bird's eye-level while you are seated. Once the hummingbirds are accustomed to your feeder, you can move it about for better lighting or camera angles. The birds will quickly reorient themselves to the new location.

You can also attract hummingbirds by offering favorite flowers either in pots or in a sunny garden location. Enticing flowers that are also good photographic props have tubular-shaped blooms and include lupines, columbines, penstemons and gilias. Nurseries normally stock a selection of hummingbird wildflowers.

Whether you plant flowers or rely on feeders to bring the subject close, you will still need potted flowers if you wish to shoot the birds amid colorful surroundings in good light. Portable flowers can be moved around to create framing foregrounds and backgrounds and coax the hummingbird into photogenic positions and poses. Look for varieties that have red blooms, sturdy stems and stout tubes to steady them in wind. Keep the flowers hidden from the hummers until you are ready to begin shooting.

A large table set up near your feeder(s) makes an ideal shooting stage. The shooting angle from your sitting position should also pick up blue sky in the background. Spread the table with a white cloth that will reflect light evenly into the shadow portion of the scene for improved contrast. Arrange the potted flowers so that some occupy the foreground and especially the background as out-of-focus color elements. Set the camera level so that blue sky and a swatch of natural vegetation (backyard trees or shrubs) appears in the distant background. With tubular species, angle the blooms so that the subject approaches and feeds while facing the camera.

Shooting will be most productive if you stay back six feet or more to permit the birds to feed without nervousness. For this you need a lens in the 500mm range equipped with an extension tube of 25 to 50 mm. Temporarily place an in-flight, hummingbird-sized stand-in at the set to make sure you have the desired magnification (this book is a good size to start with). With an ISO 400 film, you can shoot at f/5.6 with exposure times between 1/500 and 1/2000 second in early morning light, settings which provide enough depth of field to encompass the bird's body yet render the background soft and smooth, and enough speed to freeze a hovering hummer while recording its wings as

extension tubes except for the Nikon PN-11 tube, which has a handy rotating tripod collar.

Bellows are designed primarily for high magnification work. Most have a minimum extension of around 50mm. So with a 50mm lens, the minimum magnification is nearly life-size. With a

appropriately expressive blurs. (At exposure times lasting more than 1/250 second wings become so blurred that they disappear.) Manual focusing is the fastest and best way to ensure that the eyes are sharply rendered and that the composition fully integrates the hummingbird, the flower it is feeding on, and supporting elements in the background and foreground.

Once everything is ready, entice the hummingbird to your set by temporarily removing the feeder and revealing the flowers. The hummer will be confused at first but quickly spot the natural offerings and swoop in to give the real thing a thorough tasting. It should visit your set periodically allowing you a few motor-driven frames each time it appears. You can replace the feeder after a couple of visits to encourage more regular visits. The hummingbird will usually try a series of blooms before or after sipping at the feeder.

Photographing hummingbirds requires advance preparation, patience, persistence and attention to numerous details. Have fun with your hummers!

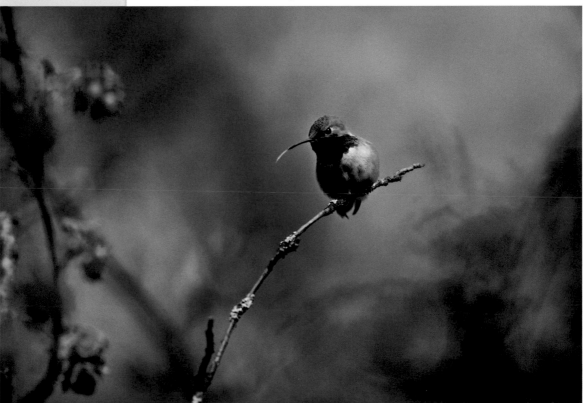

100 mm lens, it is about 1/2 life-size.

Bellows are constructed with two sets of rails — one for changing camera position, the other for adjusting the extension. When using bellows, spread the boards for the magnification desired, then adjust the position of the entire assembly on

Rufous hummingbird perched in red-flowered currant bush, Vancouver Island (above). To lure this feisty male hummingbird to the camera, I hung a feeder on one of its favorite natural springtime food sources.

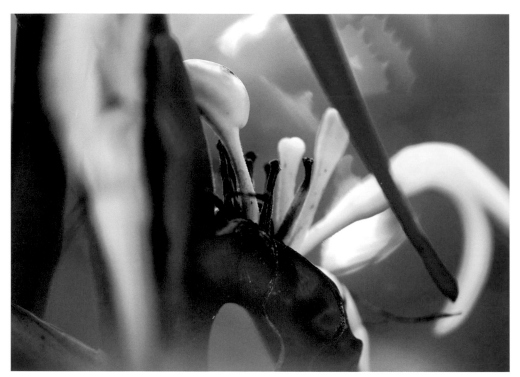

A supplementary lens is classified by its diopter rating, which is the inverse of the close-up lens' focusing distance in meters. A +1 diopter refocuses the prime lens (set at infinity) to a distance of 1/1 (one) meter, a +2 diopter to 1/2 meter (500mm), a +3 diopter to 1/3 meter (333mm) and so on. Not all manufacturers use this method for naming their lenses. Canon close-up lenses "250" and "500" focus at 250mm (+4 diopters) and 500mm (+2 diopters), respectively. The higher the diopter rating, the smaller the working distance and the greater the magnification. Close-up lenses do not provide a significant magnification increase when used with lens extensions.

Heliconia, The Big Island, Hawaii (above). At magnifications approaching life-size, floral subjects provide a wealth of graphic elements to fashion into all manner of compostions. For this magnified view I used a Pentax 645 with a short telephoto lens and bellows.

Captive red-eyed tree frog (right). Small frogs are a suitable size and temperament to record with a telephoto lens (200–300mm) and a +1-diopter close-up lens – an inexpensive, fast-working combination.

the focusing rail until the scene is sharp. If you are too tight on the subject, decrease the extension; if you are not tight enough, open the bellows further; then readjust camera position.

CLOSE-UP SUPPLEMENTARY LENSES

These lenses do not reduce the amount of light transmitted through the optical system, giving them an advantage over lens extensions when ambient light is low. They fit prime lenses with matching filter diameters, which means you likely need to acquire more than one set to fit all of your lenses, or use step-up/down rings, which may cause vignetting.

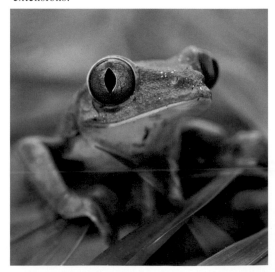

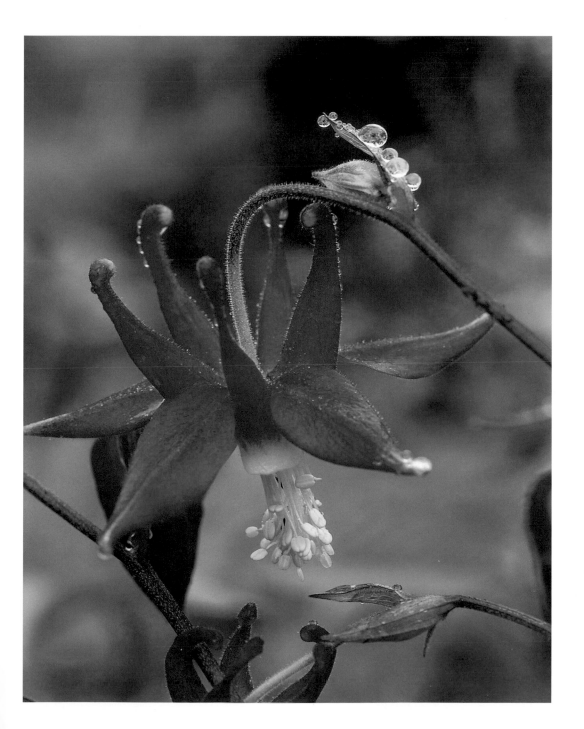

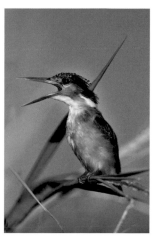

Malachite kingfisher, Lake Baringo, Kenya (above). A 500mm lens with 1.4X teleconverter provided ample close-range power (effective focal length 700mm) to capture this diminutive fisherman yawning from a favorite perch.

Red columbine, Mount Rainier National Park, Washington (left). A bellows and telephoto lens were used to make this life-size portrait. Pentax 645, Rodagon 150mm f/3.5 short mount (non-focusing) lens, Horseman VCC bellows, Fuji-chrome Velvia, 1/2 second at f/16. The fragile bloom was steadied with a plant clamp (Plamp).

Insects in a Meadow

As a nature photographer you will find few shooting experiences more enjoyable than recording insects, especially butterflies, in the field under natural light. The key word here is natural — no ghoulish flash laying low the exquisite forms of carapace and abdomen or blistering the minty tints of a spring meadow. All you need is simple equipment, a stretch of prairie, and time to savor the circling bee and clattering grasshopper.

I like to use a focal length of about 300mm with extension tube(s) attached for close focusing. The telephoto's narrow angle of view makes it easy to selectively frame blurred background and foreground colors that can be incorporated into the composition. Such a lens also allows you to work a few feet away from your subject (important with timid butterflies). I use a 25mm tube alone or two together to achieve a variety of magnifications up to about 1/3 life-size.

Make sure your lens is well hooded as you will frequently find beautiful compositions by shooting against the light. A rotating tripod collar makes it easy to switch from horizontal to vertical formats and to swap around extension tubes when you wish to modify framing.

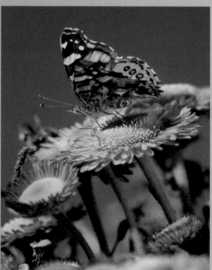

Big spaces open to the sky — prairies, meadows, and lake shores — are where you can find both plenty of insects and ample light. You won't find shooting to be as productive in forests or dense thickets though they may appear more wild. Country roadsides and ditches are good almost anywhere. They receive plenty of sun and lots of water runoff from the road, which nourishes plant growth, particularly wildflowers — the key to this approach to insect photography. Not only do wildflowers offer important design elements but the nectar and pollen they produce attract lots of insects and their predators. If you're exploring from the car, look for meadows with butterflies fluttering above (see page 133) as this indicates an active feeding area.

Few picture components breathe as much natural magic into the atmosphere of a nature photograph as do patches of empty space represented by out-of-focus washes of color, especially the vacuous blue of the sky. Using a telephoto lens at or near largest aperture is the starting point for bringing selected areas of strong color-blur into the composition. For the sky you will have to shoot from an angle lower than the flower, across an incline, or over a hump toward the open horizon. The sky shouldn't sit above the subject in one

Painted lady butterfly, Mendocino Headlands, California (right). A patch of cliff-side blooms was a magnet for these subjects. Although they flew off before I could set up, they returned shortly after I stopped moving. Once a subject began feeding, I moved about cautiously for the best angle and magnification.

Painted lady on purple coneflower, New Mexico (below). A lens hood tamed flare and a reflector brightened the shadows of this backlit specimen.

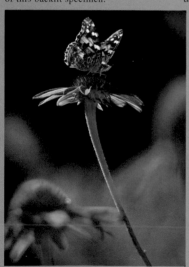

Single-element close-up lenses do not produce high quality results at magnifications above 1/3 life-size. Multi-element professional level supplementary lenses are available from Canon and Nikon for use at high magnifications with zoom and telephoto lenses.

expanse but should appear in swatches.

The key to recording a strong design is not to target the butterflies — they normally fly off at your approach. Rather note the flower(s) that they are feeding on and use this as the framework for your design. Get into position quietly. Adjust focus and framing to capture one robust bloom clearly (a healthy bloom is a source of pollen and nectar). Move the camera position forward and backward and from side to side to reposition colorful out-of-focus blooms and color patches, including the sky, until you arrive at an effective arrangement. Once you are still, butterflies should appear on the stage you have created in your viewfinder (see page 133). With butterflies, strive to bring both the eyes and antennae tips into the depth-of-field zone.

The best time is mid-morning on a sunny day. Warm temperatures stimulate nectar production and lots of bee and butterfly activity. At these magnifications, when a tripod is used with hands on the camera, a shutter speed of 1/125 second normally will yield sharp photographs. At slower speeds, you should switch to a cable release unless you are using IS or VR lenses.

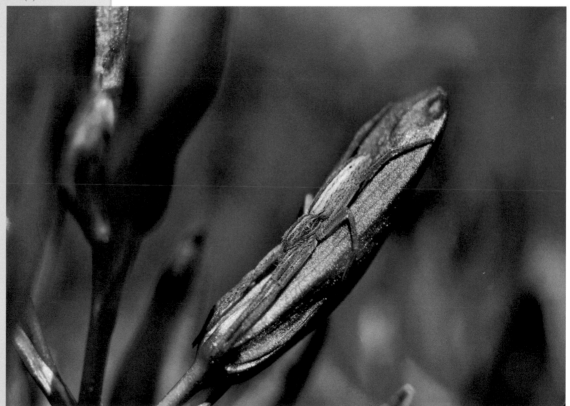

Crab spider on camas, Vancouver Island (below). This diminutive predator waited to ambush small flies that fed on these blooms. Shallow depth of field can be used to surround your subject in soft color.

TELECONVERTERS

Teleconverters conveniently increase the focal length of the prime lens by 2X or 1.4X while maintaining the lens' full focusing range. With the lens adjusted to its closest focusing distance,

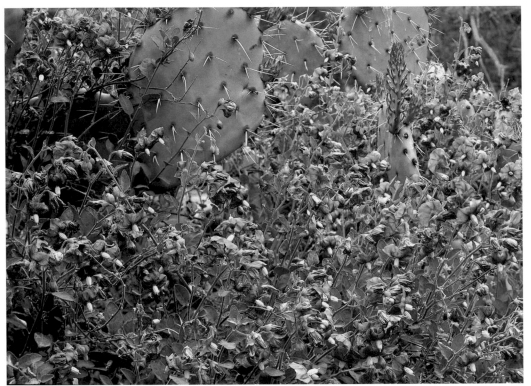

Prickly pear cactus and silver-leaf nightshade, Grasshopper Point, Arizona (above). I used a tilt/shift close-up bellows to angle the depth-of-field zone through the picture space to align with this array of blooms. Being able to tip and tilt the depth-of-field zone allows you to use larger apertures without sacrificing sharpness and consequently faster shutter speeds to arrest subject motion.

Using a tilt/shift close-up bellows (right). I'm tipping the lens forward to align with the subject.

maximum aperture. If you are using a teleconverter and an extension tube together, place the teleconverter on the camera body first, then attach the extension tube, and lastly, the prime lens.

TELEPHOTO LENSES

Telephoto lenses allow you to maintain adequate working distances from wary subjects. They can be used with teleconverters, extension tubes and bellows, and close-up supplementary lenses as well as nearly any combination of all four. One of my favorite uses of a telephoto lens in close-up work is for shooting wildflower

magnifications of about 1/4 life-size are possible with the 2X converter and 1/5 life-size with the 1.4X converter. Teleconverters work well when combined with telephoto lenses to photograph wary subjects such as butterflies, frogs, and songbirds. About ten percent loss of image quality occurs with 1.4X converters and a twenty percent loss with 2X converters. Fortunately image degradation takes place about the periphery of the frame and is usually not a problem, particularly when this area is not in the depth-of-field zone. If edge-to-edge sharpness is important, stop down one or two stops from

meadows at maximum aperture. With careful manipulation of camera position and focus distance, you can use the shallow depth of field to create dramatic abstractions organized around

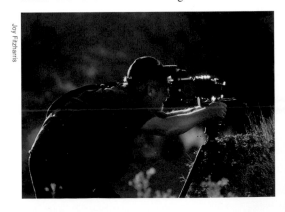

Joy Fitzharris

out-of-focus background and foreground elements (see page 188).

WIDE-ANGLE LENSES

Adapting a wide-angle lens for close-up work is best accomplished with a short extension tube (12–15 mm). At closer range it creates the same feeling of expanded perspective as at normal magnification. When using close-up supplementary lenses, vignetting may occur with focal lengths less than 24 mm. This can be checked by viewing the scene at stopped-down aperture. Most viewfinders only show about ninety percent of the picture area, so vignetting may still appear on the film even if you can't see it in the viewfinder. I like to push a wide-angle lens into a clump of flowers, with some of the blossoms even touching the front of the lens. Then, working with the camera handheld at ground level, I try various positions — changing the angle even slightly can radically alter composition.

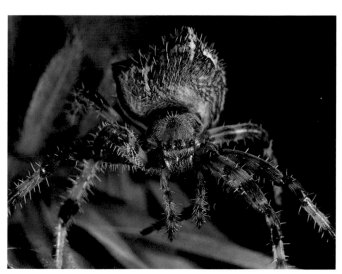

Wide-angle lenses are useful for producing magnifications exceeding life-size with minimum extension and therefore minimum light loss through the optical system. In order to focus at such magnifications, the lens is attached in reversed position on extension tubes or bellows. A reversed 24mm lens with 50 mm of extension produces 2X (2:1) life-size; with 150 mm of extension, it produces 6X (6:1) life-size.

TILT-SHIFT LENSES

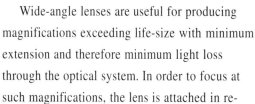

These lenses make maximum use of depth of field (close-up photography's most limited commodity) making it possible to use larger apertures and faster shutter speeds that freeze motion.

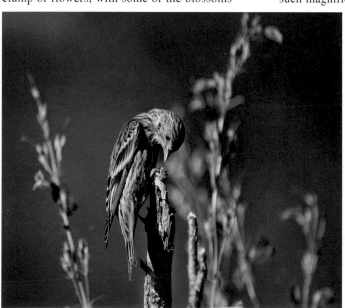

Orb-weaver spider, Santa Fe, New Mexico (above). To achieve this 2X life size portrait, I used a 28–105mm zoom lens and a 25mm extension tube, a simple combination that offers a wide range of magnification simply by adjusting the zoom control. When photographing animals at magnifications exceeding life size, it's necessary to use electronic flash to arrest subject movement and camera shake and have enough light to shoot at small apertures for adequate depth of field. This portrait was made handheld with a dual flash Sailwind unit.

Pine siskin near Santa Fe, New Mexico (left). This visitor to my bird feeder was recorded with a 500mm lens and 25mm extension tube on Fujichrome Provia 100F pushed one stop to ISO 200.

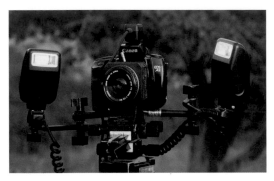

Macro flash brackets with two TTL automatic flash units (above). *This popular and impressive-looking apparatus holds two synchronized strobes in place with adjustable arms. Although flash is the best way to photograph subjects at life-size and greater magnifications, you will find that such contraptions require too much time to assemble and are difficult to adjust and transport in the field. You will get more use from a macro ring flash or a simple manual unit like the dual flash Sailwind unit pictured below.*

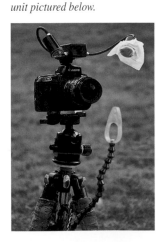

Tilt-shift lenses allow the film plane to be aligned with the subject plane with minimal framing compromise. First establish the framing desired, then tilt the lens to parallel as closely as possible the important elements of the composition, adjust the focus, and reposition the camera to capture the scene as originally framed. Finally, using depth-of-field preview, select the aperture and shutter speed combination that best interpret the scene. Keep the shift setting to zero to avoid exposure problems.

Tilt-shift lenses can be used with extensions, teleconverters and close-up supplementary lenses. They are available from Canon or Nikon in focal lengths, ranging from 24 mm to 90 mm. The longer focal lengths generally are more useful for natural subjects.

Greater Than Life-size

At magnification exceeding life-size, the image quality of standard lenses begins to deteriorate and working distances are so reduced that the light may be blocked from the subject by the lens itself. Special procedures are necessary to avoid these problems.

Reversing the Lens

Image quality is restored by reversing the lens on the camera body, accomplished by screwing an adapter to the front of the lens. Unfortunately the adapter circumvents automatic coupling devices and makes stop-down metering, manual closing of the diaphragm, and manual exposure control necessary.

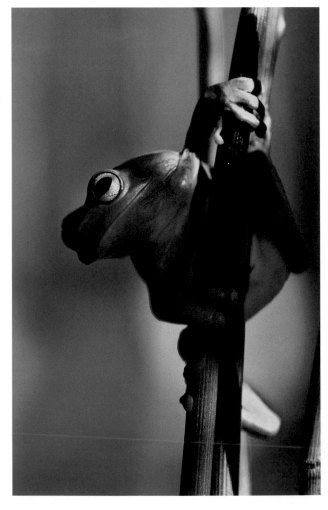

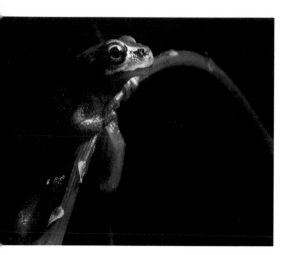

Working With Electronic Flash

The advantages of working with electronic flash include reliable automatic TTL exposure control, brief exposure times which allow handholding, and adequate illumination for exposing fine-grained films at small apertures to maximize depth of field. Electronic flash is usually the only viable approach for recording small animals at magnifications 1/2 life-size or greater. The artificial feeling of flash can be minimized by placing the flash away from the camera–subject axis and using bounce reflectors or diffusers to soften the light. An efficient diffuser is a single layer of Kleenex which reduces output by about one stop (compensate for this only if using manual flash).

In close-up work, full flash is used to light both the subject and background; usually no ambient light registers on the film. This type of lighting is thematically suited for images of nocturnal subjects in which portions of the background are black due to flash fall-off. With the notable exception of butterflies, bees and other pollinators, many insects can be included in this category, as well as many species of reptiles and amphibians. Due to its brief duration, flash also is necessary when hand-holding the camera.

Flash Position

In nature, light illuminates a subject from any direction, and so can your flash. The most convenient position for the flash is on the camera's hot shoe, but you can also place it to one side, above, or even behind the subject using a remote synchronization cord and a macro-flash bracket or light stand. If you use multiple flashes, be sure that one flash dominates the lighting scheme by reducing the power of the other flashes. Generally, the background light should be reduced by one stop and a fill light should be reduced by about two stops. Consult your flash manual to find out how to do this.

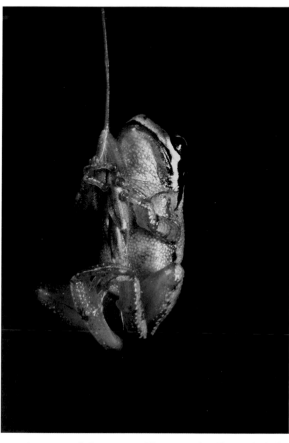

*Frog portraits. Choose the lighting effect you like. Diffused backlight creates a natural setting for a White's tree frog (**far left**). A single flash positioned for side light simulates a moody, moonlit setting for a Pacific tree frog (**left**). The same subject is illuminated more evenly with two flashes for a more contrived studio feeling (**above**).*

Wild Flora

Conventional and offbeat approaches to one of nature's most expressive subjects

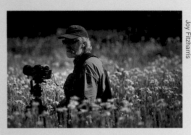

Joy Fitzharris

Yellow columbine and coral bells near Durango, Colorado (below). This detailed portrait, recorded at life-size magnification, was illuminated by an overcast sky and fill light from a matt white reflector.

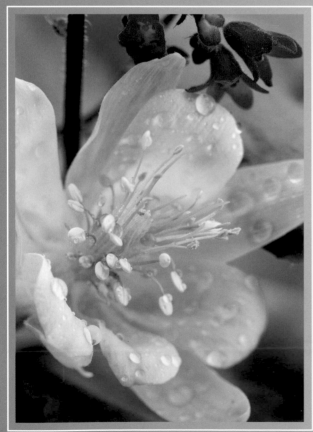

MEXICAN HAT, WILD adder's tongue, maidenhair fern — romantic names for wildflowers and other flora that comprise the intimate details of a landscape. The natural world is filled with small still-life subjects waiting for a composition. Accessible no matter where you happen to live, they offer photographers endless opportunities for creative self-expression. In this chapter, I'll outline some of the basic principles for making beautiful portraits and then offer some offbeat approaches that should help launch your own creative endeavors.

Most of your floral photography will take place close to the ground and you will usually need to use a tripod to insure sharpness. For ankle-high subjects, rest your camera on a couple of bean bags right on the ground. For taller specimens, you can usually work with your tripod legs collapsed and completely spread. The operating principle here is to position your tripod at, or below, bloom level.

WINDS OF WOE

Once you have the camera stabilized, the next task is to immobilize the subject. Keep in mind that close-ups of flowers under natural overcast light using a polarizing filter and fine-grained transparency film require exposures in the 1/4-second range and longer. When the shutter is open this long, even a breath of air will cause the blossom to shake unacceptably. A light breeze makes it nearly impossible to attain detailed, frame-filling photographs. I normally spend such periods working with solid, hard-sided subjects or scouting new areas for possible pictures. Breezy days are also great times for capturing wider views of colorful meadows in blurred motion. This method is suitable for even sunny midday conditions because shadow and highlight portions of the scene are blended together to automatically reduce contrast.

Although the atmosphere seems completely calm, once you study the subject at close-range through the viewfinder, you will discover that there is usually enough energy to jostle fragile specimens. If this is the case, you must be patient and time shutter release carefully to capture the subject between zephyrs. In such circumstances a Plamp (plant clamp — see www.tripodhead.com) comes in handy to keep the blossoms absolutely still during exposure. You clamp the jaws of one end of this articulating gizmo to something solid (avoid using your tripod whenever possible) and the other end to the plant (outside the picture frame, of course). The Plamp is also handy for adjusting the location of the flower in the frame rather than trying to move the camera itself, a cumbersome and finicky undertaking at close range.

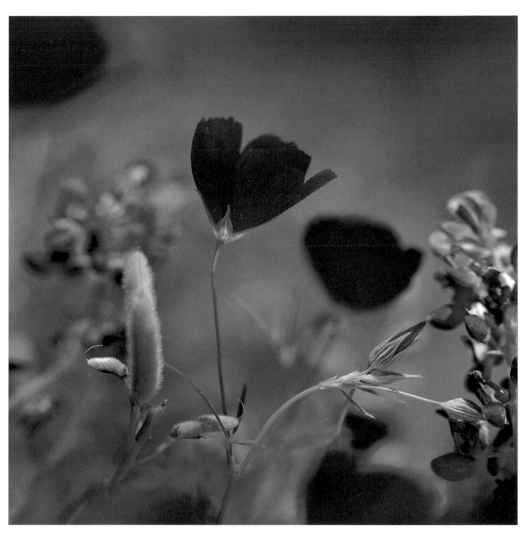

IMPROVING THE LIGHT

Although wildflowers are often photographed with artificial light, you will find natural light both more attractive and amenable to controlling the numerous features of the composition. Overcast or hazy skies provide the soft, even illumination ideal for close-up work, especially with wildflowers. Even under these conditions, matt white reflectors improve color rendition and shadow detail, although it may be difficult to notice until the film is developed. If shooting under sunny conditions early or late in the day, reflectors are essential for close-up portrait work.

Winecups and bluebonnets near Llano, Texas (above). This portrait was made with the camera resting on the ground in order to include an expanse of blue sky in the background. A matt white reflector was placed on the ground beneath the scene to spotlight this trans-illuminated specimen.

Windblown meadow, Mendo-
cino Headlands, California
(right). This ethereal capture
was made on a day too cold and
windy for standard wildflower
portraiture. A 300mm lens was
used to isolate and compress a
colorful section of the field. I set
the camera for double exposure
and recorded the first image at
1/4 second (to blur the vegeta-
tion) and f/22. Over this I
recorded the second
image at 1/250 second
(to freeze subject mo-
tion) at f/4, focusing
on the wave of grasses
in the central area of
the frame. Each take
was underexposed by
one stop so that nor-
mal exposure would
result when the two
parts were combined.

Sego lilies, Canyon-
lands National Park,
Utah (far right top).
In desert habitats, soft
light is rare. To gener-
ate your own, use a
large, neutral color
umbrella to shade the
subject and bounce
light into the scene
with a matt white re-
flector. This photo was
taken at midday under
a cloudless sky.

How to Shoot at High Noon

When working under a clear sky at midday, acceptable close-up results are only possible when you take steps to soften the sun's light. A simple procedure, customarily used by professionals, that produces naturally lit, professional-caliber imagery calls for the use of a large umbrella of neutral color (those used by golfers are ideal). Set up the parasol to block all direct sunlight from the subject and the background. Then use a matt white reflector held away from the umbrella to bounce soft light back into the scene. This produces an effect nearly identical to overcast conditions with low contrast and normal color balance. It's great to have an assistant to help out with the umbrella and reflector. If you are working single-handedly with a ground-hugging subject, set up the umbrella directly on the ground, hold the reflector in one hand, and trip the shutter with a remote release.

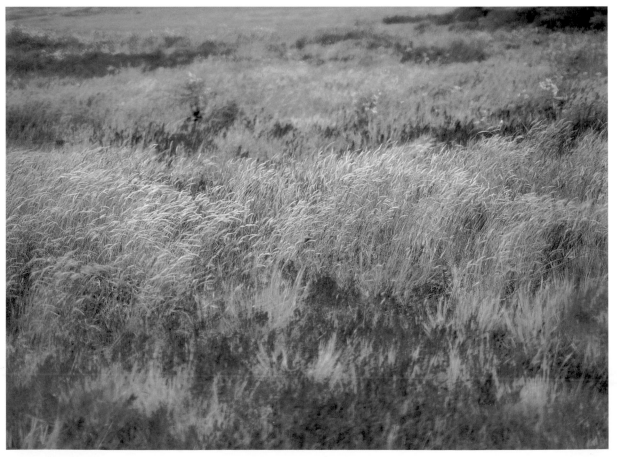

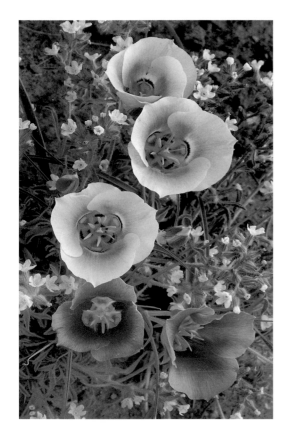

WILDFLOWER PORTRAITS

Making a simple, detailed portrait of a blossom usually represents a photographer's first attempt at expressing the beauty of the wildflower world. Effective portraiture is not as easy as you might at first think. Here are some suggestions to guide your efforts.

• Get close enough. For a portrait, the bloom should occupy most of the picture frame.

• Sharpest focus should be on the pistils and stamens unless other more distinctive features offer greater visual interest.

• Use out-of-focus patches of color to frame the main blossom.

• Check the picture area (especially about the periphery) to make sure no other elements are sharper, brighter, more colorful, or in any way more attractive than the main subject. Readjust framing as necessary.

• To simplify the composition, shoot at a large aperture for shallow depth of field to soften less important features surrounding the main subject. Once you've made a few portraits and are more familiar with the subject and working at close range, you likely want to begin to experiment with alternate imagery less anchored in this formula approach.

Aerial agave, South Rim of Grand Canyon, Grand Canyon National Park, Arizona (below). This dreamy effect was created by double exposure. The first image was made with sharp focus on the tips of the spikes. For the second exposure I shifted focus closer to the camera by a couple of inches to blur the entire scene slightly. Both takes were precisely framed from directly above with a zoom lens and extension tube.

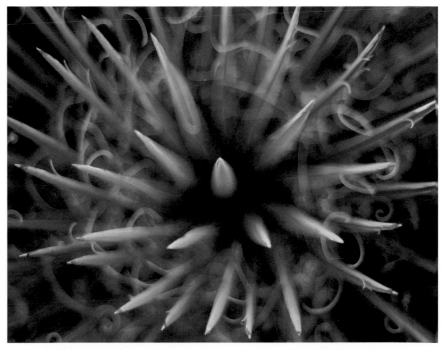

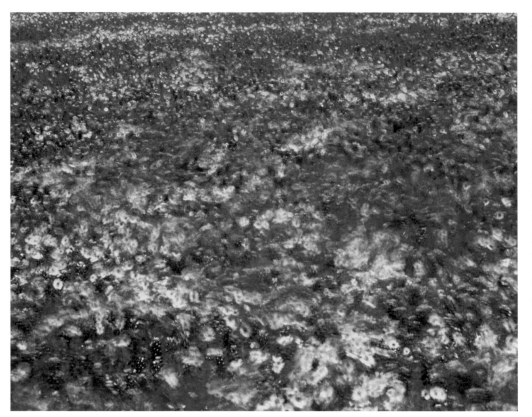

Daisies and bluebonnets near Austin, Texas (above). You can't easily judge the outcome of a blurred-motion attempt. One of several frames, this photo was chosen for the stream of yellow that traces an S-curve path through the frame. Canon EOS A2, Canon 90mm tilt/shift lens, 2X teleconverter, Fujichrome Velvia, Singh-Ray circular polarizing filter, one second at f/22.

AERIAL ANGLES

With small subjects you can take *bona fide* aerial photos without the expense of renting an airplane. You can create those arresting studies in line, form and pattern that are the hallmarks of Cessna-snapping. Your best tool here is usually a zoom lens either with macro capabilities or equipped with an extension tube for close-focusing. Your tripod must be set up so that the camera projects over the flowers far enough to keep the legs out of the viewfinder. This is easy if your tripod has a center column that can be

reinserted laterally in its collar (as with some Manfrotto/Bogen models) to cantilever the camera out away from the legs. Otherwise you need to tip the tripod forward over the subject with the two front legs spread wide to straddle the view, and the back leg stretched out and anchored to the ground with your camera bag or some other weight (a bungy cord comes in handy here). The tripod doesn't have to be rock solid, just dead steady for a second or two at a time to prevent the camera from moving during exposure. From directly above, there is no top or bottom to the composition so you can take any angle on the subject you wish. Zoom in and out to test various magnifications. Let the flowers lead the flow of possibilities until you hit upon a graphic that you like. Even with a small patch of blooms, I like to aim so that blossoms around the periphery are cut off to give the impression that the color field extends forever. Framing

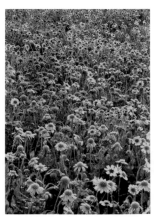

two blooms is usually a mistake as the center of interest is split, robbing the composition of its unity.

THE SLOW SMOOTHIE

This is my favorite wildflower motif. It's a blend of delicious reds, mauves and whites gently spread into a background of fresh greens. Two conditions are necessary. The first is wind — the ruin of most wildflower photographs but in this case it's essential. Next you need a colorful expanse of blooms about the size of a kitchen table or larger. A normal to wide-angle lens usually works well for mixing up the palette of color. The shutter setting depends on how much the flowers are moving around. Intermittent shakes and shudders may require an exposure of several seconds or longer (unpack your neutral density filters); while in a breeze, a 1/15 second does nicely. If the exposure is too long the blossoms will lose definition and saturation, too brief and they will look merely fuzzy as if you were not focused properly or were hand-holding the camera. Try various shutter speeds to make sure you get the effect you want and remember to compensate for the change in exposure time by adjusting the aperture. An average or evaluative meter reading normally yields accurate exposure.

Several refinements offer additional possibilities. If you are set up within a few feet of the flowers, a burst of action-stopping flash can be seared into the mix during exposure. Set both the flash exposure and ambient light exposure for one stop less than full exposure. When added together, these two values will yield the correct density. It's best to hold the flash off the camera above the flower patch for more even front-to-back illumination. This is easy to synchronize manually for exposures of a second or more (just press the flash's test button when you hear the shutter open). At faster speeds you'll need to attach a sync cord between camera and

Sand verbena and daisies, Texas Hill Country (lower left). A tilt-shift lens allowed depth of field to be aligned with the plane of blooms for a sharp rendering.

Misty meadow, Mendocino Headlands (below). This dreamscape was made by double exposure. The first take was in sharp focus, the second with slight defocus to generate halos around the highlight elements. Pentax 645 N11, 300mm f/5.6 lens, Singh-Ray circular polarizer with color intensifier, Fujichrome Velvia,

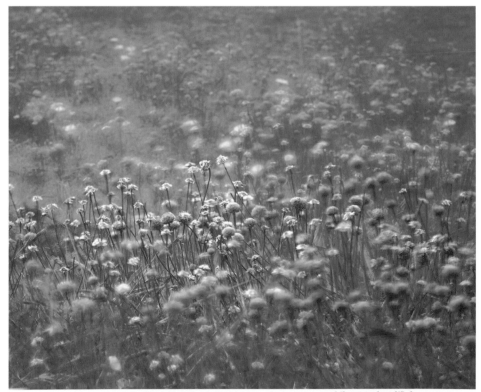

1/8 second at f/5.6.

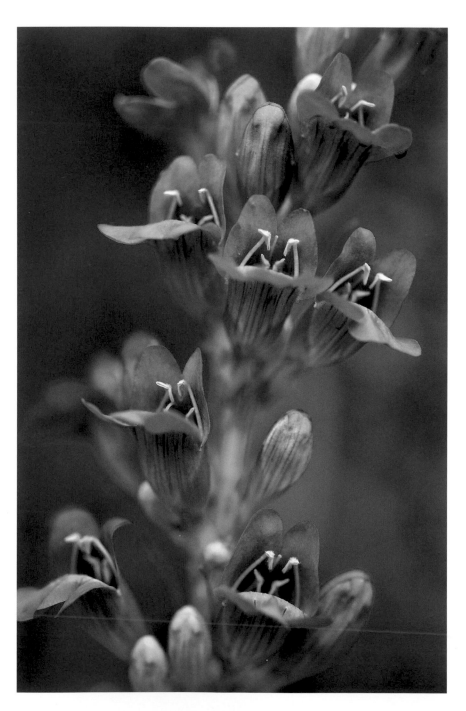

flash and use standard fill-flash techniques. Another approach uses double exposure and produces a similar effect. Make one image at a slow shutter speed for blurring effects and the other at a motion-stopping speed for fine-edged detail. Variations for generating the blurred component include defocusing, zooming to a slightly different magnification, or zooming during the exposure. Again, underexpose each take by one stop. The dreamy effects generally spring from a marriage of etched blooms haloed in dreamy color.

TELEPHOTO PROSPECTING

It's difficult to predict the results of blurred motion techniques. The viewfinder offers few clues of the impending magic. By contrast, this long lens approach allows you to savor the image in nearly full measure before you even trip the shutter. Like many good things, it's a simple undertaking with infinite possibilities. The approach is based on using the telephoto's limited depth of field to place out-of-focus blurs strategically in the composition. You can modify these dabs, blobs and washes of color in size, saturation, definition, transparency and position by judicious selection of camera angle, focal distance, camera-to-subject distance, and camera-to-blur distance. Although this sounds like formula work, it isn't. It's an artistic exercise requiring Mondrianic color sense, Pollockian

For Maximum Sharpness

- *Use a tripod whenever possible.*
- *Trip the shutter with a cable release or the camera's self-timer.*
- *Avoid using the smallest or largest lens apertures.*
- *Avoid high-vibration shutter speeds between 1/4 and 1/30 second especially with super-telephoto lenses.*
- *Lock up the mirror during exposure.*
- *Use low ISO, fine-grained films.*
- *Select fast shutter speeds to arrest subject movement and camara shake.*
- *Position the depth-of-field zone to include the most important features of the scene.*

persistence, du Champsian zeal for experimentation, and Rodinesque appreciation of form before all the lush pieces of the puzzle can be fused in the viewfinder, ready for exposure. A telephoto lens in the 400mm–600mm range fitted with an extension tube for resolving close-up blooms is the ideal brush for creating these painterly effects. You may choose to work in the abstract, devising sensuous combinations of pure colors and shapes. Or select a bloom or bouquet for sharp rendering and clear identification and let this center of interest anchor and shape the complement of blurry chromas.

It's difficult to prejudge such scenes with the naked eye — you need to analyze the picture elements through the lens. To do this, I kneel behind the tripod with the camera positioned at bloom level. If the sun is low in the sky I opt for a front-lit view to capture pure saturated colors. If shooting during midday I set up for backlighting so that petals and leaves are trans-illuminated and glow with inner color. This back-door defence against high noon's laser saves your emulsion from burned highlights and frozen shadows. Of help in further reducing contrast is the shallow depth of field that the telephoto projects into the scene to soften the edges of shadows and highlights.

Once lighting issues are settled, I begin measuring the range, precise angle and trajectory to the target blooms. Camera range is a compromise between how large I want the featured flowers to be and the size and definition of the complementary color blurs. Camera angle determines just

Narrow-leaved penstemon, Wasatch Mountains, Utah (far left). A tripod, plant clamp, calm atmosphere, strategically placed depth of field, and vibration-free shutter speed were all factors that worked to produce sharp detail in this image.

Purple asters, Texas Hill Country (below). I discovered this harmonious combination of blurred and sharp color swatches by casting about through this clump of common wildflowers with a 500mm telephoto lens fitted with 50 mm of extension for close focusing.

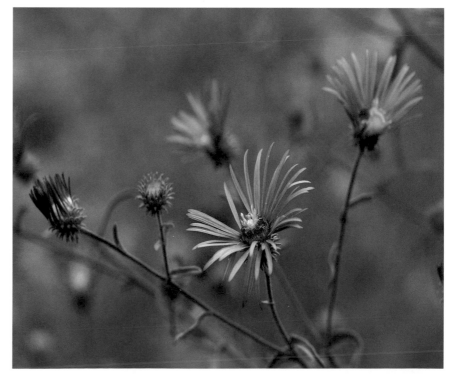

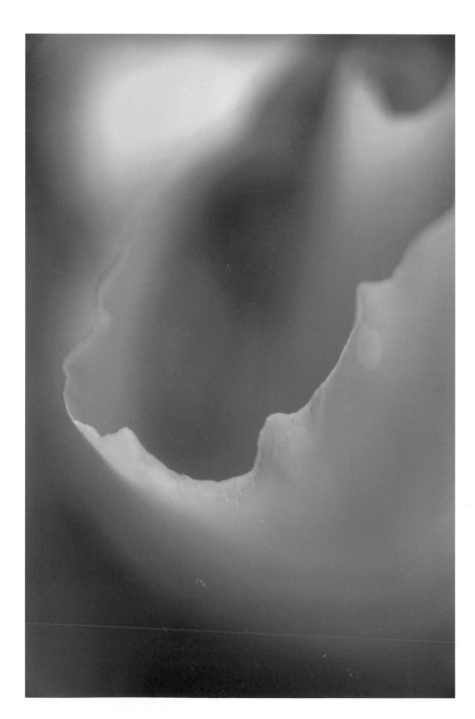

how the color patches are arranged about the main subject, and the trajectory is adjusted for both arrangement of floral elements as well as for the inclusion of blue sky (yes) or clouds (none or a few). Each shift in camera position and lens focus serves up a new composition for you to enjoy and evaluate. The process becomes less trial and error as you get a feeling for how the many factors engage one another. Set the aperture at maximum, or nearly so, with whatever shutter speed renders normal exposure at a center-weighted, average or evaluative meter reading. Warm sun and soft breeze, bird twitter and insect buzz, delicate scents of moist earth and minted grasses make it easy to linger dreamily over the beautiful sights in the viewfinder. Just remember to take a photo once in a while!

DOWN AND DIRTY

Change into play clothes for this one — no need for those pesky tripods either. For these ground-hugging shots, mother earth provides all of the camera support you'll need. The intent is to take the viewer inside the floral bouquet while setting the blooms up against the most inviting hue in the universe — the blue ceiling of a sunny day. An ultrawide-angle lens is required here, something in the range of 20mm. To get it to focus close enough, you'll need to attach an extension tube of 12–15mm (longer tubes will not bring the subject into focus) between camera and lens.

Keep a polarizing filter handy to provide more color saturation in the sky should the camera angle and timing of your shoot make this practical. Crawl up to a color patch (yellow and orange petals look most dramatic against the blue) and shove your camera right into the center of a tight bouquet. So much the better if leaves and petals brush against the front of the lens. Once you've calmed down from your first revealing peak in the viewfinder, you can begin to arrange the overload of gorgeous colors and shapes into an effective composition. Minute shifts of camera angle and position generate dramatic changes in the scene. Once the artist in you has it just right, stabilize the camera position with anything handy — pebbles, sand, your hat, a Reuben or

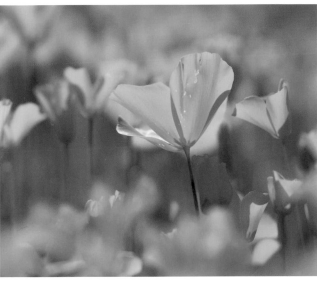

maybe the handy beanbag support you remembered to bring along. Check depth of field through the lens and then adjust focus, aperture and shutter speed for the best rendering of subject sharpness. Trip the shutter with the self-timer or a cable release, avoiding both camera-shake and wind-induced movement of the blooms. Most of the time, color and contrast improve with the use of a reflector placed on the ground right beneath the flowers. A simple sheet of white paper works as effectively as anything.

Of course, warm weather sees wildflowers sprouting everywhere. Before you set out, surf the internet for the latest information on blooming conditions and up-to-date wildflower hotline numbers. Great shooting and happy travels!

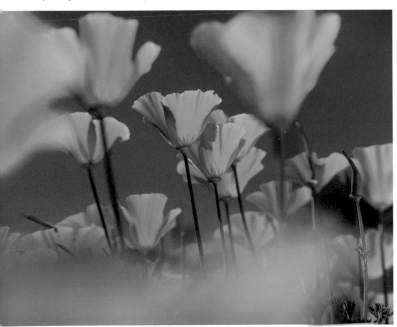

California poppies. *A favorite wildflower subject, this beautiful species is represented here by three distinct approaches. Captured at ultraclose-up range, an abstraction of form and color is created from a tiny section of scalloped petal (**far left**). A ground-level, ultrawide-angle lens (20mm) is pushed into a clump of poppies to throw them into dramatic contrast with the blue sky made more intense by a polarizing filter (**left**). Through selective focus and shallow depth of field, a telephoto lens isolates a single blossom in a sun-drenched atmosphere of orange chroma (**above**).*

Resource List

Newsletters

photograph america newsletter, Robert Hitchman, Post Office Box 86, Novato CA 94948-0086, 415-898-3736.

Photo Traveler Publications, various writers P.O. Box 39912, Los Angeles CA 90039, 323-660-8600.

These two periodic guides provide in-depth, detailed information solely for nature photographers about travel logistics, specific scenic shooting sites, and wildlife hot spots, usually focusing on one park or region in each issue. Contact the publishers for a full list of back issues and the locations that have been covered. They are invaluable for any North American nature photography destination.

Books

The Art of Bird Photography: The Complete Guide to Professional Field Techniques, Arthur Morris, Amphoto Books, New York NY, 1998.

The Art of Photographing Nature, Art Wolfe and Martha Hill, Crown Publishing Group, New York NY, 1993.

National Geographic Photography Field Guide, Peter K. Burian and Robert Caputo, National Geographic Society, Washington DC, 1999.

Nature Photography: National Audubon Society Guide, Tim Fitzharris, Firefly Books, Willowdale, Ontario, 1996.

The New Complete Guide to Wildlife Photography, Joe McDonald, Amphoto Books, New York NY, 1998.

Photo Impressionism, Freeman Patterson and André Gallant, Key Porter Books, Toronto, 2001.

Photography and the Art of Seeing, Freeman Patterson, Key Porter Books, Toronto, 1979.

Photography Outdoors: A Field Guide for Travel and Adventure Photographers, Mark Gardner and Art Wolfe, The Mountaineers, Seattle WA, 1995.

The Sierra Club Guide to Close-up Photography in Nature, Tim Fitzharris, Sierra Club Books, San Francisco CA, 1998.

The Sierra Club Guide to 35mm Landscape Photography, Tim Fitzharris, Sierra Club Books, San Francisco CA, 1996.

Websites

There are thousands of amateur and professional websites dedicated to nature photography. Here you can find everything you ever wanted to know on the topic. These three sites are especially useful and good starting points for further exploration.

Outdoor Photographer (www.outdoorphotographer.com). Basically an on-line collection of *Outdoor Photographer* magazine current and past issues. You can spend days exploring the plethora of information provided on this well-made, attractive site.

The Luminous Landscape (www.luminous-landscape.com). This small site provides authoritive reviews of equipment and film as well as informed tutorials on advanced techniques and current issues of interest to nature photographers.

photo.net (www.photo.net). This huge, mainly amateur site provides information on all manner of photographic pursuits. Forums on nature photography are helpful in getting your personal questions answered. Information on shooting locations is particularly useful.